Bible Stories

for Our Little Ones

Bible Stories

for Our Little Ones

by

W.G. VAN DE HULST

Illustrated by J.H. Isings

**INHERITANCE PUBLICATIONS
NEERLANDIA, ALBERTA, CANADA
PELLA, IOWA, U.S.A.**

National Library of Canada Cataloguing in Publication Data

Hulst, W. G. van de (Willem Gerrit), 1879-1963
   Bible stories for our little ones / by W.G. Van de Hulst ; illustrated by J.H. Isings.

ISBN 1-894666-69-0

   1. Bible stories, English. I. Isings, J. H. II. Title.
BS551.3.H84 2004   j220.9'505   C2004-901014-X

Library of Congress Cataloging-in-Publication Data

Hulst, W. G. van de (Willem Gerrit), 1879-1963.
  [Bijbelse vertellingen voor onze kleintjes. English]
  Bible stories for our little ones / by W.G. van de Hulst ; illustrated by J.H. Isings.
    p. cm.
  ISBN 1-894666-69-0
  1. Bible stories, English. I. Isings, J. H. II. Title.
BS551.3.H8513 2004
220.9'505—dc22

                                                              2004000678

Originally published as *Bijbelse vertellingen voor onze kleintjes.*
Printed under licensing from Jongbloed Publishing Group, Heerenveen, the Netherlands.

Translated by Paulina M. Rustenburg Bootsma

Illustrated by J.H. Isings
Cover Painting by Rino Visser

All rights reserved © 2004, by Inheritance Publications
Box 154, Neerlandia, Alberta Canada T0G 1R0
Tel. (780) 674 3949
Web site: http://www.telusplanet.net/public/inhpubl/webip/ip.htm
E-Mail inhpubl@telusplanet.net

Published simultaneously in U.S.A. by Inheritance Publications
Box 366, Pella, Iowa 50219

Available in Australia from Inheritance Publications
Box 1122, Kelmscott, W.A. 6111 Tel. & Fax (089) 390 4940

Printed in Canada

Contents

FOREWORD: At Mother's Knee 7

The Old Testament

CREATION 11
ADAM AND EVE IN PARADISE 13
CAIN AND ABEL 17
THE FLOOD 20
ABRAHAM 24
LOT 27
HAGAR AND ISHMAEL 31
THE FATHER AND HIS CHILD 34
JACOB AND ESAU 37
A BEAUTIFUL DREAM 41
JACOB RETURNS 43
JOSEPH 45
IN THE FARAWAY LAND 50
IN THE PALACE 54
STRANGE MEN CAME TO THE PALACE 58
FIRST GRIEF, BUT THEN 60
ALL IS RIGHT 63
POOR PEOPLE 64
IN THE REED BASKET 66
THE PRINCE BECOMES A SHEPHERD 69
THE BURNING BUSH 72
MOSES AND THE WICKED KING 73
THE RED SEA 77
THE LONG JOURNEY 79
THE GOLDEN CALF 81
THEIR OWN FAULT 84
MOSES ON THE MOUNTAIN 87
THE WHITE CITY WITH THE STRONG WALLS 89
A POOR WOMAN WHO BECOMES RICH 93
ELI AND SAMUEL 96
DAVID 101
DAVID AND GOLIATH 104
WICKED KING SAUL 108
IN THE DARK CAVE 110
THE SPEAR AND THE WATER JUG 113
ELIJAH, THE GREAT PROPHET 116
ELIJAH AND THE POOR WOMAN 119
A POOR MOTHER AND HER POOR BOYS 123
THE RICH MAN WHO WAS A LEPER 125
IN THE FARAWAY LAND 130
DANIEL IN THE LIONS' DEN 134

The New Testament

ZACHARIAS AND THE ANGEL	143
JOSEPH AND MARY	147
THE BABY IN THE STABLE	149
IN THE TEMPLE	151
THE WISE MEN FROM THE EAST	154
WICKED KING HEROD	157
WHEN THE LORD JESUS WAS TWELVE YEARS OLD	160
JOHN THE BAPTIST	162
THE DISCIPLES	164
THE WEDDING AT CANA	165
A NET FULL OF FISH	168
A SICK MAN HEALED	170
UNCLEAN! UNCLEAN!	174
A POOR MOTHER AND HER POOR DEAD SON	176
THE DAUGHTER OF JAIRUS	178
SICK AND FORGOTTEN	180
THE STORM AT SEA	183
FIVE LOAVES AND TWO FISH	185
WALKING ON THE SEA	188
THE UNFORGIVING SERVANT	191
JESUS, THE FRIEND OF LITTLE CHILDREN	193
THE LOST SON	196
THE GOOD SHEPHERD	201
THE GOOD SAMARITAN	203
LAZARUS	206
THE BLIND MAN	210
HOSANNA! HOSANNA!	213
JUDAS	217
THE LAST SUPPER	219
IN THE DARK NIGHT	222
PETER	227
CRUCIFY HIM! CRUCIFY HIM!	230
GOLGOTHA	232
THE HAPPY MORNING	237
MARY MAGDALENE	239
WHO WAS IT?	241
BY THE SEA OF TIBERIAS	244
THE ASCENSION	247
PENTECOST	249
THE CRIPPLED MAN	251
PETER RELEASED	253
PAUL	257

FOREWORD

At Mother's Knee

This book is intended to be a book for mothers. A book to be read in quiet hours, to little ones of four to seven or eight years old who sit at Mother's knee. A book to be read slowly — yes, especially slowly; very clearly with warm, loving reverence and awe which creates in little children's heart a holy reverence and a joy filled awe. It desires to be a BIBLE FOR THE LITTLE ONES, reaching out to all areas of a child's understanding. A child does not comprehend everything, yet understands a great deal. This story bible wishes to tell about the holy things in plain, clear, almost simple language, which still must never profane the consecrated happenings. It is not meant to be complete. Completeness would hinder children. This book is not meant to be anything but a modest, reverent endeavour to lead the little ones into the holy sphere of Godly things. The interest of the little ones will be the test to see whether this endeavour is accomplished. May God give our little ones His wonderful blessings in the quiet hours, listening to His voice at Mother's knee.
— The Author

The Old Testament

CREATION

Shh! A little bird is sitting in the grass. His shining eyes look about so joyfully. The sun shines brightly and the wind whispers through the leaves of the trees. It is beautiful in the garden, very beautiful! Whoosh, whoosh! The bird flies away up into a tree. There it opens its little beak and sings a song with its little head held high. Whoosh! It flies away again. It soars very high into the sky, flying far away, until you cannot see it anymore. The world is so big and the sky is so high . . . Whoosh! There goes another bird. And another. And another. They sing, and they sing, and they fly, and they fly! Look! They are like dark dots in the light blue sky. In the garden many more birds are rustling in the trees and the bushes. They play, they sing. Oh, there are so many, so very many! There are so many, no one can count them.

Hush! A little butterfly flutters by, up and down, back and forth. It sticks its long tongue deep into a pretty flower, just for a second. It may do that. The flower tastes so good! And then more butterflies come: white ones, and red ones, and gold-coloured ones. They look like flowers themselves flying about. They all taste the sweetness of the flowers. There are plenty of flowers. Oh, there are hundreds, thousands, hundreds of thousands. So many, no one can count them!

Look! A little bug climbs up on a blade of grass. Its back shines like a red bead in the green grass. How pretty! And there are many more bugs, red ones, yellow ones, black, and gold ones. There are so many, no one can count them.

Do you hear the bees humming? Do you see the mosquitoes dancing? Do you hear the rustling of the leaves in the wind? Oh, those birds, butterflies, flowers and leaves, the mosquitoes and the bugs — there are so many . . . so many! No, no one can count them. There are too many to count.

To whom do they all belong? Who takes care of them?
Do they belong to a gardener?
No.

Do they belong to a very rich man?
No.
Do they belong to a king?
No.

But to whom do they belong? And who takes care of them all?

God takes care of them. They are all creatures of God, who lives up high in heaven. He knows everything, He hears everything, and He sees everything. Yes, He sees the little bug deep in the grass. He also sees the singing bird high in the air.

Yes, and He sees the little children playing in the garden, the children playing along the road, and the very little ones who sleep in their cradles. They are God's creatures too. And God takes care of Father and Mother too. The big golden sun in the sky belongs to God. Also the tiny grain of sand blown by the wind on the window sill outside. The moon and the stars, the blue skies and the white fluffy clouds, the big, big sea; all the people, all the animals — everything belongs to God. God made them and He takes care of them.

Once, long, long ago there was not one bird or flower. There was not one man or baby. There was no sun, moon, or star. Then it was quiet and dark everywhere. Only God was there.

Then He spoke: "Let there be light!" Then something beautiful happened. There was light! All of a sudden, because God said so.

And then God made the blue sky, and the white clouds, and the wide lands, and the big, big sea.

Then the little flowers began to grow in the wide fields, just like that, because God said so. There were so many, so many, no one could count them. The rain fell out of the clouds onto the flowers, and the trees, and the green grass so they could drink. It was so very beautiful.

Then the big golden sun started to shine in the blue sky. All of a sudden, because God said so. And when that golden sun slowly disappeared behind the big world, the lovely silver moon shone, and the bright stars twinkled and shone, too. Then it was night. In the quietness of the night, the flowers and the trees could go to sleep. That was how God planned it to be. It was very beautiful. But it was still quiet on the beautiful world, very quiet, very still.

The wind whispered through the leaves, and the flowers bent their heads, but it was still very quiet. Then, all of a sudden, the happy birds flew through the sky. They sang their wonderful songs, just like that, because God said so. And in the waters came darting fish, big ones and little ones, and they played, they played their wild games. The birds could build their nests in the trees, and the fish could find quiet places along the water's side. And then it was not quiet in the world anymore, oh, no!

But it became even more wonderful, more happy. Other animals came: cows, horses, sheep, the quick squirrel, the tiny mouse, the great big elephant, and the mosquito dancing in the sunshine. There were so many, so many, no one could count them. And each found a spot to live and to play, and to sleep in the night. Everything that God had made was beautiful. God is so mighty, and good, and majestic.

But then the most beautiful thing happened — God made the first man. He could live on that world which was so beautiful and so happy. He could be king over all the animals and all the things. He could also be God's friend. The name of that first man was Adam. Oh, yes! He was the most wonderful of all the beautiful things that God had made.

Adam looked around in that great, beautiful world. He was happy, so very happy. He looked up to heaven, where God lived. The LORD, who was his Father, had given him all these beautiful things and he would always take care of him. That made Adam's heart even more happy. How beautiful, how very beautiful it was!

ADAM AND EVE IN PARADISE

Softly the wind whispered through the trees. Two people were coming near, a man and a woman. They looked so cheerful, they were so happy. And when they heard the wind softly whispering through the trees, they stopped — both of them. They listened. From heaven, God Himself spoke to them. Quietly and reverently they listened. How happy it made them! They were God's children, and they liked to listen when their heavenly Father spoke to them.

Do you know who that man was who listened so happily? That was Adam, the first man. And do you know who the woman was? That was Eve. She was the woman God gave to Adam. Adam was not to stay alone in this big world. Do you know where they lived together? They lived in Paradise. That was a beautiful garden, the most beautiful place in this beautiful world. God Himself chose it for them. And when the wind softly whispered through the trees, He spoke to them. The heavenly Father loved His children very much.

There they went again, together. The little birds darted around their feet and sang their most beautiful songs around their heads. They allowed Adam and Eve to hold them too, because they knew Adam and Eve would not hurt them. Oh, no — in Paradise, there was no pain. Look there! The little rabbits and the quick squirrels hopped and played in the green grass, right next to the big wolves. But those great wolves did not eat them. A little lamb fell asleep between the paws of a strong lion, but that strong lion kept his sharp claws very still. He would not hurt the little lamb — no indeed. In Paradise, there was no anger. Adam and Eve walked among those happy animals which were playing and playing. The golden butterflies fluttered in the sunshine. The silver fish flashed through the water. Adam and Eve knew them all. Adam had given each animal its own name. He was their master. They all listened to him.

Adam and Eve had to take care of the beautiful garden, but they never became tired or sick. They were never sad, they did not feel pain. They were always happy. They ate the most delicious fruits: the most beautiful apples, the best pears, and the sweetest grapes. They could eat as much as they wanted. Everything in this beautiful garden was for them. Everything, yes . . .

But in the centre of Paradise stood one tree of which they might not eat. God Himself had told them. But that did not matter. There were plenty of trees just as beautiful. And there were so many fruits. Adam and Eve wanted to be obedient to God — they would not touch that one tree, because if they did, they would die. God had said so. They were God's children — that was wonderful. In this lovely Paradise, everything was beautiful, everything was good. But the most beautiful thing was when their heavenly Father spoke to them. Listen! Through the trees the wind rustled softly.

ADAM AND EVE IN PARADISE

But suddenly something had happened. The wind was still softly rustling, but Adam and Eve were not listening. No, they had run away. Their eyes were filled with fear and they ran to the big high trees and the thick bushes. There they hid themselves behind the leaves. It was dark there. No one could see them. They held onto each other's hands. They wanted to help one another, but they could not. The fear in their hearts did not go away. Oh, what was it? What had happened?

Something terrible had happened. Adam and Eve had done something wrong. They had eaten from that one tree of which they were not allowed to eat. They had known that. God Himself had said that. How had that happened? When Eve was walking through the garden and had come close to that tree, she had heard a voice calling to her, a very soft and friendly voice. But it was a wicked voice. Eve did not know that. She had looked and saw a snake in the tree. He called in such a kind and friendly way.

The snake had said to Eve, "Are you not allowed to eat from any tree?"

"Oh, yes," Eve had answered. "We may eat from any tree, only not this one. Then we will die."

But that mean, wicked serpent had said, "Eve, that is not true. You can pick off this tree and eat. Go ahead — you will not die. Not at all. Just do it, then you will be as wise as God Himself. Go ahead, Eve."

Oh, if only Eve had run away quickly! If only Eve had said, "No, you wicked serpent, it is not allowed, never!" But Eve had not run away. She wanted to be just as wise as God. So she picked and ate. And then she had called Adam and he ate too.

The wicked serpent had hurried away. Actually, it was a very strange serpent. He was a wicked angel, who had once lived with God in heaven, but not anymore. That wicked angel had noticed how happy Adam and Eve were. He had seen that they were God's children, and he had thought, "If they are disobedient, they will not be God's children anymore. I shall make them become disobedient." Then that wicked angel had hid inside a serpent. Now he hurried away. He had laughed at Adam and Eve. They had sinned, they had been disobedient, and that had made that wicked one happy. That was what had happened.

The wind rustled softly through the trees. Yes, it frightened Adam and Eve. Their hearts beat with fear. That was terrible — it was such an awful pain. Before, they had not known what fear was. They had never sinned. Now they had, and they ran away. They picked leaves off the trees and covered their naked bodies. They had always been naked, but had not even known it. Now they did. Ah, they did not dare listen to God's voice. They hid deeper and deeper in the bushes. They were so frightened, so terribly afraid.

But the LORD saw Adam and Eve. He knew what they had done. He knows everything. The LORD called to Adam, "Adam, where are you?" Then Adam had to come out, and Eve too. They trembled before God's holy eyes. They were so afraid. Before it had been so wonderful when their heavenly Father spoke to them, but not anymore. Now it was terrible, and that was their own fault.

Now the punishment came too. First for the serpent, the wicked one! He would have to crawl on his belly over the ground, and he would have to eat the dust of the earth his whole life.

Then punishment came for disobedient Adam and Eve too. God had told them that would happen. Adam and Eve could not stay in the beautiful Paradise. They would have to move into the lonely world. They were not truly God's children anymore, and one day they would die. That was their own fault.

And yet, the heavenly Father still loved His disobedient children. He was sad about their wickedness, but He promised them something. Yes, now they had to move away from Him, and away from the beautiful Paradise. They had to go into the big world, and their hearts would always be afraid of Him. But someday many people would live in the world, and then the Lord Jesus would come, God's very own Son. He would bring the people back to God. Then they would not be afraid of Him anymore. Then they would be true children of their heavenly Father again. That was God's promise to Adam and Eve.

Now they had to leave Paradise. There they went, their heads bowed, sad and afraid. When they looked around once more at their beautiful Paradise, they saw an angel standing in the gate. He held a flaming sword in his hand, a fiery sword. No, they could never, never return to the beautiful Paradise. That was their own fault.

There they went into the lonely world. They had to work hard on the land now, or they would have no food, no bread. Now the sun shone hot on their backs and hurt them. They became tired, and in the night it was cold and they crawled away into a dark cave to sleep. Now the animals were angry at each other too, and had become afraid of Adam and Eve. They ran away when they saw them. Everything was sad, so very sad. Sometimes the wind softly whispered through the trees, and Adam and Eve listened again. No, they did not hear God's voice anymore. That was the most terrible thing of all.

Yet, they knew that their heavenly Father would not forget them. And someday Someone would come who would bring them back to God. Then they would hear God's voice once more as in the beautiful Paradise. Then everything would become good and happy and wonderful again. That Person would be the Lord Jesus. They waited for that, they thought about that every day, and that made their fear-filled hearts glad.

CAIN AND ABEL

Look! Very large stones were lying on top of each other in a big pile. On top of the stones were dead twigs, and on top of the twigs lay a dead lamb. It was slaughtered. A man stood next to it. He hit two stones hard against each other. A spark flew out and fell among the dead wood and the twigs began to burn. They snapped and crackled. Little red flames danced around the dead lamb, but the animal felt no pain. White smoke ascended up to the sky and high up to heaven. That man stood very quietly and reverently. He looked up into the blue sky, high into the heavens. A great happiness was in his eyes. He folded his hands, he prayed. He spoke softly to God who lives in heaven.

Who was that man, and what was he doing? That man was Abel. Adam was his father, and Eve was his mother. Abel was bringing an offering to God. He owned many sheep and goats and lambs. He was a shepherd. The LORD in heaven took good care of him. He knew that. It made him happy and thankful. Now he had slaughtered one of his sheep, but not to eat for himself, and not to give to his father or mother. No, this lamb was for God. When that white smoke was rising, it was as if Abel's happiness was going up, too. And he prayed, "Lord, I thank Thee. Thou art so good to me." Those words rose, too, much higher than the smoke, much higher than the clouds. They came to God in heaven. God hears the quiet prayers of His people. He knows everything — He knows about the happiness in their hearts, too.

A little farther off lay another pile of stones. A fire was burning there, too. Another man stood near it. Who was that? That was Cain, Abel's brother. He was a farmer. He had harvested the grain from his fields, and now he had laid a bundle of that grain on the stones. It was burning. He was bringing an offering to God too. But Cain was not happy. Cain was angry. He did not love God and he was not thankful for everything God had given him. Abel was. Then Cain's eyes looked angrily toward Abel. Cain thought, "Abel likes to give his lamb to God. I do not like to give my grain. Abel is much better than I am. I am angry at Abel." He shook his fist and walked away angrily.

CAIN AND ABEL

God knows what people think. He knows everything. He knows the anger in their hearts. The LORD spoke to Cain. "Cain, why is your heart so angry? Be like Abel; then your heart will be happy too. But if you do wrong, sorrow will come. Cain, put the anger out of your heart."

But Cain did not listen to God's voice. Cain knew that Abel was not at fault, but he remained angry with him anyway. That was very wicked of Cain.

One day, when they were in the field, far away from their father and mother, Cain became even more angry. And then . . . how terrible! He killed Abel. There Abel lay, very quiet, cold, and white, his happy eyes closed forever. That frightened Cain. He fled. He did not even dare to turn around.

But then the LORD spoke to him again, "Cain, where is Abel, your brother?"

That frightened Cain even more. He did not dare to tell the truth. He lied. He answered angrily, "I do not know. Do I have to take care of my brother?"

Then punishment came for wicked Cain. It was his own fault. The LORD said, "Cain, the beautiful grain will not grow for you in the field anymore. There will be no spot on the earth where you will find rest."

Cain cringed in fear. Now he felt how wicked his deed was, but he could never correct it. He fled far, far away, always farther. He would always remember poor Abel. That was the worst of all, and it was his own fault.

Abel was dead. His father and mother found him. They came very close to him, but he did not see them. They called him, but he did not hear them. He lay there so quiet, so cold, and so white. Adam and Eve were bitterly sorrowful. Now they had lost Abel. Abel was dead. They buried his poor dead body in the earth. But Abel himself was with God in heaven. There he could love his heavenly Father even more than on earth. There everything was very beautiful and wonderful, even more beautiful and wonderful than in Paradise. Now Abel would be happy forever.

THE FLOOD

Bang, bang. The hammer was pounding and pounding. Bang, bang. The man using the hammer worked bravely on. He was old, but still very strong. He was building a ship, a great big ship. He had three sons. They helped him faithfully. Look! They were cutting down trees in the forest, and making them into big planks. All those big boards were hammered onto the enormous ship. Nearby a cheerful fire was burning, with a big pot filled with boiling pitch hanging above it. The man took that black pitch and brushed it onto the planks on the inside and outside of the huge ship. The pitch became very hard. Then the water would not be able to come into the ship between the boards.

Yes, that ship, that great giant ship, would go into the water. It was higher than a house. It had a door and a window. It had a very high roof. That ship, that big ark, was lying in the centre of the land, and yet it would go into the water. How could that be?

The old man and his three sons continued to work steadily. For days, months, even years, they hammered and worked on the giant ship.

That old man was Noah, and his three sons were called Shem, Ham, and Japheth. Noah's wife lived a little farther away. The wives of Shem, Ham, and Japheth lived there, too. Often they came to watch. They also knew that the giant ship had to go into the water. God Himself had told them. Other people came to watch, too, many people — men, women, and children. Adam and Eve had died long ago. Cain, who killed his brother Abel, had also died. Their children had become men and women. Then more children had been born. They had grown up and now there were many, very many people on the earth. But they had forgotten God, their heavenly Father. They did wicked and evil deeds and did not think about God.

Noah did think about God. Noah loved God. And now all these people came to look at Noah's strange big ship. They laughed at Noah. They scoffed at him and they scoffed at his ship. Noah told them, "God in heaven told me it must be done." But then those people scoffed at God, too. That was terrible.

That was very sinful of them. They just laughed and said, "We do not listen to God. We do what we like. We are not afraid of God."

That frightened Noah. How did those people dare to mock God? He said, "You may not do that. God hears everything. He sees everything. He knows everything. Oh, no, don't do that ever again. Listen: if you continue to do wicked things like that, a terrible punishment will come over you. God told me that, too. A big flood will come over the earth and everyone will be drowned. Oh, no, don't do it again."

But those wicked people laughed at Noah even more, and they mocked God even more. They thought, "Noah has been building that ship for years already. Noah is a fool. He does not know a thing about it. That punishment is not coming. We are not afraid of God."

But one day, something strange happened. Animals came, just like that, from the dark forest, from the high mountains, and from the wide fields. Two of every kind of animal came, a male and a female. And they all walked toward Noah's big ship. They knew the way exactly. And they were all going in, too. Look. Elephants, monkeys, rhinoceroses, tigers, lions, and many more. Tiny little mice came, too. And birds came flying through the sky, very big ones and wee little ones. Some of each animal came to the ark. Noah gave each one its own spot, its very own pen. The ark was big, very big.

And food? Oh, yes, they would get food, too. There was enough. Noah and his three sons had brought it all inside. God had commanded it. God was also leading the animals to Noah, a male and a female of each. Now all were inside, Noah and his three sons, their mother, and their wives. And then — then God Himself shut the door of the ark. Now they were all well taken care of. The LORD would keep them safe. It was very quiet now. The hammers were no longer pounding. The little fire under the pitch pot had gone out. Everything was ready now.

For seven days the ark lay quietly closed in the middle of the land. The people, those wicked people outside, were still not afraid. They laughed and they scoffed. "Ha, now that big

ship is finished, but it cannot go anywhere. Who shall pull it to the sea? No one can do that."

Then it started to rain. First the wicked people laughed about the rain, too. It would dry up again. But the rain came faster and faster and it did not stop at all. The rain came into their houses, and then the people did not laugh anymore. Then they became afraid. It became worse and worse; the rain poured down wildly and angrily, and the water in the sea rose higher and higher. It streamed in big waves over the land.

The wild water grabbed the people. Fearfully they fled away. They climbed in the trees, they climbed up the high mountains, but the swirling water grabbed the people anyway. It rose higher and higher and higher. It grabbed them all. How they cried and screamed in fear. But it was too late now. The roaring water was everywhere. It rose higher than the houses, higher than the trees, higher than the highest mountain. The people and the animals on the earth all drowned in the deep water. No land, tree, or mountain could be seen. Everything was one big, mighty gray sea, and the fierce rain clattered on the foaming waves. Now the big, beautiful world was gone, drowned in the water.

But, there on top of the wild water, floated a dark, solitary object. That was Noah's ark. The rain poured on it, and the waves crashed against it, but the wild water could not harm that ark. God Himself was taking care of Noah. The rain and storm

could not hurt him. Inside the ark, everyone and everything was safe and warm and well. Those whom God keeps are always safe.

After many, many days, weeks, yes, even months, everything became still. The rain stopped. The waves went down. The dark clouds were no longer blown throughout the sky, and the good sun began to shine again. The ark gently floated along on the stilled waters. Slowly, very slowly, the water went down.

One day there was a boom! What was that? Everyone and everything was shaken up inside the ark. What had happened? The ark bumped hard onto the top of a mountain. Now it could no longer float along. It had stopped. The water went down farther and farther.

Look! One day Noah opened the window. He had a black bird in his hand, a raven. He let it fly away. A little while later he let a dove fly out. But the dove was not as strong as the raven, she was tired of flying all day. Everywhere there was water, and no place for her to rest. She came back. Noah opened the window and the dove flew back onto his hand. Noah put the dove back in its own spot. Seven days later the dove was let out again. It flew far, far away, all day long. Then in the evening when it came back, the dove had a little twig with green leaves on it in its beak. She had picked that twig from a tree sticking out above the water. That was how far the water had gone down. It made the people in the ark very happy. And then seven days later the dove was let out again. That day it did not come back again. The earth was dry.

Then the LORD opened the ark. Noah and all the others could come out into the beautiful sunshine. The animals could go out to the fields, the forests, and the mountains. The birds could go and build their nests in the trees. The flowers began to bloom on the green land and the earth became beautiful once more.

Noah and his family thanked God. Their happy eyes looked up to heaven. The LORD had taken care of them so wonderfully. There in the sky they saw something very beautiful. High in the clouds stood a lovely bow with seven colours. A rainbow! And God said to Noah, "Now I will never drown the world again. Do not be afraid; look at the rainbow in the sky."

Noah and his sons built a new house on the new earth. They lived long, happy years there. They knew God would take care of them, always.

ABRAHAM

It was very quiet on the road, and very lonely. The birds sang in the trees; the flowers bloomed in the grass. The sand and the stones on the road were warm from the sunshine. No one was there. It was very quiet and very lonely in the wide land around the road, too.

But look! There, far away in the distance! What was it? There were people and animals coming along the road. Look how many! They came very slowly. In the lead came a big animal — a camel. It had a tall hump on its back. Way on top of the hump sat a stately old gentleman. He was the master of all those people and animals. Beside him rode his wife, very splendidly, on a big camel, too.

They rode on slowly, very slowly, because following them came sheep, cattle, donkeys, camels, and little lambs skipping along. All those animals often stopped to nibble on the grass growing along the roadside. Sometimes they walked into the fields, or climbed onto the green hills. But all those men and women were taking care of them. They were shepherds. They were all servants of that one rich master riding up in front. Indeed, that man and his wife were very rich. They had servants and maids, cattle and sheep, silver and gold; but — they did not have children. Not one. That was very sad.

On and on they went along the hot road, very slowly. When evening came, all those people and animals looked for a place among the hills to rest. Then the servants prepared a warm tent for their master, made of long sticks and animal skins. They put up tents for themselves, too. Then they went to sleep. But not everyone; some servants had to take turns watching the animals. In the dark night a lion or tiger could come to hurt them.

When morning came, they continued their journey. Whenever they reached a spot where the grass grew green, they would stop. All the animals could graze there. Whenever they reached a creek where fresh water streamed, the animals would drink. And so they journeyed on, very slowly, very patiently.

The rich man's name was Abraham. His wife's name was Sarah. They came from a faraway land. They had taken everything they owned along — their servants, their livestock, their money, and their goods. Where were they going? They did not know. Abraham did not know. Sarah did not know. The servants did not know at all. They journeyed steadily on, farther and farther.

Did no one know where they were going? Yes, God in heaven knew. He had commanded Abraham, "Come out of your land and journey to another land that I will show you." Abraham had listened to God's voice. He loved God. He had thought, "I shall do what my Father in heaven tells me. I shall be obedient." And now he was going on through the lands, along the roads, over the hills, and over the mountains, always farther. He did not know the way. His servants did not know the way at all. But Abraham thought, "My Father in heaven knows the way. He will show me where I must go. He will take care of me. I will do everything that God tells me to do." Obeying God filled Abraham's heart with happiness.

One day they came to a broad river. They had to cross the river to the other side, but there was no bridge anywhere. Then the servants searched for a shallow spot. Very carefully they crossed over to the other side, Abraham and Sarah, the servants, the maids, and the livestock. The big animals could cross alone. The little lambs were carried. It was very dangerous, but Abraham was not afraid. He knew that God would take care of him and the animals, too.

And when they came to the other side, the LORD said to Abraham, "This is the land I will give you. Here you may live and I shall always take care of you."

There were very many people on the earth, but God had chosen Abraham. There were very many lands on the earth, but God chose this land, and the LORD Himself brought Abraham to this beautiful land.

That was wonderful for Abraham. Abraham could stay there, and later his children could live there, too. They would grow up and more and more children would be born. So many would be born that there would finally be a great nation living in that land, all children of Abraham. That nation would be God's people. But God promised something else to Abraham. That was the most beautiful promise of all. One day in that land the Lord Jesus would be born — God's own Son.

Abraham listened reverently. God's words filled him with joy. But the LORD spoke about children, many children, and Abraham and Sarah had no children — not one. How could that be? Abraham did not know.

One beautiful evening, God said to Abraham, "Look up, Abraham." Abraham did and saw the dark sky. He also saw the stars that twinkled everywhere.

The LORD asked, "Can you count the stars?" Oh, no, Abraham could not do that — no one can count them. Then the LORD said, "One day as many people as the stars shall live in this land. No one shall be able to count them."

Now Abraham did not have children, not one. But he believed what the LORD said, and he was very happy and content. He waited. He built his tents near a great forest. His sheep and his cattle and his camels could graze in the beautiful green meadows. His servants would be the shepherds. And Abraham waited. He waited quietly and patiently. What God promises always happens.

LOT

Standing on a high hill stood a man peering into the distance, looking very sad. That man was Abraham. But why was there so much sadness in his heart? Why were his eyes looking into the distance so full of fear?

Far, far away lay a beautiful land, even more beautiful than Abraham's land. The grass grew greener there and the flowers bloomed prettier. The water was very fresh there. It was a beautiful, rich, wonderful land. Lot lived there.

Lot was Abraham's nephew. When Lot spoke to Abraham, he called him "Uncle Abraham." Lot was rich, too. He also had many sheep and camels. He had come along with Abraham on his great journey, but he had not stayed with Abraham. Lot had gone to that beautiful land in the distance. Lot had wanted to become very, very rich. He had thought, "In that beautiful land the grass grows tall and the water is fresh. My sheep and cows and camels will grow quickly there. I will get many more, and I shall become very rich."

So Lot went to that other land, to the city of Sodom. Was that why Abraham looked so sad? No, not because of that. Abraham was sorrowful because of Lot. Something terrible was going to happen. God had told that to Abraham.

Why was something terrible going to happen?

That land in the distance was a rich and beautiful land. But the people living there were wicked. They did bad things. They were disobedient to God. And now God had told Abraham that the beautiful land was going to be destroyed, and the wicked people would all die. That was their punishment. It was their own fault.

Abraham looked into the distance. He thought of Lot. That made him so sad. Poor Lot! He had wanted to become rich — now he would become poor. "Why did you want to live near those wicked, bad people? That was not according to the will of God, Lot. You should not have done that."

Abraham was very sad. He returned home. He knew that whatever God says will surely happen. God's holy eyes did not want to see the sin and wickedness of the people.

It was a beautiful evening. Lot was sitting in the gate of the city of Sodom, where the wicked people lived. He noticed two men coming in the distance, two strangers. Lot did not know them. But Lot was a friendly man. He immediately went up to them and said, "I would like to help you. Come to my house. Eat and sleep in my house. Look, the evening is coming. The road is lonely and the night cold. Come along with me. I shall take good care of you."

The men did. They went along to Lot's house. But then what happened? Those wicked people from the city came. They banged on Lot's door. They shouted, "There are two strangers in this house. We saw them. We want to have them. Bring them outside. Bring them outside right now, Lot!"

Lot became frightened. Those wicked people wanted to hurt the two strange men! Lot went outside himself and said, "Don't do that. You may not do that."

But those people became very angry at Lot. They scolded him. They wanted to grab him. But suddenly something strange happened. They tried to grab Lot, but they could not find him, and they could not find the door of his house either. They had suddenly become blind.

How could that be? Those two strange men had done that. They had pulled Lot inside and made those wicked people outside terribly confused. Then Lot looked reverently at those two strangers. He was afraid. These were not ordinary men. They were two angels from heaven, and they had come into his house. Yes, that scared Lot. But when they explained why they had come and what they had come to do, it frightened Lot even more.

Outside, the wicked people shouted and screamed. Lot was not afraid of those people any longer, but he was very afraid about what the angels had told him. They said, "This beautiful land where you are living will be destroyed by fire. God in heaven does not want to see the sin and evil of the people any longer.

All will die, but you, Lot, you and your wife and your daughters may escape."

That was a terrible message. That was a frightening night.

Very early in the morning, when it was still dark outside, the angels said to Lot, "Hurry, get out of here. Go quickly away, for now the punishment is coming."

Lot thought it was so dreadful, so very terrible! Everything he owned — his money and his goods — everything, he had to leave behind. Oh, he couldn't, he didn't want to hurry away. He waited and he waited.

But finally the angels grabbed his hand. They said, "Hurry; quickly flee, or you will die, too." They brought him outside the gate of the city, along with his wife and his two daughters. "Go, go now! Hurry!"

Morning dawned. The soft, golden sunshine shone over the beautiful land. The flowers bloomed, the birds sang, the grass swayed in the wind. But still Lot had to leave. He had to leave quickly. In the distance were the mountains. That was where they would go.

There they went, Lot, his wife, and his daughters. Hurry, hurry! The sky was turning a strange red, and it was thundering, and bolts of lightning were flashing down. Fire was falling from heaven everywhere. Away, away, as fast as they could run. Away! The city, the beautiful city with the beautiful land was on fire! The houses and the steeples, everything was on fire.

"Away, hurry!" the angels had warned. "God will take care of you. But do not turn around to look! Not even once."

Lot did not turn around. Oh, no! And his daughters did not turn around either. But Lot's wife did. How she wanted to stay in the city of Sodom! She thought it was too bad that they had to leave, and then she became disobedient to God. She wanted to look back. She stopped and turned around to look at the city. She looked and then she died on the very same spot. That was her own fault.

Lot and his daughters fled away. Oh, that fire, and that smoke! Everything was burning, the beautiful land, the beautiful city, everything! But God saved Lot and his daughters just as

He had promised. The angels had done their work. Now they went back to heaven.

On that same morning, Abraham stood on the high hill again. He looked into the distance, and his face was very sad. He saw the flames and the smoke. Yes, now that beautiful, rich land was destroyed. Those sinful, wicked people were punished. That was their own fault.

Lot was saved, but he had become poor, very poor. He had wanted to become rich and had gone to live with wicked people. That was wrong. Now he had lost everything, so he went to the mountains. He no longer had a house. He had to live in a cave, just like a very poor man. That was his own fault.

HAGAR AND ISHMAEL

One day there was a celebration in the tents of Abraham. It was a big, happy celebration. Do you know why? A baby was born. Abraham and Sarah were very old, and yet they received a little child from God, a son. It was a wonderful reason to have a happy celebration. Abraham and Sarah had waited such a long, long time. God Himself had promised it, and what God has promised always happens. Abraham had been very patient, but now the wonderful event had come. Now a son had been born in the tent, a dear little boy. His name was Isaac.

But there was another boy in Abraham's tent, a big boy. Abraham loved him very much, too. His name was Ishmael, and Hagar was his mother. That boy and his mother were not happy. They were not happy at all. The boy thought, "Now Abraham will love little Isaac more than me. And Isaac will get most of Abraham's lovely things, not me." Ishmael was angry in his heart at Isaac. His mother Hagar was angry, too. She thought, "If only Isaac had not been born. Now Abraham will love Isaac much more than my Ishmael." And on that big happy celebration, Ishmael teased little Isaac.

Then old Sarah, the mother of little Isaac, became very angry. She called Abraham. She said, "Send that Ishmael and his mother away. They are angry at little Isaac, and Isaac is our very own child. That boy Ishmael belongs to a strange woman. Send them away."

Abraham did not want to do that. He loved Ishmael very much. But God spoke to Abraham: "Abraham, do it!"

Then Abraham obeyed. He thought, "If God tells me, it must be right. God will take care of Ishmael, too." Abraham gave Hagar and her son food for the journey, and a jug of water. Then he let them go to a faraway land, where Hagar had lived a long time ago. "God will take care of you, Ishmael," he softly whispered.

There they went — the mother with her son. They travelled the long, hot journey to the faraway land. Their backs were scorched by the sun. Their bare feet were burned by the sand. Often they became thirsty. Then they drank from the good, cool water out of the jug. But the road was so very long and quiet and lonely. Not one tree grew alongside the road, not one house could be seen. They were travelling through the desert. Everywhere there was sand and stones, with here and there a small shrub. The sun beat down. The sand was hot and dry. Their feet burned in that hot sand. And they were so tired. They were thirsty again, so they drank from the cool water out of the jug. Again and again they drank.

"Mother, I am so thirsty," Ishmael said. And Hagar let him drink again. Oh, but there was only a little water left.

"Mother, I am so thirsty. Give me water, just a little bit." And Hagar gave it to him. How tired her son was. He could hardly go on.

"Come along," she said, holding onto him. They went on once more in that burning sand and scorching sun.

"Mother! Water!" Ishmael begged. She gave it to him, the last drop. Then they walked on, their feet dragging through the hot sand.

Then Ishmael could not go on. His knees trembled. "Mother, I am so thirsty . . . so thirsty." But Hagar had no more water. She had given him everything she had. Not one drop was left in the jug. And nowhere, nowhere was water to be found. She could not see a brook or stream or well anywhere. There was no little house where they could ask for water. There was no tree to rest under.

"Mother . . . thirsty!" Ishmael sank down. He could not walk any farther. Hagar wanted to carry him, but she could not. He was too big, and she was tired herself.

"Ishmael, Ishmael," she cried.

He did not answer. His eyes were closed, his cheeks were pale, his arms hung limp, and he groaned with pain.

Ishmael would die. If she did not find water, Ishmael would surely die. He would die of thirst. But there was no water anywhere. Not one drop.

Then Hagar took hold of her son anyway, and she carried him just a little way, laying him down under a small bush. His head was in the shade. Then she ran away, crying and weeping with sorrow. "Oh, Ishmael, Ishmael. My son, my dear son. Now you are dying, dying of thirst." She fell down in the hot sand. She kept her hands in front of her eyes. She did not dare to look at Ishmael any longer. How sad, how terribly sad it was!

Then suddenly — what was that? Who was calling? Was someone calling? Was someone there? But where? Listen. A friendly voice was calling. It said, "Hagar, fear not. God has heard Ishmael."

Who was that? Who was saying that? It was an angel from heaven speaking to Hagar. He pointed to a well filled with fresh water, right nearby. She had not even seen it. Hagar jumped up, she filled her jug, and ran to Ishmael. Wonderful, oh, wonderful!

She put the jug to his lips. Oh, how wonderful! Then Ishmael was better again. His cheeks turned pink, his legs became strong, and together they could continue their journey. They took their jug along, filled with cool water.

Their heavenly Father had taken such good care of them. He had sent His angel to help them. Abraham had said, "God will take care of you, Ishmael." That was what had happened. God never forgets His promises.

That mother and her son arrived safely in the faraway land, and God always took care of them. Ishmael became a big, strong man. He was not angry any longer at Isaac, who now lived far, far away in Abraham's tent.

THE FATHER AND HIS CHILD

Isaac had grown into a big boy. He was a good boy. His father, Abraham, loved him very much. Abraham was extremely rich: he had cattle and sheep, donkeys and camels — thousands of them! He had silver and gold. But Isaac was his greatest treasure. He would not mind to give away all his tents, his money, or his goods. But to give Isaac away to someone else? No, never! Isaac was such a loving son. Abraham cherished him most of all.

But one day God called to Abraham. Abraham listened. Abraham liked to listen when God spoke to him. But this time Abraham was startled. He was terribly frightened. God said, "Give me your son, your only son, whom you love so much. Go to the land in the distance, to one of the mountains which I will show you. And there give me your son."

It was dreadful. Abraham often gave offerings. Then he would slaughter a sheep and burn it on a pile of stones. The smoke would rise up, and then it would be as though Abraham had given his sheep to God.

But now . . .? Must he now give Isaac, his dear son, whom he loved above everything else? Must he slaughter Isaac and then burn him on one of the mountains? If God had asked for all his animals, all his money, and all his goods, he would gladly have given them. "But now, oh, my Isaac, my dear, dear son."

Yet Abraham was obedient. He thought, "God gave Isaac to me Himself. I will give Isaac back to God. It is very awful, but I want to do everything that God asks of me."

And God's heart rejoiced because of Abraham's obedience. The heavenly Father knew what He would do.

It was early in the morning when Abraham arose. He called two of his servants and fetched a donkey. He prepared everything for the journey. He did it all very quietly. And then he called Isaac. When he saw his dear son, he became very sad. Yet they went away together. Where to? The two servants did not know. Isaac did not know either. Yes, they could see that Abraham was going to burn an offering to God, but Abraham was so quiet, he seemed so sad. And they were going so far away. Why?

They travelled one day, then another day.

On the third day they arrived at a mountain. Abraham stopped. He told his servants, "You stay here with the donkey. I and my son will climb the mountain."

There they went, the father and his child. Abraham carried the pot of fire and a sharp knife. Isaac carried a large bundle of wood on his shoulder.

"Father?"

"Yes, my son, what is it?"

"Father, you are carrying the fire, and I am carrying the wood. But where is the lamb that needs to be slaughtered and burned?"

Abraham felt the great sorrow burning in his heart. He did not dare to tell Isaac: "Isaac, my son, you must be that lamb." No, Abraham did not dare. He said, "God will provide an offering, Isaac."

Then they went on together, the father and his child.

When they reached the top of the mountain, they built a pile of stones together. Together they laid the wood on top of the stones. And then? Then Abraham told Isaac what God had said. He took Isaac in his arms and pressed him against himself. His dear, precious son! He wanted to keep him so very much. But God had said it. And what God says is always good.

"Isaac, you must be the lamb."

"Oh, Father, me?" Isaac was afraid, but he did not pull himself loose, he did not run away. Isaac knew that God loved him. He wanted to be obedient, just like his father. It was dreadful, so terribly dreadful. But Isaac said very quietly, "Yes, Father."

And then Isaac was laid upon the wood and tied down with ropes just like when a lamb was slaughtered. And then — oh, that knife!

"Abraham! Abraham!" a voice called. "Abraham, do not hurt Isaac!" That was God's voice. No, the LORD did not want Isaac to die. The LORD wanted to test Abraham, to see if he would give Him everything. And now God saw that Abraham would even give Him Isaac, his beloved son. God's heart rejoiced because Abraham was obedient. "Do not hurt Isaac! You do not have to do it."

Then the sharp knife quickly cut the ropes loose. Isaac jumped off the wood, and his father pressed him close in his arms. He was allowed to keep him.

Suddenly something rustled in the bushes. What was it? A ram! It had gotten stuck in the branches of the bush. Abraham caught the ram. Now it was just as Abraham had told Isaac — God provided the offering. Here was a ram to offer to God.

After they sacrificed the ram, Abraham and Isaac went down the mountain, back to the servants and the donkey. Together they went home, to Mother Sarah. How happy, how very happy they were! At first it had been so awful, but now everything had become wonderful. Their heavenly Father loved them. He would always take care of them.

God spoke, "Abraham, you have been obedient. You were willing to give Me everything. I shall bless you and make you happy. You shall be My faithful servant. I shall never forget you and your children."

JACOB AND ESAU

Now Isaac was living in the tent of Abraham. Mother Sarah had died, and Father Abraham, too. And Isaac had become a grown man. Now he was God's servant, just as his father Abraham had been before. Outside the tent two boys were playing. They were two brothers, Isaac's children. Their mother was Rebekah. But they did not play with each other. No! Look, one little boy played quietly with the lambs. He was very careful, and took good care of them. The other one, the big boy, climbed in the trees and chased the wild birds away. The quiet one was called Jacob, and the other, the wild one, was called Esau. They were two brothers but they did not look alike at all. Esau's skin was rough and hairy. Jacob's skin was soft and smooth. Esau was the oldest. Jacob was the youngest.

When Father Isaac would grow old and die, who would become God's servant, Esau or Jacob? God said Jacob would become His servant, but Isaac loved Esau the most: he was so strong and wild. Mother Rebekah loved Jacob the most: he was obedient and quiet. Father Isaac sometimes thought, "I so wish Esau could be God's servant." Mother Rebekah thought, "I wish Jacob would be God's servant. God has told us, but will it happen?" That was not right of Isaac and Rebekah. They had to believe what God told them. Whatever God says always happens.

Jacob and Esau grew up and became men. They were two brothers, but they were not alike at all. Look, Jacob took care of the sheep. He was a quiet man. He liked to stay near home and help his mother in the tent. He was very thoughtful to her. Rebekah loved him the most.

But what about Esau? There he went. He did not stay near the tents and the sheep and his mother. He went far away into the fields and the forest and climbed the mountains. He was a hunter, a wild, big, and strong man. He carried big sharp arrows with him, a bow to shoot, and a big knife. He hunted the animals in the forest. He was not afraid of the wildest animal. And when he returned home, he would roast the meat of the animals that he had caught. That smelled good, and tasted delicious. Father Isaac got the best piece. Father Isaac enjoyed it so much. Yes, Father Isaac loved rough Esau the most.

Sometimes Jacob thought, "If only I was the oldest, then someday I could live in these beautiful tents and be a rich master. And I would be God's servant, just like my father Isaac is now. I would like that very much. But my brother Esau is the oldest. He will become God's servant. How can that be? Esau is so rough. Esau never thinks about God."

One day Jacob sat in his tent cooking a big pot full of lentil soup. It looked good. It was red and smelled delicious. Listen, footsteps sounded outside the tent. Roughly the tent door was shoved open and Esau came in. He had walked and hunted through the forest and fields all day. He was tired and so terribly hungry. Now he smelled that good food, and he saw that big bowl full of red stew. He wanted to start eating it right away. He dropped onto a bench and said to Jacob, "Give me some of that red food there! I am so hungry! Give it to me!"

But Jacob did not give it to him. Jacob was clever. He said, "Oh, you may have it, the whole bowlful, but then I must be the oldest." That was wrong of Jacob. That was not right.

Esau said, "Do you want to be the oldest? Do you want to have most of the things when Father dies? All right! Just give me some of that red food there." That was wrong of Esau, too. He should not have done that. But he did it anyway. He was

JACOB AND ESAU

careless. He gobbled the whole bowl empty, then he left. He did not care who was the oldest.

Jacob thought, "Now I will be the oldest. Now I will get the most. Now I will be God's servant." He quietly laughed about Esau's carelessness. That was wicked of Jacob.

Many years passed. Father Isaac was very old and blind. He lay on his bed in the tent most of the time and his eyes could not see anymore. One day he called Esau.

Esau came. "What do you want me to do, my father?"

"Listen," Isaac said. "I am the master of all the servants and the sheep and the tents. I am very rich. But I am very old and shall soon die. Who shall then be master of all? You must be, Esau, you are the oldest. Go to the forest, Esau. Hunt a deer and roast it for me, I like that so much. Then bring it to me to my bed, and then — then I will bless you. I shall lay my hands on your head and then you shall be master over all the servants and the sheep, and the tents will be yours. Then you shall be master over your brother Jacob, too. You are the oldest." That was what Isaac said. But did he not know what God had said?

Someone was standing outside the tent. Who was that? Who was listening? Isaac did not notice. Esau did not notice either. Esau left. He got his bow and arrows and went to the forest. He was very cheerful, but he was not honest. Esau had promised Jacob that he could be the oldest. Now he wanted to be the oldest anyway. He wanted the blessing from his father himself. Esau knew what he had promised, but he did not care. He laughed about it. Esau was always careless. Briskly he went into the forest.

But who had been listening outside the tent? It was Mother Rebekah. She had heard everything. She was afraid. She thought, "Now Esau will get the great blessing and not Jacob, and I wanted Jacob to have the big blessing." She went to her own tent and called Jacob. "Jacob, come here quickly."

When Jacob came, he asked, "What is it, Mother?" Rebekah said, "Quickly, Jacob, get a baby goat and slaughter it. I shall prepare the kid as your father likes it and then you must bring it to your father Isaac. He will think you are Esau, and give you the big blessing. Quickly, Jacob."

Jacob was afraid. He did not dare. He said, "Esau's skin is so rough and hairy but my skin is so soft and smooth. Father cannot see me, he is blind, but he will feel that I am not Esau."

Rebekah said, "Do it anyway, Jacob, I know what to do." That was wrong of Rebekah and Jacob. They were going to deceive old, blind Isaac.

Rebekah made a savoury roast. Then she took the skin of the kid and put it on Jacob's hands, and dressed him in Esau's best clothes. Those clothes smelled like the forest. Then Jacob went to his father. It was very, very wrong of him to do that.

Isaac heard someone coming in. He could not see. He asked, "Who is there?"

Jacob said, "I am Esau."

But Isaac did not believe it. "You have returned so soon and you sound strange. Come here. Let me feel your hands."

Jacob knelt beside his father's bed. Isaac felt all over Jacob's hands and neck. Yes, they were hairy and rough. He said, "Your hands are Esau's hands but you speak so soft. You speak like Jacob. That is so strange. Are you truly Esau?"

"Yes, Father, I am truly Esau." That was very wrong of Jacob. He deceived his old, blind father.

Then Isaac believed that Esau was kneeling there by his bed. He laid his old hands on his son's head and said, "I give you the big blessing. You shall be master of all the servants and the sheep and the tents. You shall also be master over your brother. You shall be very rich, and God in heaven shall take care of you."

Jacob arose and left quickly. Now he had received the big blessing, but he was not very happy. He had done a great wrong. He could not be happy.

But who was coming now? It was Esau. He was so happy, he had shot a deer. Now he was going to roast it as good as he could. Then he opened the tent where his father Isaac lay on his bed.

Isaac asked, "Who is there?"

"I am your son, Esau."

Isaac trembled. "Esau?" Yes, this was Esau. This was the real Esau. Isaac heard it in his rough voice. "O Esau, Esau, I do not have the big blessing anymore. I gave the big blessing to

Jacob! Jacob was here. I thought it was you here beside my bed! Oh, Esau, Esau!"

Esau shouted angrily. He fell beside his father's bed and cried, "Have you no blessing for me? Bless me also, my father!"

Then Isaac laid his old hands on Esau's head. He said, "Your brother Jacob shall be master of all the servants and the sheep and the tents. But you, Esau, will not be poor. You shall have many servants, too. But your brother Jacob will be the richest. He will be first."

Esau left. When he was outside the tent he shook his fist, he was so angry. He was angry at Jacob. "I will kill him," he said.

Mother Rebekah heard it. She was very frightened. "Jacob, go away quickly to that far land where I lived as a girl, to your Uncle Laban. Esau will kill you. Go away, far away. Esau is so angry, he is so strong and so rough."

Jacob went. Quietly he sneaked away. Now everyone was sad. No one was happy. Isaac, Jacob, Esau, and Mother Rebekah were all very sad. Rebekah watched Jacob walk out of sight. She was very sad. She thought, "Now Jacob is gone. I have lost my son." Yes, but it was her own fault.

Jacob walked on and on. He was so alone. He was so poor. He was so sad. Yes, but it was his own fault. They had all sinned. They could not be happy. That was their punishment.

A BEAUTIFUL DREAM

A man was walking along with his head bowed. His eyes were sad. It was quiet and lonely in the vast land. He was so alone. He was so tired. It was Jacob, who had deceived his father. He had wanted to become rich, but now he was poor. He had wanted to become God's servant, but now he had done such a great wrong that his heart was afraid of God. Would he never return to his mother, or his father, or his sheep?

He walked on and on very sorrowfully. Darkness set in. He could not see the way any longer and he was so tired and sleepy. But there were no houses here where he could sleep. He was all alone in the dark night and he could not go farther. Some big stones were lying in the field. Jacob took one, and then he lay down on the ground with his head on the stone. He fell asleep — he was very tired from walking so far.

But when he was asleep, he dreamed something wonderful. It frightened him, and yet it was beautiful. Look, the dark sky opened and everything became light. What a beautiful light! Then angels came down from heaven, more and more angels. They came down a ladder to the earth. They shone like the sunlight. Their clothes seemed to be sunbeams. It was wonderful! Then they climbed back up to heaven again, a long, long row of angels. And up in heaven was God Himself. Jacob's heart was afraid. God knows everything. God knew what had happened. Then a voice spoke. The LORD Himself spoke to Jacob. It was not an angry voice. No, the LORD said, "I am the God of Abraham and Isaac. I shall be your God, too. You shall be My servant and I shall always help you. I shall always take care of you. And later you will return to this land and live here with all your children."

Jacob listened. He was ashamed. He had done such a great sin, yet he was allowed to be God's servant. How he wished he had not committed that great sin!

When Jacob awoke, he looked up at the sky. The beautiful angels were gone and he did not hear God's voice anymore. It had been a dream. Jacob had dreamed, but Jacob was no longer afraid. He looked up to heaven and prayed,

"O LORD, I wanted to be Thy servant so much, but I did a great wrong. Please let me be Thy servant as my father is. Help me, LORD, take care of me. Let me live here again someday, and let me love Thee always."

Jacob took the stone and set it upright. He had a little jar of oil with him which he emptied on the stone. He thought, "God sees that; He sees everything. Later, when I return from that faraway land, I will come back to this stone. I must never forget this place. When I return from that faraway land I shall thank God at this very same spot."

Then Jacob continued his journey. Did he go home? No, that was not possible. He could not. Jacob had to go to that faraway land, poor and alone. That was his punishment. It was his own fault. But he was no longer afraid. He always remembered his beautiful dream. He thought, "God will take care of me. Yes, I will always do what God tells me. I want to love God with my whole heart."

So Jacob travelled happily the long, long way to the faraway land where his Uncle Laban lived.

JACOB RETURNS

Camels, sheep, cattle, and donkeys were slowly moving along. It was a big, enormous flock, a long, long caravan of animals. Servants carefully lead them on. On one of the camels rode the master of the caravan and on other camels rode his two wives and his sons and daughters. Who was that rich master? Where did he come from? It was Jacob. Many long years had passed since he fled from Esau and had slept with his head on the stone. Then he had been poor and sad, now he was rich and happy. God had taken care of him. Jacob had stayed with his Uncle Laban in that faraway land. He had married Laban's two daughters and had received children and sheep and camels and cattle in great numbers. But he had wanted to go back to his own land very much. He always remembered, "In my beautiful dream, when I slept with my head on the stone, the LORD promised that I would return. It shall surely happen." And now after many long years, Jacob was returning.

As he came very near his own land his heart filled with fear. Why? He was thinking of long ago. He remembered Esau. That made his heart afraid. He thought, "I deceived my old blind father. I deceived Esau. I did much wrong. Esau will be angry when he sees me."

And Esau was coming. Far in the distance he could be seen coming with his servants, riding on camels and carrying swords and spears. They were wild, strong men. What would happen when Esau saw Jacob? Who would help Jacob?

Jacob knew he had done a great wrong and he was so sorry. He thought, "I was very wicked. I deserve severe punishment. It is my own fault that I am so afraid." In his fear he started to pray. "God, help me. Forgive me my wrong." Then in the dark night, when Jacob was outside all alone, the LORD came to him and said, "I will help you. I promised. Do not fear." Then Jacob's heart was filled with joy.

The next morning Esau came riding along, with all his strong, wild men. Dust flew up from their speeding camels. Sharp spears flashed in the sunlight. Jacob saw him coming, but he remembered what God had told him. He walked up to Esau and bowed down before him. Then Esau jumped off his camel and walked up to Jacob. Was he looking angry? Would he grab his sword? Oh, no, Esau was not thinking about the past. Esau was no longer angry. Esau opened wide his strong arms, and he pressed Jacob to his chest and kissed him. He was so happy to see his brother again. How wonderful! God had done that. He had made Esau's angry heart into a friendly heart. The LORD can do anything. How happy the two brothers were!

Esau left with his wild, strong men again. Jacob went to live in Isaac's tent. That no longer angered Esau. Father Isaac was still alive, but he was very, very old. Soon he died. Mother Rebekah had died long ago.

One night, long ago, Jacob had lain in the dark night and slept with his head on a stone. Then he had dreamed that beautiful dream about the long ladder and the angels climbing on it. Then he had heard the voice of God, who said, "Jacob, you will become My servant. I shall take care of you, and later you will return and live in this land with all your children."

Now that promise had been fulfilled. Jacob lived in this beautiful land with all his children. His heart was so happy. He lived on the same spot where first Father Abraham had lived, and then Father Isaac. They had been God's servants and now Jacob was God's servant. He had desired that with all his heart. Now it was so. What God promises always happens.

JOSEPH

Along the quiet road a young man walked. He kept looking into the distance, but would then shake his head. No, he did not see anyone. He appeared to be a rich young man, wearing a beautiful many-coloured robe. He looked like a prince. What was he searching for on that quiet road? He saw someone coming, and the young man asked, "Have you seen my brothers? I am searching for them, but cannot find them. My ten grown-up brothers and their sheep. Have you seen them?"

"Yes, but they are not here anymore. They have gone on farther into the hills," the stranger said.

So the young man continued farther, too. Through the wide lands, over the hills, and through the valleys he went. All the time he was thinking, "I wish I could find them. Where could they be?"

That young man wearing the beautiful robe was Joseph. He was one of Father Jacob's sons. Father Jacob had twelve sons, but they did not all wear beautiful many-coloured robes. Oh, no. Only Joseph did, because Father Jacob loved Joseph the most. Only Joseph had received such a beautiful robe.

The brothers were not happy about that at all. They were angry with Joseph. Joseph was a little proud, too. Sometimes he dreamed in the night, strange beautiful dreams.

Once he dreamed he was in a wheat field. They all had bound sheaves of wheat and stood them straight up in the field. And then? It was a very strange dream — then the brothers' sheaves all bowed down to Joseph's sheaf as if it was the king. Joseph told that dream to his brothers when he awoke. It made them angry. They said, "Must we bow down to you? We are much older than you. No, we will never do that." Oh, it was only a dream.

But another time Joseph dreamed again. It was a strange and wonderful dream. He dreamed he was a star in the heavens. Then eleven other stars came to bow down before him; yes, even the sun and the moon bowed down to him as if he was the king. Again Joseph told his dream to his brothers when he awoke. But that made them even more angry. They said, "Must we bow down before you? And must our father and mother bow down before you, too, just like the sun and the moon? No! Do you hear? We will never do that. You are a master dreamer. That is what we will call you — Master Dreamer."

The brothers did not love Joseph. Their hearts were resentful toward him. They always had to leave home to shepherd the sheep and cows far away, searching for grass for the animals. They went here, and then they went there but Joseph stayed home with Father Jacob. Sometimes Joseph would hear bad things about his brothers; he would tell them to his father. How the brothers disliked Joseph! They hated him!

Now Joseph was walking along the quiet road, searching for his ten brothers. One of Father Jacob's sons was still at home. He was only a small boy. His name was Benjamin.

The ten big brothers had gone far away with the sheep, and stayed away such a long time. Father Jacob had said, "Joseph, go see where your brothers are. Ask them how they are doing and bring back a report to me. I am rather concerned about them."

That was why Joseph was walking such a long, long way.

But finally he saw sheep and cows and donkeys grazing on the hills. And even farther away he could see his brothers. They were lying on the grass under the trees. How wonderful — there they were! Joseph was so happy. He hurried to reach them sooner.

The brothers saw him coming. "Look," they said to each other, "There comes that master dreamer!" Their eyes were not happy at all — their eyes were angry. "See, he is wearing his beautiful many-coloured robe, and we don't have any. He thinks he is the most important of us brothers. Likely that master dreamer is coming to see if we are doing something wrong!" Their hearts were so angry at Joseph.

Then one of them whispered, "I know what."

The others listened.

He said, "We'll kill him — that master dreamer. Then he will be gone."

But Reuben whispered, "No, don't kill him." Reuben was the oldest. He felt a little sorry for Joseph. He thought, "Our poor father will be terribly grieved if Joseph does not return home." He said, "No, let's not kill him. I know something better. We will drop him into an empty well. He will not be able to get out of there anyway." Reuben was a little afraid of his other brothers.

"All right. We will drop him into an empty well," the others agreed.

There came Joseph. He was very close. His eyes shone with happiness and friendliness. He stretched out his hands to his brothers.

But . . .

What was the matter? Oh, what was it? His angry brothers jumped up. They shouted angry words at him. They grabbed him with their rough, hard hands. They ripped off his beautiful many-coloured robe.

"No, no!" Joseph cried. "Why are you doing this?"

But his angry brothers pushed him along and pulled on his arms. They dragged him to a deep well and pushed him in. Thud!

Joseph cried, Joseph pleaded, "Let me out! Please let me out!"

But they laughed at him. They ate their bread under the trees in the shade. Reuben, the oldest, quietly left. He thought, "After, when it is dark, I will pull Joseph out of the pit. Not now, I do not dare." Reuben was afraid of the other brothers.

Poor Joseph. There he lay, deep in the pit, afraid and so alone. It was very dark and damp in the well and he could not get out. The well was too deep. He called, he cried, he pleaded. It made no difference, none at all. Would he have to stay down there forever? And what if his brothers would go away? Would they leave him alone? What then? Oh, what then? Joseph looked up. High above he could see a little patch of blue sky. Up there was a little bit of heaven. Joseph folded his hands. He prayed.

Joseph knew that God lives up in heaven. God knows everything. He sees everything. Yes, He knew how wicked the brothers were. He saw poor Joseph, even though the well was very dark and very deep.

Father Jacob had often told Joseph about God. He would tell him how good God had been to him in his life. Joseph thought, "The LORD can do anything. He can take care of me, too." Then Joseph quietly sat down. "I shall be content. I do not know what is going to happen to me, but God does. I shall be still."

The brothers ate their bread. They talked and they laughed. And Joseph's beautiful robe lay torn in the sand. Suddenly they saw something coming in the distance. It was a caravan of camels carrying large packs on their backs, and men, too. The brothers knew who they were. They were Ishmaelites. They had bought goods in another land and they were going to Egypt to sell their goods.

"We can sell Joseph to them!" Judah whispered, as he pointed to the pit Joseph was in. "Those men can take him along, and he can be their slave! Yes, let's do that. Then we are rid of him, and we will get some money for him, too." They called the traders with their camels and asked them to stop. A few of the brothers went to the pit. They dropped ropes down and Joseph grabbed them. How happy he was! He could get out! They were pulling him out. But what was this?

Up came those strange men with their camels. They looked at Joseph. They could see how afraid he was, but they did not care. They only looked him over to see if he was strong and healthy. They only calculated if he would make a good servant. Then they said, "All right, we will buy him. We will give you twenty pieces of silver for him."

The brothers laughed. "Sure. Yes, take him along. Then we will be rid of him."

The strange men took hold of Joseph as if he was an animal. They tied his hands with one end of a long rope, the other end they tied to a camel's saddle. One of the men climbed on the camel. "Get up," he commanded.

Poor Joseph. The strong camel dragged him along. He didn't want to. He called, he pleaded, "I do not want to go away. I want to go to my father."

But those wicked brothers laughed. They had received their shiny pieces of silver. Poor Joseph. There he went. Far, far away was his father's house, but he was unable to go there. He might never go there again. He was being dragged away to a faraway land. Father Jacob would be waiting for him. Father Jacob would be looking down the road to see if Joseph was coming. But Joseph would never come again.

"Get up!"

The road was long, the sand was hot and those strange men were so rough. Joseph walked along, his head bowed down. But then — then he looked toward heaven again, to God. He thought, "My father had much sorrow in his life, but the LORD took care of him. God will take care of me, too." And Joseph walked along like a good servant.

When evening came, Reuben went to the pit. He did not know that the brothers had sold Joseph. He called, "Joseph! Joseph!" He did not hear anything. He called louder, "Joseph! Joseph, where are you? Are you dead?" He did not hear anything.

Then he went to the other brothers, and they told him that Joseph was gone to a faraway land and would never return. Reuben was dismayed. "Our father will be very sad. He will be filled with terrible sorrow. He loved Joseph so much. He loved Joseph most of all. He will be angry with us, too."

"No, no," the brothers said. "We know what to do. We have slaughtered a sheep and dipped Joseph's robe in the blood. Now a servant has taken the dirty robe to Father."

That was what happened. Father Jacob waited at home for Joseph, but Joseph did not come. Instead of Joseph, a servant came. He showed him the robe covered with sand and blood. How it frightened Father Jacob!

"That is Joseph's beautiful robe!" he cried out. "Where did you find it? Oh, a wild animal must have killed my precious son. I have lost my dear, dear son. Now I shall never be happy again." Father Jacob wept and was terribly sad. Then when the brothers came home, they pretended to be sad, too.

Those deceivers! They deceived their father. Yes, but long, long ago Jacob himself had deceived his blind father, Isaac. Now Jacob was being punished, but he did not realize it.

IN THE FARAWAY LAND

The journey lasted very long. The sand was so hot. Joseph, the poor slave, grew so tired. Finally the tradesmen came into the faraway land of Egypt. There they sold their beautiful purchases on the market. They sold Joseph, too. A rich ruler bought him for some money, just like men bought camels or donkeys. Then Joseph had to come along to the house of the rich man to work there as a slave. That rich man was Potiphar.

Joseph thought about home where he had been the rich son, the favourite of his father. There he had the best place and the most beautiful clothes. But here? Here he was only a servant. He had to do everything that his master commanded. But Joseph still thought, "I will be quiet and obedient and very patient. I will do my work well. I must. God in heaven sees me. God shall take care of me."

The rich lord Potiphar noticed how obedient Joseph was and how well he did his work. Potiphar thought, "This is a good servant." And one day he said to Joseph, "You shall be in charge of all my slaves." That was wonderful for Joseph. His master

IN THE FARAWAY LAND

loved him, and Joseph thought, "God is caring for me. I shall do my best even more."

But then something terrible happened. And it was not Joseph's fault at all.

Potiphar's wife was a wicked woman. She deceived her husband, and she wanted Joseph to deceive him, too. But Joseph would not do it. Then one day she grabbed Joseph by his robe, speaking friendly words to him. She wanted them to deceive her husband together. But Joseph did not want to. He pulled himself away. He did not want to do bad things against his master Potiphar. That was not allowed. That would be a great sin before God, who sees everything. No, Joseph did not want to do it. He pulled himself loose, but the wicked woman held onto Joseph's robe. Then Joseph fled out of the room.

How the woman's wicked eyes flashed with anger! She began to scream very loudly. All the servants came running. And then? Oh, that wicked, deceitful woman! She said, "Joseph wanted to deceive his master Potiphar! I became angry and wanted to hang onto him, but he ran away! Look! I still have his robe in my hand."

That was what she said, but it was exactly the other way around. She told Potiphar that lie, too, and Potiphar believed his wicked wife. He became dreadfully angry at Joseph. He said to his servants, "Bring that wicked servant Joseph to prison!"

Poor Joseph! It was not his fault at all.

Now Joseph sat between dark walls. His feet were locked in a big wooden block. There were heavy chains around his arms. He thought about home. He remembered his father. He remembered the beautiful dreams. He was not proud now. Oh, no. He was not proud at all anymore. He felt so poor, so unhappy, so very alone.

But then he remembered God who knows everything. "God will take care of me. I shall be quiet and content. The LORD sees me here even in this dark prison," Joseph thought, and he prayed quietly.

The jailer who watched over the prisoners observed how quiet and content Joseph was. He thought, "This is not a wicked man." One day he said to Joseph, "You may help me. I shall loosen your feet from the wooden block, and your arms from the heavy chains. You may bring the food to the other prisoners. But you may not go out of prison."

That was pleasant for Joseph. The jailer liked him a little bit. Joseph thought, "God is taking care of me. I shall be very obedient and do my very best." So Joseph was allowed to walk around free in prison. But he could not get out. That was not allowed.

One day two men were brought into prison. They were important men. They came from the king's palace. The one had to pour the wine for the king. He was the chief butler. And the other was the king's chief baker. One of the two had done a great wrong, but the king did not know who. Now the king was angry at both of them. Joseph brought them their food every day. The one was wicked, the other was not. But Joseph did not know who the wicked one was either.

One morning they both appeared very afraid and sad. They looked distressed. Joseph noticed it right away. He asked, "What is the matter with you?"

They said, "We each had a dream last night, and our dreams are somewhat alike. Maybe our dreams will come true, but it makes us so afraid. We do not know what will happen to us. In the king's palace there are many learned men who might be able to help us. But who can help us here?"

Joseph felt sorry for them. He said, "I cannot help you either. But God in heaven knows everything. I shall pray to God for you. Maybe God will tell me what your dreams mean."

And so Joseph did.

When he came back to the two men he said, "Tell me your dreams. God in heaven shall give me wisdom and I may tell you what will happen. Tell me your dreams."

The chief butler told his dream first. "My dream was a beautiful dream. I saw lovely clusters of grapes growing on three large vines. I picked them and pressed them into a cup, and gave it to the king. It seemed to me I was back in the beautiful palace. Then I awoke."

IN THE FARAWAY LAND

Joseph listened. His eyes shone and he said, "That was a good dream. You dreamed about three large vines. After three days you will return to the king."

Next the chief baker told his dream. "My dream was such a strange dream. I was walking outside, carrying three baskets on my head, one on top of the other. Delicious baked goods were in the baskets, like the ones the king always eats. But the top basket was open, and then birds came and picked the basket empty. I awoke in fear."

Joseph listened. His eyes looked serious. Now he knew that the chief baker was the wicked one. His dream was a bad dream. Joseph said, "You spoke of three baskets. In three days you will be killed and the birds will come to pick your flesh."

Three days later was the king's birthday. Then it happened exactly as Joseph had said. The chief baker was taken from prison and killed. He was the wicked one, and received his punishment. But the chief cup bearer was allowed to return to the king in the beautiful palace and pour the wine into the golden cup. He had not done any wrong.

Joseph had not done any wrong either. But he had to remain in prison. He asked the chief butler, "Please, Sir, tell the king I am in prison and have not done anything wrong either. Then perhaps the king will set me free, too."

"Yes, yes, I shall do that. Certainly I shall do that," said the chief butler. He was so happy that Joseph had explained the dream so well, and that he could return to the king. "I shall tell the king everything."

But — the butler forgot. When he was living in the beautiful palace again, he did not remember the poor slave in prison. That was not very kind of him.

Joseph waited. He waited a very long time, until he realized that the butler had forgotten him. That was a great sorrow for Joseph.

And yet, Joseph did his best every day again. He remained patient and very obedient. He thought, "God in heaven knows why I must experience so much sorrow. God will take care of me." And Joseph was quiet and content.

IN THE PALACE

The king of Egypt lived in his beautiful palace. Whatever he said was done.

One night, the king dreamed two strange dreams. In the first dream he stood near a broad river, the Nile River. Suddenly seven cows walked out of the water onto the land. They were beautiful, fat animals. But then — seven more cows came out of the water. They were ugly, skinny animals, and they ate up the seven beautiful fat-looking cows. It frightened Pharaoh awake. Oh, it was only a dream.

Pharaoh fell asleep and dreamed again. It was almost the same dream. He stood at the Nile and saw seven beautiful ears of grain growing, full of kernels of grain. But then seven thin ears of grain grew and ate up the seven beautiful ears. It was a dream again, but it frightened the king. He thought, "Maybe something will happen. Will it be something good? Will it be something bad? I do not know."

All the learned men of Egypt were commanded to come and explain the dream to the king. Whatever the king said had to happen.

There they stood, very upset. Oh, yes, they read many strange books, and they said many strange words, but they did not know the meaning of the king's dreams. Then the king became angry. Yes, but how could they know and tell what would happen, because of the king's strange dreams?

Then . . . only then, the chief butler remembered Joseph. The chief butler was standing behind the king, and all of a sudden he said, "O my lord the king, I know who can tell you about your dreams. Joseph, who is in prison. He can do it. He explained my beautiful dream, too."

"Then Joseph must come here," the king said.

Immediately servants ran to the prison to get Joseph. How poor and dirty Joseph looked! His hair was long. His clothes were dirty. His cheeks were pale. He could not appear before the king in this condition. But the servants knew what to do.

IN THE PALACE

Joseph was washed and his hair was cut. They dressed him in a clean linen suit, and then they hurried him to the king, who was very impatient.

In the king's palace everything was beautiful, very beautiful. The king himself, in his royal clothes, was the most splendid of all. Joseph stood before him. Joseph only had a linen suit on. He was only a poor slave. Yet this mighty, rich king had something to ask of him. Did Joseph look proud? Oh, no, Joseph was not proud anymore. Long ago, in his father's house, he had been. But not anymore. He had endured so much sorrow that he had learned not to be proud any longer.

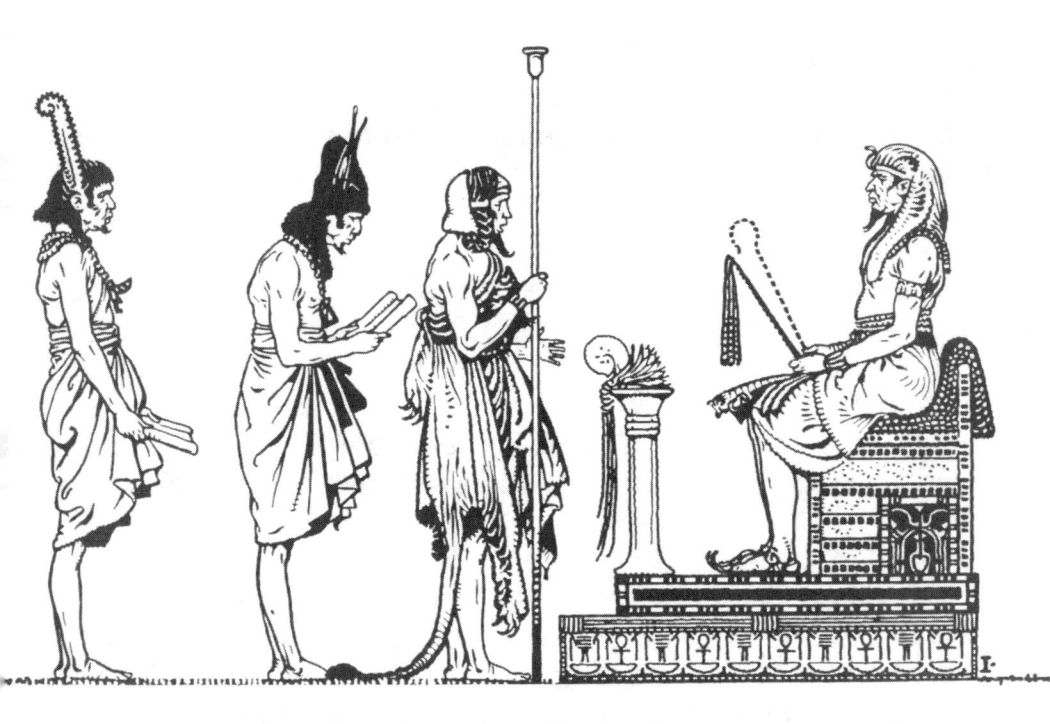

The king asked, "Can you tell me what my strange dreams say will happen?"

Joseph answered, "No, my lord the king, I cannot. But God in heaven knows everything. The LORD in heaven can tell you. Tell me your dreams."

The king told first about the dream of the seven cows, the fat and the lean ones. Then he told about the seven ears of grain, the full and the thin ones. Joseph knew what it meant. God was telling him and he told the king.

Joseph said, "My lord the king, they are beautiful dreams but they are also sad dreams. Something is going to happen. First something wonderful, but then something sad. First seven good years are going to come, seven beautiful years. The grain will grow wondrously in the fields. There will be so much grain, the people will not be able to eat it all. But then seven lean years will come. The grain will shrivel up on the land. There will be so little grain that the people will be hungry. First seven years of plenty, and then seven years of famine.

"You dreamed two times. First about the cows, then about the ears of grain. It shall surely happen.

"O my lord the king, when the grain grows so wonderfully in the land, and when there is so very, very much, you must save it in your barns. Then when the famine comes, your people will have grain for bread and the seven lean years will not be so bad."

That was what Joseph said.

The eyes of the king shone with relief. Now he knew what would happen. This young man, this slave, was a wise man. He had given good advice. The king loved him very much. He said, "Yes, that is right. That is very good. We shall save the grain." But the king said more. He said something wonderful. He said, "I am the king. But you Joseph, you shall be the ruler under me. You must help me. You must make sure that barns are built to save the grain, and everyone must be obedient to you."

And then the king gave Joseph a golden ring on his finger, beautiful clothes, and a golden chain around his neck. Then Joseph rode in the king's chariot, so that everyone would know that Joseph, the poor slave, had become ruler over Egypt.

"Kneel! Kneel!" the servants called. Joseph stood in a royal chariot, beautiful horses pulled him along. He was wearing royal clothes. "Kneel! Kneel!" the servants cried.

The people outside fell on their knees and bowed before Joseph, the ruler of Egypt. All over the land Joseph rode along the streets and roads as if he was king himself. Quietly Joseph stood in the chariot. He watched the people kneel and call to him, but he was not proud.

IN THE PALACE

Now his robe was even more beautiful than the many-coloured robe of long ago. Now he was rich, much richer than Potiphar. But Joseph's heart was quiet and happy. He thought, "God in heaven has taken such good care of me. He has never forgotten me. All my sorrow has suddenly disappeared."

Joseph looked up to heaven, where God lives. Quietly he prayed, "LORD, I thank Thee. I am so very happy. Help me to be a good ruler. I want to do my best. Please help me, LORD."

STRANGE MEN CAME TO THE PALACE

Joseph lived in a beautiful palace. That was only right, for he was ruler, next to the king. He was rich, much richer than Potiphar. He had many servants and slaves, many more than Potiphar. Everyone had to do what he commanded. Joseph commanded good things. He said, "Take care of the grain. Sow it, and reap it, and bring all the grain into the barns. Let none go to waste."

Much grain grew in the fields. The people baked delicious bread, but much was left over. Joseph told them, "Bring it to me. I will pay you for the grain, and I shall save it." And Joseph's servants built large barns, and filled them with grain. Joseph said, "Build more barns. Do not waste any of the grain." For seven years the beautiful grain grew in the land of Egypt. The people brought it to Joseph and Joseph built more and more barns. It seemed like one large city full of grain.

Then came the seven lean years. The seven sad years. The sun burned on the land and the grain dried out. No kernels grew on the grain in the lean years. The people could not bake bread anymore. They became hungry. But that did not matter, not at all. "Come to me!" Joseph said. "I have grain. Barns full of grain." And the people bought grain from the good ruler, as much as they needed. The people loved Joseph. They said, "He has saved our land."

Also from other countries people came to buy grain from Joseph. He had enough — he had barns full of grain. He sold them grain in their hunger. He helped everyone.

One day, strange men came to the palace. They came from the faraway land of Canaan, and they asked for grain, too. They were allowed in. There were ten men. They were brothers. Respectfully they bowed before Joseph. Who were they? Joseph looked at them. He knew them right away. It startled him. Yes, oh yes, it was them! All ten of them! His very own brothers.

STRANGE MEN CAME TO THE PALACE

Joseph wanted to stretch out his arms to them. He wanted to cry, "I am so happy, so very happy to see you again. Is my father alive?" Yes, he wanted to, but he did not. "No," he thought, "They do not know that I am Joseph. Maybe they think I am still a slave. Maybe they think that I have died. But they do not think at all that I am a ruler. I shall pretend to be angry, but I do not mean it. Are my brothers still as wicked as long ago? I will test them."

Joseph looked at them fiercely, and asked in a harsh voice, "What are you here for?"

"My lord, we have come to buy grain. We will give you money. Give us grain for our money. We come from Canaan. Our aged father sent us here."

"That is a lie!" Joseph shouted. "You are spies. You have come to search out the way here, and then you will return later with the soldiers of your land, and you will take away our grain and kill us!"

The brothers became very frightened at those angry words.

"No, my lord," they said. "We are not spies. We are shepherds." And they told him that their father was very old, and that his name was Jacob. And that there was one more brother at home, the youngest, and that his name was Benjamin. And yes, they even said that they had one more brother, but he was gone. His name was Joseph. They did not know that this one brother was sitting before them as a ruler on a throne.

"I do not believe you," Joseph said gruffly. "Go away to your home and fetch your brother Benjamin. I want to see him. Then I will believe that you are not deceivers. Go home, but one of you must stay here. Otherwise you might not come back again."

How distressing! What an angry ruler this man was! Quietly the brothers said to each other, "Our father will be terribly sad. Now we are being punished. We were angry like this to our brother Joseph. He begged but we laughed at him. Now this ruler is angry with us. It must be God's punishment for our wrong."

They thought that Joseph could not understand what they said quietly to each other in their own language. But he understood everything. It made him sad, too. But he continued to be harsh to them. "Go on. One of you, Simeon, stay here."

There went the nine brothers, afraid and sad. Yes, they each had received a sack full of beautiful grain along. But when they opened one of the sacks along the way to roast some grain on a fire, they became very afraid. The money that they had paid to the angry ruler was lying in the sack on top of the grain. How could that be?

They said, "Now that angry ruler will likely say we are thieves and that we secretly took that money along again. But that is not true at all." They became even more afraid and sad.

And when they came home . . .

"No, no!" Father Jacob said. "I will not do it. I will not send Benjamin along to that angry man. Joseph is dead, Simeon is gone; if Benjamin did not return I would die of sorrow. No, I will not allow it."

They ate the good grain. Their hunger was gone. Yet no one was happy. Their hearts were afraid and sad.

After a while, the grain was all used up. Hunger came, and hunger hurts. Then Father Jacob had to let his dear son Benjamin go along anyway. "Take good care of him. Do take good care of him."

The brothers went away with their donkeys and their empty sacks. They went to get grain. Benjamin rode on a donkey too. He had an empty sack too. Father Jacob watched them go. His old heart was torn with grief.

FIRST GRIEF, BUT THEN . . .

It was a long, hard journey. The sand of the desert burned hot. But finally the brothers arrived in the beautiful land of Egypt, where there was grain to fill their hungry stomachs.

They were so scared. They were afraid of that ill-tempered, angry ruler. What would happen this time?

But everything went well. How wonderful! The ruler was very friendly, especially toward Benjamin. They were served a delicious dinner, and Benjamin received the most food. Again they had to tell about home, and their father. The ruler wanted to know everything. Then they were allowed to go home again with sacks full of grain. Simeon was allowed to go home, too. Good!

There they went. All eleven, cheerful and content. "How happy Father will be when we all arrive home safely. Hurry! Let's go home!" The ruler had taken the money that was in their sacks. He had not said they were thieves. Good! Joyfully they journeyed on.

But suddenly, looking back, they saw a cloud of dust above the road. It was made by soldiers on wild horses! They called and shouted, "Stop, stop!" They told the brothers to wait.

What was the matter now? When the soldiers came near, the leader said angrily to the brothers, "You are wicked men. You have taken my master's silver goblet. You are thieves."

In fear, the brothers looked at the man. They said, "We did not take the goblet, honestly, we didn't. We did not take it. We are not thieves, Sir. We returned the money that was in our sacks the first time — we are honest men. Search through our sacks, Sir. Search, and whoever has the goblet you may put to death."

The soldiers searched. They looked in every sack. No, Reuben did not have the goblet. But there was double money in the top of each sack. Who had done that? How could that have happened? But the goblet? No. It was not in Simeon's sack, it was not in Judah's. The brothers started to smile. Of course not, no one had it. "Go ahead and search, soldiers." Another sack with no goblet, and another. Only Benjamin's sack was left. It was opened. Horrible! There lay the beautiful goblet on top of the grain and on top of the money. The brothers grew terribly afraid.

"Benjamin did not do it, Sir. No, honestly, he did not!"

But the officer said, "Benjamin must come along. That is the command of my master."

"But then we will all come," the brothers answered. And there they went, afraid and sad. What would happen to poor Benjamin? Would he be put in prison? Would the ruler put him to death? Oh, when Father Jacob heard this . . .!

They came back to the ruler. He looked at them angrily. He said, "What are you all doing here? Only Benjamin must stay. He shall be my slave. You go away!"

But the brothers fell down on their knees before Joseph. "Oh, my lord! Please let Benjamin come along with us," they asked and they pleaded.

Joseph's face looked very angry. "No!"

Then Judah said, "My lord, our father will die of sorrow. Our father loved our brother Joseph so very much. But Joseph is dead. Now our father loves Benjamin. If Benjamin does not return, he will die of grief. Let me be your slave, my lord. Do with me whatever you will, but let Benjamin go. We dare not return to our father without Benjamin. Let him go, the poor boy. Let me be your slave."

Joseph listened. Deep in his eyes was a great joy. The brothers loved Benjamin so much, and they loved their father so much too. They were not wicked men anymore. Joseph saw it. Joseph heard it. It made him very happy, and he was not truly angry.

There were the brothers, bowing low before him. He remembered his beautiful dream from so long ago, when the eleven sheaves bowed before his sheaf. The dream had now been fulfilled. The brothers looked at him, afraid and sad. Then Joseph could not wait any longer. He could not pretend to be angry anymore. He commanded with his hand, and all the soldiers and servants left the room. He wanted to be alone with his brothers. Then — then he stretched out his arms to them. Tears filled his eyes and he cried, "I am Joseph. Is my father alive? I am Joseph, do not be afraid!"

The brothers were terrified. Was that Joseph? They bowed even lower. Was that Joseph himself? They did not dare to look at him, they had been so cruel to him. What was he going to do? How afraid they were of him.

But Joseph was not angry. He cried with joy. He walked up to them. He hugged Benjamin and kissed him. How different that was from putting Benjamin in prison or putting him to death! Joseph kissed him, and he kissed all his brothers. He said, "Do not be afraid of me, I will not harm you. God in heaven has been very good to me. Now I can take care of you and Father. I am very glad to do that. The LORD took care of all of us. You meant to harm me, but God meant it for good.

"All of you go home now, Benjamin too. Let Father Jacob come here to live with me. You come to live with me, too, and take your wives and your children and your servants. Every one of them. No, I am not angry. I put that goblet into the sack myself. But I did not mean my harshness. You are not wicked men anymore. I can see that. Go home to Father, and tell him everything. He will be so happy."

ALL IS RIGHT

There the brothers went again, travelling the long way home. All their sadness and fear was gone. They journeyed quickly. Father Jacob saw them come with Benjamin. Now his heart was content. But they appeared so joyful. What were they saying? They ran up to Father Jacob.

"Oh, Father, Joseph is alive! That ruler in Egypt is Joseph! He is our very own brother!"

But Father Jacob could not believe it. He said, "That cannot be. Joseph is dead. He was killed by a wild animal."

Then the brothers told him everything. They told him of their wickedness long ago, and Father Jacob believed them. He said, "The LORD has made everything right. I shall come along and see Joseph. That will be wonderful."

Joseph waited, but it took so long. He told his servants, "Bridle the horses, prepare my chariot. I shall go to meet my father." There he rode like a king. The horses pranced, the golden reins shone in the sunlight. Far, far away in the distance came the wagons, and the camels, and the sheep. Joseph saw them. He drove even faster. He wanted to be with his father so much. There came Father Jacob. Joseph jumped off his chariot and ran to meet his father. They embraced each other and wept. They cried with joy. It was beautiful, so wonderful!

Father Jacob went along with Joseph to live in the beautiful land of Egypt. Joseph's brothers, too, and their wives and their children, and their servants. Everyone! Joseph would take good care of them. Now they were all happy. God had taken such good care of them. Father Jacob became very old. Then he died. Once long, long ago he had slept with his head on a stone. And dreamed a beautiful dream of angels and heaven and God. Now he could live in that beautiful heaven himself, near God. That was the most wonderful thing of all.

POOR PEOPLE

"Hurry up! Go faster! Work harder! Hurry up!"
The poor people were already going fast, and they were already working hard. But that angry man was still not content. He hit the bare backs of those poor people with his stick. "Hurry up!"
They all had to bake clay bricks. They had to carry them away and pile them up the whole day long. The sun burned on their naked backs and they were so tired, and the sand was so hot. They wanted to rest but they were not allowed because those angry men would not let them. Oh, they could hardly go on any longer. There in the distance stood the beautiful palace

of the king. He had commanded it. His wicked servants forced those poor people to work the whole day.

Who were those people? They were all Father Jacob's children. There were so many, so very many! They were the Israelites. But Father Jacob had died long ago, and Joseph the ruler of Egypt, had died long ago, too. And all his brothers were dead, and the good king Pharaoh was dead as well.

Now another king was sitting on the throne. He was a wicked king. He was very harsh with the Israelites. He thought, "If enemies come to my land, maybe the Israelites will help them. Perhaps they will chase me away. I do not want that. I will make the Israelites work very hard. They will have to bake bricks, more and more bricks. They will become tired and weak and sick. Then they cannot help my enemies. Yes, they must bake more bricks, and I will build high towers, big, wonderful, strong towers."

That was why those Egyptians drove the poor people along. The wicked king had said so.

In the distance stood the small white houses where those poor people lived. Oh, look! The mothers and the children were hiding away fearfully in their little houses. An Egyptian was coming, an evil servant of the wicked king. Did he want to beat those mothers and children, too? No, it was worse, much worse. He was searching for little boys who had just been born. And when he found them, he would take them along to the big deep Nile River. Then he would throw those dear little boys into the water, and they would drown. The wicked king had commanded it. All the little boys of the Israelites had to be drowned. The king thought, "Then they cannot help my enemies later. The little girls may stay with their mothers. They cannot fight anyway when they grow up. They can be our slaves." And so he sent his servants to the little white houses where the poor Israelites lived. They would look and search, and they would listen at the doors for the cries of little babies. Then they would come in and seize them. Poor little boys!

Father Jacob did not know of it. And Joseph did not know of it either, but Someone knew. God can see everything. He saw that wicked king and his evil servants. He saw those poor people and their fearful children. He knew their grief and their hurt. He did not forget them. Once God had told Father Jacob, "I will take care of you and your children." And what God says always happens. He would not forget them.

IN THE REED BASKET

One day a baby boy was born in one of the little white houses, a sweet beautiful little boy. His mother hugged him close to her breast. His father and sister watched. They reached out their hands to him. How they loved him! But . . .

Mother cried. Father looked so sad. And Sister listened, afraid for the noise outside on the road. Hush! Outside, the servants of the wicked king were coming. They were searching for little boys. They listened at the doors for a baby's cry and then they would grab him and drown him in the great deep water of the Nile River.

The soldiers also listened at the door of the little white house where the boy had been born. What if they heard him? Mother trembled with fear. She pressed her dear son close to her breast. She did not want to give him to the wicked men outside. She put her hand on his mouth so he would not cry out loud. The bad men listened, but they did not hear anything. They passed by. Good!

But that little brother was growing bigger every day, and he cried louder every day. His father and mother were so afraid and so sad. What if those wicked servants heard him? No! No! Mother did not want to give up her little one. She hid him in a back corner of her house. The wicked servants did not know it and they did not hear him.

But the little boy grew bigger and bigger. Sometimes he cried so long and so loud. His father and mother could not hide him any longer. The servants of the king would hear him anyway and then . . .!

IN THE REED BASKET

On a quiet evening Father went to the river. He picked an armful of reeds and quietly went home again. What would he do with those reeds? He wove them into a basket. It was like a little reed cradle. Then Mother laid her dear son in the reed basket. It looked so precious, the little brother in the reed cradle. But Mother cried, and Father looked very sad and scared.

Very early in the morning Father left the house. He carried the reed basket in his arms. And in the basket lay the child, his dear little son. Where was he going? To the Nile River! Was he going to drown his baby himself? Oh, no. He put the basket among the reeds. Far into the reeds, close to the water's edge.

Poor little boy! There he lay in his reed cradle, all alone. Who would take care of him? The wind whispered through the reeds. Would the wind sing him to sleep? The reeds swayed up and down. Would the reeds rock him to sleep? What if the water rose? What if the water tipped the little cradle? Poor baby boy!

But look, behind some trees a girl was hiding. She waited, and she listened. She was so afraid and there were tears in her eyes. Who was it? It was Miriam, the little boy's sister. Often she would look in the distance toward the little reed basket. What if the water rose and took her brother away? Her heart thumped with fear. What was she waiting for? What was she listening for? Hush! She heard something. She looked and quickly hid behind the trees. The princess, the daughter of the wicked king, was coming! She was beautifully dressed, and her maids followed her respectfully.

Every morning she came to bathe in the clear water of the Nile. Miriam hiding behind the tree knew that. She saw that the maids stayed on the shore, but that the princess walked into the water. She passed through the reeds, but then — then she saw something. She looked and looked, and then called her maids. "Come, come quickly. Something is here. It is a reed basket. What is in it? Come quickly, fetch it for me."

The maids pushed through the reeds. They took the basket and brought it to the princess. Carefully they opened it. A baby! A little baby boy! He was awake. He kicked with his legs, and he grabbed with his hands. His little mouth opened and searched for food. Then he began to cry. He cried so sadly because no one was feeding him.

The princess felt sorry for him. She thought, "He is such a sweet, beautiful boy." She understood that he was a little boy from the small white houses in the distance. He was a little Israelite boy. He had to be drowned in the Nile River because her father, the king, had commanded it. But she felt so sorry for him. She found him so lovable. No, she would not let him be drowned. She looked at him! He stretched his little hands toward her and his mouth asked for food.

"Poor little boy! You can be my little boy." Her father, the king, would not mind when she asked him. "You will be my little boy. I shall take care of you. You need not be drowned in the water. You are mine. Hush, little boy."

But the baby did not understand. He was too little. He was hungry but no one was giving him anything. Wait, who was coming from behind those trees? It was Miriam. She was so happy, but she was afraid, too. She dared to go right to the princess and said, "I know someone who can feed the little baby." Miriam's heart was thumping. What would the princess say? Yes, oh yes, she said, "Let the woman come to me immediately. Let her feed my little boy. He is so hungry."

Oh, how wonderful! How wonderful! Miriam ran off quickly. And who did she get? She went to get her own mother, the mother of the baby boy. There came Mother. She was allowed to take her baby in her arms again. She was allowed to cuddle him very close to herself again, and she might feed him. Then the baby did not cry any longer.

The princess smiled. She said, "He is my boy, but he is so little. I cannot take care of him very well. Later when he is bigger, he will come to live with me in the palace. He is my boy. I shall give him a beautiful name. He shall be called Moses. That means, I have found him in the water."

Then Mother could take her son home again. How wonderful! There she went. And Miriam ran ahead to tell Father. What joy!

Yes, and now the wicked servants could come and listen at the door, but they could not take little Moses away. He belonged to the princess. And later he would live in the palace. He would become a prince. How wonderful! That was what God had done.

Father and Mother, and Miriam, too, thanked God. He had taken care of their little son. First everything had been so sad, now everything was happy.

And what about when Moses grew up? When he became a prince? When he became very rich? What would happen then? Would he forget his own father and mother? Would he forget his own people in the little white houses? No one knew. But God in heaven knew.

THE PRINCE BECOMES A SHEPHERD

When little Moses grew up into a strong boy, his mother brought him to the princess. Then the little boy became a prince. He lived in the beautiful palace. He received lovely clothes and delicious food. He was allowed to learn everything. He became very educated.

But he did not forget his poor father and mother. He did not forget the people in the little white houses, either. No, he thought, "I am an Israelite. I live in a palace, I look like a prince, but I belong to the poor people who work so hard for the wicked king. I love them the most. If only I could help them. I feel so sorry for them." Often he went to visit them, but he could not help them. The evil servants drove those people with sticks and whips. The evil men laughed about their weariness and pain.

Every time Moses visited his people and returned home to the beautiful palace, he was very sad. He thought, "I am so rich and my people are so poor." Then he would pray to God in heaven: "O LORD, help those poor people. The Egyptians are so cruel to them."

Many years passed and Moses became a grown man. He was a rich prince. He thought, "Oh, I wish I was poor, too, so I could live with my own people. But I must always remain a prince." That was what Moses thought. But God in heaven did not think that way.

One day Moses went to see his people again. He noticed how hard they had to work. How the sun burned on their naked backs! How tired they were, and how sad! But he saw something much worse. An Israelite stood between some stacks of bricks. Then a cruel Egyptian came with his whip. He beat that man on his bare back as if he were an animal. Moses saw it. He became angry. He ran up to that Egyptian. He grabbed him, and he hit him. He hit him so hard that the Egyptian died.

But that was wrong. The Egyptian was a servant of the king. What if the king heard about it? Moses was frightened! Quickly he dug a hole and put the dead Egyptian in it. Then he filled the hole with sand. No one had seen it. No one knew. No one could tell the king.

The next day Moses went to walk among the brick piles again. Hush! He heard something. He heard yelling. Angry, bad words. Was another Egyptian beating the poor Israelites again? Moses went to see. Oh, no! There was no Egyptian. There were two Israelites. They were angry at each other. They shouted bad words at each other. They were fighting with each other.

That saddened Moses. He said, "You should not do that. You must be friends. You have so much grief already. You make your life more sad by fighting with each other. Do not do that."

But one of the men became angry at Moses. He cried, "What! Do you want to be master over us, too? Do you want to kill us as you killed the Egyptian yesterday?"

Moses was startled. "Oh, no! Those men know about it. If they tell the king, the king will put me to death!" Moses became terribly afraid. He did not dare return to the beautiful palace. What if the king had heard about it? Moses ran away. He ran far, far away into the desert. It was quiet and lonely there. The king and his servants would not come there. But now Moses was not a rich prince anymore. He had become a fugitive. Who would help him now? Where would Moses live?

He walked on and on, always farther, until he came to a well. It was almost evening. As he sat there, seven girls came to the well. They led a huge flock of sheep. The sheep were thirsty. They wanted to drink from the water in the well. But the well was very deep and on top of the well lay a big heavy stone. The girls could not lift the heavy stone off the pit. Moses thought,

"I should help those girls. I am big and strong." He lifted the big heavy stone. Wonderful! There deep down in the well was the cool water. The girls were so glad. Quickly they went to draw water in their jugs and poured the cool water into the stone basins which stood by the well. All their sheep could drink from it.

But then some other shepherds came. They were big, strong men. They had sheep, too. They laughed wickedly and said, "Come, we will chase those seven girls and their sheep away. Then our sheep can drink first."

But Moses heard it. He became furious with those shepherds. He said, "That's not going to happen. These girls were at the well first, they drew the water, and their sheep may drink first. That is fair."

The shepherds looked at Moses. They were afraid of that strange man. They dared not chase the girls away. The maidens were soon finished. Moses helped them draw water, too. Delighted, they went back to their father's house.

Their father asked, "Why are you home so early this evening?"

The girls told him of the stranger at the well. "He was so friendly, Father, he helped us. And the shepherds did not dare to chase us away."

But then their father said, "Where is that friendly man? Is he still at the well? Go quickly and bring him here. Maybe he is hungry. Maybe he does not have a place to sleep tonight. Go quickly and call him."

Moses came. He ate with them, and slept in their house. And in the morning when he awoke, he was allowed to stay. Yes, Moses was allowed to always stay with that man and his seven daughters. Now Moses was not unhappy anymore. He went out with the sheep and took good care of them. He married one of the seven girls and continued to live in that strange land.

And so, the rich prince became a poor shepherd. He thought, "Now I cannot help my people at all anymore. I cannot even come near them. I am also becoming old. I will probably always be a shepherd." That was what Moses thought. But God in heaven did not think like that. That was not His plan for Moses.

THE BURNING BUSH

A shepherd was roaming through the lonely land. He was searching for fresh grass for his sheep. Quietly they followed him. He took good care of them. He wandered farther and farther. In the distance stood a high mountain, surely there would be some nice places there. That shepherd was Moses. He had gone far, far away from home with his sheep. But at the base of the high mountain there had to be some nice grassy spots. And it would be so quiet there, so very quiet.

Suddenly Moses saw a strange thing. There were flames of fire at the base of the mountain. How could that be? All those green bushes were on fire. How strange! He looked at those flames. How strange, the leaves and branches were not burning up. They remained green. The fire was not damaging those leaves. It was very strange. Moses looked and looked.

Then he heard a voice, but he could see no one. The voice came out of the burning bush. The voice said, "Moses! Moses!"

Moses listened. That was not the voice of a human being, it was the voice of God! It frightened Moses. He bowed his head and put his hand in front of his eyes. Very reverently he listened.

The LORD said something wonderful to Moses. The LORD spoke to him about the poor people living in the little white houses in Egypt. How they had to work so hard for the wicked king, and that they were whipped so often.

No, God had not forgotten the Israelites. They were the children of Abraham, Isaac, and Jacob. The LORD had promised to take care of them, therefore it would happen, too. Listen. God said to Moses that the wicked king was not to hurt the poor people any longer. They were to go away. They were to travel to the land of Canaan. That was where Abraham and Isaac and Jacob had lived. Now they had to go there to live, too, and then they would be free. There would be no wicked king to persecute them any longer. It would be a wonderful land for them. How happy Moses was! How wonderful this was for his poor people.

Yes, but the LORD said more. "Moses, you must go to the land of Egypt. You must tell this to the Israelites, and you must tell the wicked king, too." That frightened Moses. Did he have to go to the king? He did not dare. The wicked king of earlier days, when Moses had lived in the palace, had died long ago. But the new king was just as wicked. No, Moses did not dare; he would rather remain a shepherd. But he had to go. He was not allowed to be afraid. God would help him and keep him. He had to be God's servant.

Then God's voice could no longer be heard. Moses dared look up again. The flames and the fire were gone. The bushes were not burnt, and the green leaves were rustling softly in the wind. Moses went home, and his sheep followed him faithfully. Moses thought, "I shall do what God told me to. I may not be afraid. It is so wonderful for my poor people. I shall go to the king."

MOSES AND THE WICKED KING

On a throne sat the king. He was rich and majestic. The room in which he was sitting was beautiful and his servants looked splendid, standing respectfully behind him. Two men stood before him. They were not rich and splendid like the king and his servants. They looked plain and poor and wore linen robes. They had come to ask the king something. Who were these men, and what had they come to ask?

The one man was Moses. He had come to bring the message that God Himself had given to him from the burning bush. His brother Aaron, who lived in Egypt, came along. The king listened, but he became angry. Had those two men come to ask him to let those poor Israelites go away from Egypt? No! He would not allow that.

The king said, "I want to build towers and strong cities. I need bricks. They must make bricks for me. They must be my slaves. They may not leave."

"God in heaven said to let His people go," Moses and Aaron exclaimed.

Then the king became even more angry. "No, no!" he shouted. "I will not do what God in heaven said. I am the boss, not God. I will make the Israelites work even harder, and my servants will drive them even faster, and whip them harder. I am the boss. I will not do what God says. Go away! Go away!"

Then Moses and Aaron left very sadly. That wicked king! How dare he speak in that way?

But after a while, Moses and Aaron came before the king again. This time the king had called for them. Something had happened. Something terrible. The water in the River Nile had turned into blood. No one could drink it. Then later, frogs came into the land. Multitudes of frogs! The streets and roads were full of frogs! And the houses and the palace, too. And when the frogs had gone away, vicious flies came and bit the people.

Many times terrible things happened in the land. They were plagues. They were punishments for the wicked king and his wicked servants. One day while it was thundering fiercely, very big hailstones fell from the sky, killing the people and animals in the land. Another time grasshoppers came flying through the sky. They looked like tiny birds. The grasshoppers darkened the sky because there were so many. They fell on the land and ate everything, the grass, the grain, the leaves from the trees, and the flowers in the meadows. Everything.

Another time it became dark in the middle of the day. That darkness lasted three days. The sun did not shine, the moon did not shine, and the stars did not shine either. Indeed, it made the people very afraid. That was how God punished the Egyptians.

The king became scared, too. He called for Moses and Aaron. How angry he was at them! He thought it was their fault. But he did not act angry. He did not dare. He acted very friendly. He said, "Please pray to your God. Ask him to take the punishment away, then your people may leave. Then all the people may go free."

Moses prayed and God took away the punishment. But then the wicked king laughed, and mocked God. He said, "I will not do it. I will not let the people go away. I will do what I want and I will not listen to your God!"

MOSES AND THE WICKED KING

That happened each time again. Every time there was a plague the king would call for Moses. He would promise to do what God required, and let the people go free. But when the plague was over, he would say, "I will do what I want. I will not let the people go. They must stay here." That was very sinful of that wicked king.

But then the worst thing happened. Moses went to the little white houses. He told the Israelites something strange that God had instructed him to tell them.

In each house a lamb was to be slaughtered. Then each father was to go outside, with a bowl filled with the blood of the lamb in one hand, and a branch of hyssop in the other. He was to dip the hyssop in the blood and smear the blood on the door posts and above the door. That was what they had to do. Moses had commanded it.

Evening came, but the Israelites did not go to bed. Instead they baked bread and roasted a lamb. The fathers prayed, the mother and children prayed along. Everyone was dressed in their best clothes and all their possessions were packed. The sheep and cows stood ready in the barns. How strange! It seemed as if those people were prepared to go on a journey. Yes, they were ready — that was God's message which Moses had told the Israelites.

During that night the worst plague happened. An angel from heaven went through the land of Egypt, and everywhere, in each house, the oldest son died. But when the angel saw the little white houses, he passed by because he saw the blood on the door posts. How terrible it was — in every house someone had died. But not in the little houses of the poor Israelites.

There was sorrow throughout the whole land of Egypt. Everywhere! This was the great punishment of God. The king called for Moses and said, "Go away! Go away right now! Get out of my land. Take your people along with you. They can be free. Take every one of those slaves! Hurry! Now I know it is your God who has punished us so heavily. Your God is the mighty one, not me. And what He says must happen. Go out of my land, otherwise we may all die!"

Moses went back to the Israelites. They stood waiting, ready for the journey. Now it had happened just as God had said. They would leave that very same day. There they went. It was a long, long procession of very happy men, women, and children. The people of Egypt came and gave them gifts, beautiful gifts of silver and gold. They said, "Go away! We are so afraid. Hurry and don't ever come back. We are so afraid of your God. We are afraid that we will die, too!"

So the poor people from the little white houses went away. No one came to hurt them with a stick or whip any longer. Oh, no. And they were no longer poor people. They were no longer slaves. They were free, wonderfully free! God Himself would take care of them. He would bring them to a wonderful land. He had promised that. They had suffered much sorrow and pain, but now everything was turned into gladness. God never forgets his children.

THE RED SEA

There went the Israelites, telling each other, "How wonderful! Now we are not being beaten. We are free. We are going to the beautiful land of our fathers Abraham, Isaac, and Jacob. We will always be able to live there. How wonderful! And God in heaven will take care of us."

They were travelling through the desert. They went very slowly because all the children and the sheep and the cattle could not travel very fast.

Suddenly! Hush! What did they hear behind them? Look, far behind them in the distance they could see dust rising from the road. Horses and chariots? Yes, listen. Who was that? It was the wicked king of Egypt. He had come with his horses and chariots as fast as he could go. Dust billowed up. Swords and spears glistened in the sunshine.

"Forward! Forward!" What did he want to do? Why was he so angry? Why did he urge his horses on so excitedly? He was sorry he had let the Israelites go. He wanted to get them back to be his slaves again.

"Forward! Forward! We'll catch up to them. They are going slowly and our horses are very swift. Forward!" The wicked king laughed. He said, "The sea is ahead of them. They cannot go through the sea. They will be caught. Hurry! Forward!"

How afraid the Israelites were! They saw the horses coming. They heard the fierce soldiers yelling. They were so afraid. Who would help them? The sea was ahead of them, the great, deep water. They could not go on. They would drown. Would they have to go back to Egypt? Would they have to work so hard again, and be beaten like animals? Who would help them?

But Moses was not afraid. He knew God in heaven would help them. God would not forget His people. So Moses said to all those frightened people, "Onward!" Yes, but they were so near the sea. Moses said it anyway, "Onward." He reached the sea first. Then he took his tall shepherd's staff and hit the water. Oh, look! The water streamed away just like that, as if it was afraid of Moses' staff. A path was made through the middle of the sea. How could that be? Had Moses done that? Had his shepherd's staff done that? No, a man could not do that. God in heaven had done it. He had made the sea dry to save His people.

See, there they went, all those frightened people. They went over the dry path through the deep sea. The men and the women and the children, the sheep and the cattle — everyone. Beside them the water stood like a wall. It did not fall over them. It did not even make them wet. Safe and well they travelled because God in heaven looked down on them. He was taking care of them. Forward, slowly forward, they came to the middle of the sea. And then they reached the other side. How wonderful! All those people and animals climbed up the other shore.

And that wicked king, where was he? He was coming. He saw the dry path through the sea. He saw that the water stood like a wall. He drove his wild horses and his fierce soldiers into the sea, too. "Forward, forward! Hurry, forward!"

The horses jumped, the chariot wheels crunched, and the soldiers yelled. There they went after the frightened Israelites. But then! Terrible! The walls of water started to fall over the king and over his servants. He screamed, "Go back, go back!" And his servants yelled, "Go back, go back!" But they could not return. Never again. The water swished and foamed, and the deep dry path was gone. The waves rolled over the heads of the soldiers, and then they were gone. All of them — the soldiers, the horses, and the chariots, and the sharp swords and the spears, too, all were gone. The wicked king and his wicked servants drowned together in the deep sea. That was God's punishment.

But there on the other shore was happiness. Moses and Aaron and all the people thanked the LORD. He had saved them, He alone. He had performed a great miracle. The LORD had made the sea dry for His people. No one could do that except God.

THE LONG JOURNEY

Now the Israelites joyfully travelled on, no longer afraid. The LORD would always take care of them. Now they knew it. They were going to the beautiful land of Canaan. Everything would be so happy there, so wonderful!

But that beautiful land was far away, and the journey was terribly long and difficult. All those people and animals went step by step through the hot sand of the desert. The hot sun burned on their heads. It was so warm and they grew so tired. They became so thirsty, but there was no water. There were only stones and sand. What would they do? Suddenly, in the distance they could see something glistening in the sand. Water! A big pool of water! The thirsty people ran toward it. They scooped up the water in their hands. They wanted to drink with big gulps. How awful — it was bitter!

"We cannot drink this bitter water!" They became angry, they cried and complained. They told Moses, "We will die of thirst! Who shall help us?"

That was very sinful of those people, very wicked. They knew God would help them. They had to be patient.

Then Moses went toward the bitter water. He threw a piece of wood into the water. God had told him to do that. Moses said, "Now you may drink."

They did — they drank and the water tasted delicious. They gulped it down. They filled their jars and pots full of water. They could carry all that fresh water along on their journey. Now that their thirst was quenched, they went on once more. The LORD had helped them once again. Would they now stop being impatient?

But another time they had no meat, and they could not buy it anywhere. They also had no bread. Grain, with which to bake bread, did not grow in the desert. Once again the people became angry, very angry at Moses. They said, "We have no meat and we have no bread. The journey is lasting so long, and the sand is so hot. We shall never reach that beautiful land. We shall die of hunger. Oh, if only we had stayed in the land of Egypt!"

That was very wrong of those Israelites. They should have been patient. They forgot about God in heaven, but God remembered them.

Evening was coming and darkness began to fall. "Look, what is that?" the people said to one another. Birds were flying through the sky in the distance, coming toward the Israelites. There were many, very many, and they flew very low. The Israelites could just grab them, as many as they wished. They fried the birds and ate them. It was delicious meat. God was taking care of them.

Then morning came and light dawned. Look, what was on the ground? The people slept in their tents, but when they came outside something was lying on the ground. It was white, and looked like little white flakes. What could that be? They did not know, but Moses did. He said, "Take those flakes. It is manna. It is a delicious flour. Take it and use it to make bread." The people gathered the flakes. They ground it and baked it over the fire. Oh, yes, it was wonderful, sweet bread. It tasted like honey cakes. The next morning, more beautiful manna was on the ground. Every day the people could take as much as they needed. Now they had bread. God was taking care of them.

The LORD had led the Israelites out of the land of Egypt. He had made a dry path for them through the sea. He had given them water and meat and bread. Would they stop being impatient now? Would they trust God now? God had been so good to them.

THE GOLDEN CALF

A celebration was going on in the Israelite camp. But it was a strange, quiet celebration. There went the Israelites. They had clean white clothes on and they walked quietly and reverently. Their sheep and cattle and donkeys and camels stayed near the tents. They did not belong at this celebration. Moses and Aaron walked ahead. In the distance was a high mountain. That was where they were going. At the mountain they waited quietly and reverently. Why? What kind of celebration was it?

Oh, look! High up! A great cloud covered the top of the mountain. It thundered, and then the Israelites heard the voice of God speaking to them, even though they could not see Him. They listened to what God told them: They must be obedient; they must love God, and they must love each other, too. If they did that, they would always be happy and content. Then God would always take care of them, and they would always be God's people. Now God Himself had told them.

The people had to stay at the bottom of the mountain, but Moses was allowed to climb up. Moses was not afraid. Moses was God's servant. There he went, climbing higher and higher. The people saw him go. He climbed still higher. He came near the big cloud, and then he climbed higher still. The people could not see him anymore. Now Moses was with God. He could hear God's voice. After, when he came down, Moses would tell the people what God had said.

The people waited quietly and reverently. Oh, yes, they would be obedient. They would love God. They would love each other, too. They would do everything that God had commanded. But Moses stayed away so long. They waited and waited. But Moses did not come back. Night came. The people went to sleep. When morning came, Moses still did not return. They waited. It had already taken two days, three days, a whole week. Would Moses never come back? It took longer, still longer. Was Moses dead? The people became afraid and sad.

They said, "Moses is gone, now we are all alone in the desert. Who will go with us to the beautiful land? We are so afraid. We are so alone. Who will help us?" But then those people said even more. It was wicked. They said, "Our God in heaven is so far away. We cannot see Him. Let us make ourselves a god we can see. The Egyptians made gods of gold, and they prayed to those gods. Let us make an image, too, and pray to it. Maybe it will help."

So the people went to Aaron and said, "You must make an image for us. Then we can pray to that image. Maybe it will help."

Aaron was shocked. "No, no!" he said. "You may not do that. You may never pray to an image. You may only pray to God who is in heaven. You must be obedient and love God. You know that. The LORD Himself has told you."

But the people became angry at Aaron. They said, "You must."

Then Aaron became afraid. "I have no gold," he said.

But the people cried, "We do!"

They went to get their beautiful golden earrings and golden bracelets and golden rings, and they brought them to Aaron. All their beautiful golden treasures they brought to Aaron. The people cried and shouted at him, "Make a god for us, a god of gold! You must!"

Aaron did. He was so afraid of their angry eyes and faces. He made a golden calf; it was a beautiful calf, made of gold. Then he put it on a high platform in the midst of the people so everyone could see it. The people fell on their knees, and bowed their heads. They prayed to that golden image. But when they stood up again, they sang and they jumped and they danced. They had a big wild feast. Those foolish, wicked people! They were not allowed to pray to images, but they did it anyway. They were disobedient. They were to love God in heaven, who had taken such good care of them. But they did not think of God in heaven at all. They sang and they jumped and they danced.

Suddenly — Who was that? Oh, who was that coming down the mountain? He heard the singing and the shouting. He saw the jumping and the dancing. He saw that image of gold, and

THE GOLDEN CALF

his eyes filled with anger. He came down the mountain. He ran up to the people. Who was that man? It was Moses. No, Moses had not died. Moses was not gone. He had been very near to God on the mountain. He had heard God's voice. Now he was supposed to teach the people what God had told him. But those wicked, foolish people had forgotten God.

He was so angry with them. He ran up to them, and he cried, "Stop! Stop! This is not allowed! This is a great sin before God!" Aaron had been afraid of the people. Not Moses. Look what he did! He pushed that golden calf over. It fell down. Then

Moses broke it in pieces. "Away with it! You may not pray to an image! You are a wicked, disobedient people."

All those people were very quiet. They wanted to walk away, but they did not dare. If only they had not done this great wickedness! If only they had not forgotten God in heaven! They were so afraid of Moses, so afraid of God. What would happen now?

God in heaven forgave their sins. Moses prayed for them and Moses still loved his people very much.

THEIR OWN FAULT

Now the Israelites journeyed on. The hot sun burned on their heads, and the hot sand burned under their feet. The journey was taking so long, so very long. But look, in the distance there were mountains, and behind the mountains was the land that God had promised them. There was the beautiful land where Abraham and Isaac and Jacob had lived long, long ago. And Joseph, too, when he was a little boy. Now they would all enter it. How wonderful! Then they would not live in tents any longer, but in beautiful houses. Then their cattle and their sheep could graze in the beautiful green meadows. Then they would no longer walk step by step through the hot sand. There would always be water there. Grain would always grow there. The most delicious fruits would be hanging on the trees. Here in this hot desert they were so tired and poor. But there, in that beautiful land, they would be happy and rich. How wonderful!

Moses picked out twelve brave, strong men. Why was that? He said, "You must go to the beautiful land. We will wait here. You must go and search it out, and when you return you must tell us all about it. But be careful — strange people are living in that land. Watch out."

Those twelve men were brave. There they went, and all the people watched them go. In a short while, they, too, would be able to go over the mountains to that beautiful land. How wonderful that would be! The people waited. Every night they went to sleep, and every morning they looked again to see if the twelve men were returning.

One morning a shout was heard. "There they come! There they come!" All the people came running from their tents. They were so happy, so excited! And then those twelve men had to tell everything about the beautiful land. The people listened, and they looked and laughed. Oh, yes, it was a wonderful, beautiful land! Look! Two men were carrying a stick on their shoulders. On the stick hung a large cluster of grapes. The people had never seen such marvellous grapes, so big and delicious. Oh, yes, it had to be a wonderful land.

But big, strong men lived in that land. They looked like giants, angry giants. When the Israelites heard that, they were frightened. "Giants? Angry giants? Then we do not dare to go there. They will kill us when we come. We do not dare. We are not going to do it."

"Quiet! Be quiet," said one of the twelve men, whose name was Caleb. "Be quiet and do not be afraid. It is true — big, strong men live in that land, but God Himself has promised us that land. We may not be afraid. God will help us. God has always helped us."

But the people did not listen. They did not want to listen, they were so afraid. They said, "We are not going. We do not dare. We are not going to do it. Come on, we will not listen to Moses anymore. We are going back to Egypt. We are such poor, miserable people!"

"Come," said Joshua, who was alos one of the twelve men. "That is not true. We are not poor — we are God's people. The LORD will help us. The big strong men will not be able to harm us. We may not forget God. Stay here."

"No, no!" the people shouted. "You are deceiving us." And they became so angry at the two men that they picked up stones, big heavy stones. They wanted to throw them at the two men to kill them. How wicked those discontented people were!

But then something happened. God spoke to Moses, and those wicked people received a severe punishment. They were not allowed to enter the beautiful land. They would have to remain always in the desert and there they would die. They would never see the beautiful land. The little children would, after they had grown up in the desert. When they were men and women, they would be allowed to enter the beautiful land. But that would be a long, long time from now. Then their fathers and mothers would be dead. That was the punishment. Those people had forgotten God, who had always taken such good care of them. That was wicked. Now everyone was sad, but nothing could be done about it. What God says always happens.

But the two men who had said, "God will help us," were allowed to enter the beautiful land. It would take many, many years and they would be very old, but one day, they would enter it. Not the others. How sad! They were so near the beautiful land, yet now they had to turn around, back into the desert. It was so sad, yes, but it was their own fault.

There they went again. The sun was hot. The sand burned their feet, and they were so thirsty and tired and so afraid. Yet the LORD took care of them. He did not forget them. He gave them water again, and He gave them meat. And every morning the white flakes lay on the ground around the tents. Even so, they became discontented again. They were angry at Moses again and again. It was so sad. And so they journeyed on, here and there, throughout those long years.

One day the grumbling of the people became very bad. Those disgruntled people said, "We don't like that manna anymore! Oh, no!" And they kicked away the little white flakes. Yes, that was very, very bad. God sent a severe punishment for that. Fierce serpents came crawling through the desert. They bit the people and there was poison in their sharp teeth. The poison was hot like fire, and it killed the people. The deadly snakes were everywhere. They were crawling outside in the sand, they crawled inside the tents. Those poor men, women, and children! They could not run away. The serpents were everywhere, and they were so fast and cruel. They bit and bit and bit. Poor men, poor women and children! They shouted and cried in fear.

Again it was their own fault. They had forgotten God. But God never forgot those miserable people. They called and cried to Moses, "We are sorry about our wickedness. Pray to God for us! No one can help us, except God. We will all die. Pray to God! We are so afraid, so terribly afraid!"

Moses prayed to God, and the LORD did not forget the sinful people. Look, there went Moses, climbing a hill. He put a tall pole in the ground. And on top of the pole? How strange! On top of the pole hung a serpent. Not a live serpent — a serpent made of bronze. It shone and glistened in the sunshine. God had commanded Moses to make it. The bronze serpent would help the people.

How could that be? There came the sick people crawling out of their tents. They looked at the bronze serpent, which shone in the sun. The mothers carried their sick children outside. The strong boys carried their sick fathers. Those wicked serpents had bitten them, and their poison burned like fire. But they all looked up at the serpent on the pole, and then they became better. Moses told them: "Look at the serpent and you shall be healed. You shall not die. God in heaven will help you." They looked and then those wicked serpents with their poisonous fangs could not hurt them anymore.

Again, God had saved His people. Then the serpents slithered away, and the people were so happy. They thought, "Let us never be wicked and discontent again. We may not. God is so good to us." So they journeyed on from one spot to another in the desert, because they would never enter the beautiful land. That was too bad, yes, but it was their own fault.

MOSES ON THE MOUNTAIN

Moses had become very old. His hair was white, and so was his long beard. Then God said to Moses, "Now you may rest. Another man shall lead my people. You may go from earth to heaven." But what about that beautiful land behind the mountains? The discontented people were not allowed to go, but what about Moses? Was he not allowed to go to that beautiful land either?

No! One day Moses had been disobedient to God. The Israelites had been very thirsty. The LORD had said to Moses,

"Go to those rocks and say that water must come out." But Moses had not done that. He had not spoken one word. He was so angry at the people, that he hit the rock. Yes, that was disobedient of him, and that was why he could not enter the beautiful land. Now that Moses had become very old, the LORD said to him, "Your work is finished. You may go from earth to heaven. Climb the mountain. You may look at the beautiful land, but then you shall die."

There went Moses. He climbed higher and higher. He was very old, but he was still very strong. He could easily climb that high mountain. The people below watched him go. They were sad. Now Moses was leaving them. They would never see him again. They loved him so very much, yet they had hurt him so often. They were sorry, they were very sorry, but it was too late now. He was going away forever. He had said goodbye to all the people. He had said, "You must always love God and be obedient to Him; then you will be happy. But if you are disobedient, and do not love God, you will not be happy, and then punishment will come."

Moses climbed higher and higher. Finally he was hidden by the big rocks, and the people below could not see him anymore. How sad they were. What about Moses? Was he sad, too? No, he was happy because God had called him up the mountain. He went as a faithful servant. The LORD had always been so good to him. He knew that very well. The LORD had taken care of him when he was a little baby and he lay in the reed basket in the water. The LORD had taken care of him when he was a rich prince and when he was a poor shepherd. The LORD had helped him all the time when he was leading the people through the desert. The LORD would take care of him now as he climbed the mountain, too.

No, Moses was not sad. There he was on the very top of the mountain. He could see very far. In the distance lay the beautiful land. Green trees and delicious fruits grew there. Golden grain for the people and grass for the animals grew there also. How wonderful it would be to live there! He was not allowed to go there, but that did not matter. The children of the Israelites would. That filled Moses' heart with joy. God showed Moses everything of the beautiful land. Then God took his faithful servant away from the earth. Now Moses would live in heaven near God and the angels. It was much more wonderful there than in the beautiful land of Canaan. In heaven there is no sadness. In heaven there is no pain. No one will be sick there, and no one will be angry. Oh, to live so close to God in the beautiful heaven, that was most wonderful of all! Now Moses was happy and would be happy forever and ever.

THE WHITE CITY WITH THE STRONG WALLS

Who would bring the people into the beautiful land now? Joshua would. Joshua was one of the men who long ago had brought back the grapes from the beautiful land of Canaan. Joshua was a brave man. He loved God. He had said, "We may not be afraid of the giants in the beautiful land. God will help us."

That was long, long ago. All of those men and women who were so dissatisfied had died, and their children had grown up. Now they were allowed to enter Canaan, and Joshua would show them the way. God in heaven would help them.

They had come very close to the beautiful land. Joshua chose two men out of the people. Brave strong men. He said, "There is the big white city with the strong walls. Do you see it? You must go there. You must look around very closely. When you return, tell us all about it. But be careful. The people living there are our enemies. Will you be brave?"

Yes, there went the two men. They came to the white city. The walls were high and broad. On top of the walls were high and strong towers. Where soldiers kept watch. They would drive the Israelites away when they came.

The two men came near the gate of the city. The gate was open. Quietly they entered. They walked through the streets and they looked and listened. They told each other, "The walls are broad, and the towers are high. The soldiers are strong, but we may not be afraid. God is going to help us."

Evening came. On top of the wall stood a house, which the men entered. They wanted to sleep there during the night. The woman of that house looked at them and thought, "These two men look like Israelites. They want to take our city." Did she become angry at them? Did she go to the king and his soldiers? Did she say, "Grab them, they are our enemies!"? No, she did not do that. She was friendly and said, "Come in, I will give you a nice spot where no one can find you."

She brought them on top of her house, on the flat roof. Stalks of flax were on the roof, drying in the sun. The woman told the men, "Hurry, hide under the stalks. It is a big pile. I will cover you, and when the king's men come to search for you, because they know you are in the city, they will not find you." Then the woman went downstairs again, leaving the men on the dark roof. What would happen now?

THE WHITE CITY WITH THE STRONG WALLS

Hush! Downstairs someone was banging on the door. The soldiers of the king had come. They asked the woman of the house, "Have two men come in here, two strangers, men of the Israelites?" But the woman did not tell them that they were on the roof. She fooled them and said, "Quickly, go outside the city. Maybe you will still find them there."

Quickly the soldiers left. They hurried out of the city gate into the dark fields. They searched everywhere but found no one. But what would happen if those soldiers returned? What if they came and asked again — what then? But the woman was very clever. She climbed on the roof, and whispered, "Come quickly. You must run away before the soldiers return."

"But where can we go? The gates are closed, and everywhere soldiers are searching for us."

The woman knew that. She said, "Come." Her house was built on top of the wall. On the one side was the city, but on the other side were the dark fields. She said, "Come!" She tied a strong rope on the windowsill. It hung outside far down to the ground. Now the men would have to lower themselves by that rope. They would land in the dark field outside the city. There they would be able to slip away in the dark, and the soldiers would not be able to find them. Yes, she was a clever woman. She was a good woman.

The men grabbed the rope, but then the woman said, "I helped you, I took care of you. Will you help me when you return with all the Israelites? Yes, I know you are coming back with your people. You are coming to conquer our city. Your God is a mighty God. He led your people through the sea. I know. And when you come, will you promise not to hurt me, or my father, my mother, my sisters, or my brothers? Will you promise me that? I want to love your God, too."

The two men said, "Yes, you have been so good to us. We shall not hurt you when we return, and we will tell all our men about you. But our men do not know where your house is, and they do not know you. You must leave this red rope hanging from your window. Then we will all see it, and we will all know where you live. And not one of us will hurt you. We promise."

Then the men lowered themselves down the rope, down to the dark fields, and they fled away into the dark countryside. The woman left the rope hanging from the window.

When the two men returned to Joshua and the Israelites they told them everything. They told them about the good woman who had helped them, too, and Joshua said, "We shall not hurt her, or her father, or mother, her sisters, or brothers. We will look for the red rope hanging from her window."

Then all the people prepared themselves to enter the beautiful land. They were not afraid as their parents had been in earlier times. They were not afraid of the white city with the strong walls. They believed God in heaven would help them. He had promised them the beautiful land, and what the LORD says always happens.

There went the Israelites, up to the beautiful land. But what about that white city with the strong walls? The gates were closed, and soldiers were on watch in the high white towers. They would want to stop the Israelites. But the Israelites kept going. They came very close to the strong city. And then? Did they climb up the high walls? Were they going to fight the king's soldiers? No, not at all! Look! They walked around the city in a big circle. How strange! That was all they did. Then they returned to their tents.

The next day, they walked around the city again in a big circle. They did the same on the third day, and the fourth day. How very strange! The king and the soldiers in the white towers watched them go. They laughed. They thought, "Oh, let those Israelites walk around our city. That won't hurt us. They will not be able to get in anyway. They are afraid of us." The fifth day and the sixth day the Israelites came again and walked around the city. And on the seventh day? Then they walked around the city one time, and another time. And again. First came men in long white robes. They were the priests. They carried trumpets with them, but they did not blow them. Not yet. They were just walking along quietly. They did that seven times.

Then . . ? Then the priests blew on their trumpets.

Oh, how terrible! Look! The strong walls of the white city rocked back and forth, back and forth. All of a sudden then those strong walls fell down. The stones tumbled down on top of one another. The white towers crumbled down and the closed gates fell apart. Now the Israelites could climb into the city. The king and the soldiers and all the people could not stop them. The walls had just tumbled down. That was a great miracle. God had done that. He had helped the Israelites. He had promised that the whole beautiful land was for them. No one could stop them when God helped them.

Oh, look! One piece of the wall remained standing. On that wall stood a house. And what was hanging out of the window of that house? It was a red rope. The whole wall had fallen down. The stones were lying in heaps everywhere. But that one piece of the wall was still standing. The Israelites already knew why. In that house lived the good woman who had helped the two men. Her father and mother, her brothers and sisters were with her. No, the Israelites would not hurt them. They had promised that.

Now they continued on into the beautiful land where they were allowed to live. No longer would they need to live in tents. Oh, no, now they could build houses to live in. Now they did not have to eat manna anymore either. In this beautiful land grew delicious grains. There was water and meat and bread, as much as they needed. There was plenty of grass for their sheep and cattle. They did not need to walk through the hot sand of the desert anymore. They were home in their own land. How wonderful! Now they would have to be very obedient to God in heaven, and love Him very much. He was so good to them.

A POOR WOMAN WHO BECOMES RICH

Ripe grain stood in the field. Tall stocks wearily waved their heads back and forth. The heads were heavy with all the kernels, and when the sun shone, the grain looked like gold. When the breeze came through, the grain waved gently back and forth.
Listen, men and women were coming. They sang so cheerfully about the beautiful grain that God had grown for the people. The joyful men would cut it down with their sharp sickles,

and the joyful women would gather the stalks of grain in armfuls, and bind them into sheaves. From those thousands and thousands of kernels of grain they could bake bread and cakes, for days and weeks and months. Swish, swish! the sickles of the mowers went. The stalks fell and the women bound them together. Swish, swish! It was a celebration. A celebration of harvesting the ripe grain that God had given to His people.

But look! Who was walking there alone? It was a young woman. She was very poor. She worked far away from the mowers, far away from the women. She was searching for the stalks which were left behind on the field. She was shy and a little afraid. There, she found one, and another one. She picked them up. That was allowed — yes, she might do that. Already her hand was full. Now she would be able to bake some bread that night. She bent and she searched.

The owner of the land came along. His name was Boaz. He was very rich, but he was a friendly man, too. Boaz went up to the mowers. Swish, swish! they went with their sickles. Swish, swish! He was so happy with that beautiful grain!

But then he saw that poor young woman. "Who is that?" he asked. And the mowers answered, "Oh, don't you know? Do you see that little white house in the distance? A poor old woman lives there. Her name is Naomi. She has been away for a long, long time. Ten years. But now she has returned, and she brought this young woman with her. Together they live in the little house in the distance. They are very poor."

"What is her name?" asked Boaz.

The mowers told their master everything. They said, "Once, long ago, no grain grew in the fields. Naomi had no flour to bake bread, so she left for a faraway land, she and her husband and two sons. In that faraway land there was bread, and they did not have to go hungry there. In that land her two sons married two women. But then things became very sad for Naomi. Her husband died, and then her two sons died. Now she has returned and lives in her own old little house. But one of the two women from the faraway land came along. Her name is Ruth. She loves Naomi very much. She told her, 'I will always stay with you. I will not let you go back alone. And I shall go to find grain on the fields for you.' "

Boaz looked at Ruth very kindly. He thought, "She is a good woman. She takes such good care of old Naomi." He walked up to Ruth. That frightened her. But Boaz said kindly, "You may search for grain, as much as you want. No one will hurt you."

Then Ruth fell on her knees. She said, "You are so good to me. I am not even a woman of your own people. I am a stranger from another land."

Boaz smiled kindly. He said, "I know, I know it all. But when the mowers eat and drink on the field, you may sit with them, Ruth, and eat with them."

The mowers roasted kernels of grain on the fire until they crackled. They tasted good. Ruth ate too, and was also allowed to save some food for Naomi.

Then the mowers and the women returned to work, and Ruth continued searching. Quietly Boaz whispered to the women binding the grain, "Drop a few extra stalks, and just walk on. Ruth only has so little, and then she will find much."

Ruth noticed how friendly the women were to her. It made her very happy. How surprised Naomi would be when she came home that evening! She already had so much — arms full of grain.

That was a happy evening in the little house. Naomi said, "Now we are not poor anymore. We can bake cakes and bread.

Yes, the LORD does take care of us. The LORD has made Boaz's heart friendly toward us." And Ruth said, "I will always stay with you. I shall love your people. Your people are my people, and your God is my God. Tomorrow I shall go back to the field. Boaz said I may return every day until all the grain is harvested."

"Yes, you must," said Naomi.

Ruth went every day. And when all the grain was harvested, something wonderful happened. Ruth married Boaz, the rich man. Now she was a rich woman. Boaz loved Ruth very much. He had said, "She has been so kind to Naomi. She is a good, precious woman." Now Ruth could live in a beautiful house, and Naomi went along with her. Later a little boy was born. Boaz was his father, Ruth was his mother, and Naomi was his grandmother. When that dear little boy played on his grandmother's lap, the old woman was so very, very happy. She said, "I have had much sadness in my life. My husband died and my two sons died. But now? Now I have a little son again, a dear boy. God has been very good to me, and to Ruth and Boaz. The LORD shall always take care of this dear boy, too." God takes care of everyone, all the time.

ELI AND SAMUEL

Quietly a woman walked along beside her husband. She was so sad. There were tears in her eyes. Why? Her husband was very good to her. He loved her very much. He was rich. He would give her anything. But still she was very sad. Why? She wanted to have a child. A dear little boy. But she had no children, not one. She was so alone. She could not buy a child either. You cannot buy dear little boys, not with all the money in the world. That was why she was so sad.

The woman's name was Hannah. Her husband's name was Elkanah. They lived in a village, but now they were travelling together to the city where the tabernacle was. That tabernacle, or church, was the house of God. They went there once every year. Then Hannah would get a present from her husband. But she never got that one thing she wanted more than anything else. You cannot buy that. Not for all the money in the world. That was why she was so sad.

There was God's house. Reverently Elkanah entered. He brought an offering. He did that once each year. Elkanah loved God. And Hannah? She went inside, too. But she was so sad. Tears filled her eyes. Near the doors sat a man, a very old man. He was the priest. He had to take care of God's house. People who did wicked things could not go inside. The old priest was God's servant. His name was Eli.
Oh, yes, Hannah was allowed to go inside. She searched for a quiet corner. And then, what did she do in that quiet corner? She fell on her knees. She closed her eyes and folded her hands. Hannah prayed. She prayed quietly for a long, long time. She told God in heaven everything. She told Him that she did not have one little baby, and that she was so sad. She would like to have a little boy so very much. She said it very quietly. No one could hear it. But God in heaven heard it. He hears everything.
She pleaded, "Please, God, give me a child. A little boy. Other women have so many children and I do not have one. How sad I am! If Thou wilt give me a little boy, then he will always be Thy servant. I will tell him about Thee. I shall tell him that Thou hast given him to me, and he shall love Thee, too. Then he shall always be Thy servant. O LORD, please give me a son." That was what Hannah prayed, quietly, for a long time. She knew little boys cannot be bought with money. Not for all the money in the world. God in heaven gave the people their children. God can do anything, and that was why Hannah was praying so quietly and so long in that little corner.
Eli, the old priest, sat by the door. He noticed the woman in the corner. What was she doing? He looked. She was on her knees, but she was there for so long. What was she doing? He looked again. Her lips were moving, she was saying something, but Eli could not hear one word. He became a little angry at her. He thought, "That woman acts so strange. Is she a bad woman? Is she drunk? That is not allowed in God's house!" He stood up and went to her. He said, "Shame on you! Are you drunk? That is not allowed in God's house. Go away, quickly."

Hannah became afraid. She said, "No, my lord, oh no, my lord! I am not drunk. I am very sad, and I was telling God all the grief in my heart."

Then Eli was not angry anymore. He said, "Did you pray to God? That is good. God will give you what you have asked of Him."

Hannah left. She journeyed back with her husband Elkanah to their village. She told Elkanah everything. She was not sad anymore. There were no tears in her eyes anymore. She thought, "God will not forget me."

It took a long time — a whole year. But then a little baby was born in Hannah's house. The LORD had listened to Hannah's quiet prayer. He gave her a son, a dear little boy. Hannah was so very happy. She said, "I have asked the LORD for this boy. I know a beautiful name for him. His name shall be Samuel." How happy Hannah was!

Samuel grew up into a big boy. Then something special happened. Hannah took Samuel along to the old priest, and she said, "My lord Eli, may my little son stay with you? May he help you here in God's house? Remember when I prayed in that corner? I said, 'LORD if Thou givest me a little boy, then he will always be Thy servant.' And the LORD gave me a little boy. Now I am bringing him to you in God's house. May he help? Then he will always be a servant of God."

Samuel was allowed to stay with the old priest. He liked that. He wanted to be God's servant. Hannah went back home. But every year she came back and brought a new linen suit for her son. Then she would ask Eli if Samuel was a good boy, and the old priest would answer, "Yes, Samuel is a good, fine boy. He helps me faithfully. He may always stay here in God's house." When Hannah heard that her heart filled with joy. She thought, "My son may always be God's servant. He loves God. That will make him happy always. The LORD is so good to us, to me and to Samuel, too." And joyfully Hannah would go home. She was not sad anymore.

Once, in the middle of the night, Samuel woke up. He heard someone calling, "Samuel, Samuel!"

Quickly he jumped out of bed and went to the other room where Eli slept. Eli was very old. His eyes could not see well anymore. Samuel thought, "Eli must have called me. I shall go there right away to help him."

But Eli said, "No, my son. I did not call you. Just go back to sleep."

Samuel went back to bed. But a little while later, he heard someone calling again, "Samuel, Samuel!"

"Now, surely Eli called me," he thought. Quickly he went to the old priest and said, "Here I am!"

But Eli said, "No, my son, I did not call you. Go back to sleep."

Samuel went to bed again. Then he heard the call a third time. "Samuel, Samuel!"

He jumped up and went to Eli and said, "Here I am. Surely, now you called me. I heard a voice."

"No, my son, I did not call you. But now I know whom you hear. I am not calling you, but the LORD in heaven is. He needs to tell you something. Go back to bed. Listen carefully. When the voice calls you, you must say, 'Speak, LORD, Thy servant hears.'"

Samuel went back to bed. He listened. There was the voice again, calling, "Samuel, Samuel!"

Softly and reverently Samuel said, "Speak, LORD, Thy servant hears."

Then God Himself spoke to Samuel. It was a sad message. It was a message for Eli, the old priest. Eli had two sons whose names were Hophni and Phinehas. They were priests, too. They were supposed to be God's servants, too, but they were wicked men. They had no respect for God's house. They did bad things. Eli knew that, but it did not even make him angry. He did not punish them.

Now God came to punish those wicked, bad men Himself. God said to Samuel, "Hophni and Phinehas shall die together on one day." Yes, that was a sad message. Then it was very quiet again in the room where Samuel slept.

But morning came. The cheerful sun shone through the windows. Samuel was not cheerful. He arose early and opened the doors of God's house. He did not dare to go to Eli. What if Eli asked about what God had said? But Eli was calling him, and Samuel went to him. Then Eli asked, "Samuel, what did God tell you last night?"

It frightened Samuel, but he had to tell the sad message. Eli was shocked. It was his own fault. He had never punished his wicked sons. Now God would come to punish them. Eli said, "The LORD is God, He may do all He wills."

It took a while yet, but then the punishment came. Hophni and Phinehas died in the war. They died together, on the same day. That was what God had said to Samuel. That was what happened. It was their own fault.

Eli, the old priest, heard of it. He got such a shock that he died, too, on that very same day. Then there were no priests in the house of God anymore. Who would be God's servant now?

Samuel would. He loved God. He would be God's faithful servant his whole life. That was what happened. Samuel often heard the voice of God speaking to him. Then he would listen reverently, and tell the people what God had said. The people listened to Samuel. They said, "We must do what Samuel says. Samuel is God's servant. We must be obedient and love God. Then we will be happy just like Samuel."

DAVID

Look, what a large flock of sheep! They were all grazing quietly in the green meadow. The sun shone warm and the grass tasted good. The little lambs skipped along with their mothers. They were not at all afraid. The shepherd was there and he took care of them. He took very good care of them. Sometimes one of the sheep would wander away. But the shepherd knew, and he would go to find it and bring it back. And if the sheep was tired he would carry it in his arms. Oh, yes, he would take care of them. He was a good shepherd. His sheep knew him.

That good shepherd was called David. He was only a young man. Far in the distance stood some little white houses where his father Jesse, his mother, and also his brothers lived. David's brothers were big, strong men and were all older than he was. He was only a young man. Every day he herded the sheep. He was a cheerful and happy young shepherd. The sky was blue, the flowers bloomed, and the birds sang in the trees. Everything was so beautiful. The shepherd looked up. He thought, "God in heaven has made everything so beautiful. He takes care of the flowers and the birds. He takes care of me, too." That made David cheerful and glad.

Hush! Listen! How wonderful! It was music, very soft music. Who was making that music? How beautiful it was! David, the young shepherd, was making the music. He was playing a harp. He had made the harp himself. His fingers plucked the strings gently. They were very fine strings. When he plucked them, it sounded so beautiful. It was very soft, wonderful music. David sang with it, too. His eyes looked up to heaven. He wanted to tell God how beautiful everything was. He wanted to tell God how happy he was, and how much he loved God. That was why he was making such beautiful music.

The sheep were grazing; they did not listen. No one heard what David was singing. But God in heaven heard it; He knew that David loved Him.

One day, when evening came, something terrible happened. A lion came out of the forest. It was a terrible animal with large jaws, and sharp claws. Quietly the lion came stealing along, silent and cruel. Suddenly he leaped and grabbed a sheep with his sharp claws. He was about to bite it with his big jaws. Poor little lamb! That lion was so fierce. That lion was so cruel. Who would help the sheep?

But the shepherd saw it. He ran up to it. The lion roared loudly. He dropped the lamb and leaped at David, mouth wide open and sharp claws forward. It wanted to rip David to pieces. Poor David! That lion was so big. That lion was so strong. Who would help David? But David was not afraid of that big lion. David knew that God in heaven saw him. He thought, "The LORD will help me." Then, with a heavy club he hit that cruel lion on the

head. He killed him, and the little sheep was saved. David was saved, too. He thought, "I take care of my sheep. God takes care of me. Fierce lions kill people, they are so strong and big. But God made my arms stronger than the lion's cruel claws. God takes care of me."

One day something strange happened. David was called to come to his father. One of the servants came to tell him to go home right away. David did not know why, but he went home. He came into the room. Oh, look. Who was that? A very old man with a long beard stood in the centre of the room. That was Samuel.

Yes, long, long ago that same Samuel had lived with Eli. Then he had been just a little boy. Now he had become an old man with a long beard. He had a little jar in his hand, a jar of oil. David's father and his strong brothers looked at him respectfully, because Samuel was God's servant. But what was he coming to do here? Why was he carrying that little jar with him?

Samuel knew. God Himself had told Samuel. Yes, it was very strange. God had said, "Samuel, go find one of the sons of Jesse. One of them must be king." Which son was the right one? Samuel had let all David's big, strong brothers come to him, one by one. Each time he shook his head. No, none of them could become king, none of them. And Samuel had kept the jar of oil in his hand. Then he had asked Father Jesse, "Do you have any more sons?"

Jesse had said, "Yes, I have one more son, David. He is herding the sheep. He is still very young."

But David had to come. And now David had arrived. He bowed to Samuel. He knew Samuel was God's servant. And then? Oh, look. Samuel went up to David. Carefully he poured oil out of the jar onto David's head. Samuel said, "David shall become king. God has said so. It shall surely happen. Not David's big, strong brothers, but David. God Himself has chosen David. That is why I poured the jar of oil onto David's head. Now he has been anointed as king."

How strange. Would David now receive royal clothes? Would a golden crown be placed on his head? Would he go to live in a big palace, and sit on a beautiful throne? No, David would go back to his sheep. Later, much later, he would become king. Now he would have to wait, for someone else was king in the land. This king's name was Saul. But King Saul was disobedient to God. That was why God chose a different king, a king who loved God. That king would be David. But not yet.

Samuel went back home. He had done what God had commanded him. David went back to his sheep. He was not proud at all, and he did not tell anyone what had happened. His father and brothers did not tell anyone either. If King Saul heard it, he would be very angry. No one should know about it. But it would surely happen; God Himself had said so.

DAVID AND GOLIATH

There was war in the land. Wicked enemies had come into the land of Israel. They wanted to take everything away. King Saul was frightened. But all the big, strong men went to help their king. They would chase those wicked enemies out of their land. Three of David's brothers went to war too. Not David — he was too young. He stayed home to take care of the sheep. But he often thought about his brothers. They were away so long.

One day Father Jesse said to David, "You must go and see how your brothers are doing in the war, they have been gone so long. Maybe they are sick. Maybe they have died. Go and inquire. I am so concerned."

David did not mind doing that at all. David thought, "I would like to see my brothers and all those brave soldiers. And I would like to see our brave king, too." So David left.

Far away, early in the morning, King Saul and his brave soldiers were among the mountains. That was where their wicked enemies were, too. David came near the battlefield. He listened, but he did not hear anything. He went farther. Oh, there they were! The strong king and his strong men were on a hill. They were waiting. What were they waiting for? Shouldn't they have been chasing those wicked enemies away? Did they not dare? Were they afraid of them? David came nearer. All those men looked afraid and sad. Why?

He saw his three brothers, too. No, they were not sick, they were not dead. But they were afraid and sad, too. Why? He asked, "Why are you so afraid? Why do you look so sad?"

They answered, "Don't you know? Have you not heard? Look, there he comes, that wicked giant. We are so afraid of him."

DAVID AND GOLIATH

David looked — yes, a huge giant was coming. He wore a bronze helmet on his head, and a suit of shining bronze. He had a huge sword with him and a tremendously heavy spear with a sharp iron point. His name was Goliath.

The giant came very near. He mocked King Saul and his soldiers. He swung his sword and cried, "Who dares to come and fight with me? Let him come if he dares."

But no one dared. King Saul did not dare. David's strong brothers did not dare. That giant was so big, so strong, so wicked. He laughed at the fearful king and his frightened soldiers. And he mocked God, too. He swore. That was the worst of all. David heard it. It made him very angry. That giant was not allowed to mock God!

David's brothers said, "That wicked giant Goliath comes here every day. He mocks, he swears, but no one dares to fight with him. Whoever will fight with him may marry the king's daughter. But we are all so afraid of him. He will kill us if we go near him! He is so big and so strong and so mean."

The giant left. He went back to his friends on the opposite side of the hill. David could still hear him laughing in the distance. David was very angry at that wicked giant. Suddenly he said, "I will fight with him."

The soldiers stared at David. He was still very young, and he was not even a soldier. He was just a shepherd who took care of sheep. They thought, "If David dares to go near the giant, the giant will kill him right away." Yet David said, "I shall fight with him."

Then David had to come before the king. King Saul asked, "Do you dare to go and fight with Goliath? Are you that strong?"

David said, "No, my lord the king, I am not that strong. But God in heaven will help me. Once I killed a lion. Another time I killed a bear. That lion was much stronger than I, but God helped me. That wicked giant Goliath mocked God. That is not allowed. I shall fight with him. The LORD will take care of me."

"But then you must wear a suit of armour. Only then will you be a soldier," King Saul said.

David put on the armour, but that suit of bronze was so heavy, his arms felt stiff. He could not even walk properly in it.

Quickly he took it off again and said, "I shall fight in my shepherd's robe."

Then David went to the brook. He found five smooth stones and put them in his shepherd's bag. Then he waited, and he prayed.

"The giant is coming! The giant is coming!" the soldiers cried.

David was not afraid.

Yes, there came Goliath, swinging his terrible sword. A man came along with him to carry his shield. Goliath mocked and swore. He shouted, "Who dares to fight with me? I am not afraid of anyone!"

David came down the hill. He walked right up to that terrible giant. In one hand he carried his shepherd's staff, in the other hand a leather sling. He did not even have a sword. He did not even have a spear.

Goliath the giant saw David come. He became furious at David. The boy was not even a soldier! And he did not even have a sword! He was coming with a stick. Goliath shouted, "What do you think you are doing? Do you think I am a dog, that you have come to hit me with a stick? Come here! I will pierce you with my spear. I will kill you, and wild animals will eat you. Come here, if you dare!" He roared, and he lifted his spear high.

But that did not frighten David. He came closer and said, "You have mocked God. That is terrible. God will help me."

How the giant roared in anger! He stalked up to David. He was so big, and David was so small. He was so strong, and David was so weak. One stab with that spear . . .!

But David did not run away. David put a smooth stone in his sling, he swung the sling around, and the stone flew out. That stone flew into the giant's head. And then . . .? Then the giant fell down on the ground. It made the ground shake. David ran toward him. He took the giant's sword and killed him.

King Saul and his soldiers on the hill saw it happen. They gave a joyful shout. The enemies on the other hill saw it, too. They cried out in fear, and ran away as fast as they could go. King Saul and his soldiers chased after them. They drove those wicked enemies out of the land. They had won the war!

Joyfully the army went back home. David went along, walking beside the king.

DAVID AND GOLIATH

But the people did not look at the king, they looked at David. They had heard what David had done. They cheered and sang, "King Saul is brave, but David is braver!"

The king heard it and it made him angry at David. He thought, "The people love David more than me. I do not want that to happen. I am the king. They must love me the most." He did not say anything, but his heart was very annoyed. That was bad, that was very wrong of the king. He was not allowed to be angry with David.

Quietly David walked beside the king. He heard what the people were calling and singing. He thought, "The giant was much stronger than I. I could not have killed him, but God helped me. I want to be God's servant forever."

And David quietly went back to his sheep.

WICKED KING SAUL

It was very quiet in the king's palace. The servants walked quietly through the beautiful rooms. They looked so sad and whispered to each other when they spoke. They pointed to the room where King Saul was and said, "See how angry he looks! Our poor king. Who will help him?" King Saul was lying on his couch. He was wearing beautiful clothes, and on his arm he wore a bracelet of gold. Bowls full of delicious fruit stood on a table beside him but he did not look at them. Outside in the garden the sun shone brightly. Flowers bloomed there, and birds sang cheerfully but he did not listen to them. Angrily, he looked straight ahead. His eyes were dark and filled with wrath. His eyes were filled with fear, too. His hands were clenched into fists of anger. Why?

In earlier days, King Saul had not been afraid and angry. God had made him king, and he had been God's servant. He had been happy and content. But King Saul had been disobedient, time and time again. He had become proud and had done what he wanted to do. Now he could not be happy anymore. So God had said, "I will choose someone else to be king over My people." Now King Saul was angry and afraid. Sometimes it was very bad. Then his eyes would look so dark and his fists would clench, and anger burned in his heart. That poor king! But it was his own fault. He did not want to listen to God.

His servants felt sorry for him. They whispered quietly, and they said, "We know something! We have an idea. We will let someone play beautiful music when the king is so angry and afraid. Then he shall listen, and maybe forget about his anger. Yes, we will do that."

The servants went to David. They said, "You can make such beautiful music on your harp. Sometimes our king is so afraid and angry. Come and live in the palace and play your beautiful music for him. Maybe he will listen. Maybe it will make him better for a while."

Yes, David wanted to do that for the poor king; he felt sorry for him. So he went to the palace and took his harp along. King Saul was lying on his couch, alone and angry. Who could make him happy again? David quietly came into the room. He sat near the wall and put his harp between his knees. He thought, "I shall play my most beautiful music. Poor king! Maybe then the anger will leave his heart."

Softly David plucked the strings of the harp. How beautiful, how very beautiful it sounded! The king looked up and listened. David played and played. It sounded more and more beautiful. The king listened. His eyes which had been so dark became happy. He forgot his anger, and the fear left his heart. He listened and listened. It sounded so wonderful.

When the music was finished, David quietly left. But King Saul's servant asked David, "Will you come again when the king is so afraid and angry? Will you play for him again?"

"Yes, certainly. I always want to help the king if I can." And David returned again and again.

But one day, when David was playing his beautiful music for King Saul, the king's eyes looked so dark, so terribly dark and angry. He looked at David, and King Saul thought, "That is David, who killed Goliath the giant. Oh, yes, I remember. All the people looked at him and not at me. And all the people loved him more than they loved me. He dared to fight. I did not. He is God's friend; I am not."

Then King Saul became angry, terribly angry with David. Beside his couch lay a spear with an iron tip. King Saul jumped up and grabbed the spear. He lifted it high, pointed it at David, and then threw it. The spear sped away. What if it hit David!

He missed! Thankfully the spear missed David. The sharp point drove into the wall, but it did not hit David. David jumped aside just in time. That angry wicked king! David had not hurt him at all.

David fled from the palace. But he was not angry with the king.

But wicked King Saul did not love David at all. He thought to himself, "Just wait, I shall kill David anyway! Just wait!"

IN THE DARK CAVE

Far away were the mountains. The wind blew gently through the grass there. It was quiet, very, very quiet near the mountains. Some men were coming along. They were in a hurry, and often turned to look back. Were they afraid? Of what?

"Come along," they said to each other. "Faster, faster! In the mountains we can hide." Again they looked around with fear in their eyes.

Who was in the lead? It was David. All those men were his followers; he was their leader. "Come along," he urged, "I know where there is a dark cave in the mountains. It goes far and deep into the mountain. That is where we shall go to hide. No one will see us there. Come quickly."

They climbed up the mountain, and there was the dark cave. David went inside. It was dark and damp there. But David went inside anyway, and his friends came along, all of them. They looked around once more. How frightened their eyes were! "Come on," they encouraged each other. "What if he sees us! Come!"

That dark cave was very big and deep. David and his friends crawled far away, all the way to the back. Then it was very quiet again among the mountains. The wind gently blew through the grass.

IN THE DARK CAVE

Why were these men so afraid? Who were they running away from? And David, wasn't he supposed to take care of his sheep? Shouldn't he have been playing on his harp when the king was angry? Why was David there? Had he done something wicked? Was that why he was there? Oh, no, David had not done anything wrong. But wicked King Saul wanted to kill him. That was why David had to flee. If David went to the palace, the king would say to his soldiers, "Seize him!" If David stayed with his sheep, the king would send his soldiers and command, "Seize him! Kill him!" That was how angry the king was at David. Yet David had not done anything wrong at all. Now he was running away. He hid in a dark cave in the mountain, and the other men were hiding, too. They were afraid of angry King Saul, too. They had all become David's friends.

But why did they look back all the time? Far behind them Saul himself was coming with a large group of soldiers. What if he found David!

Saul and his soldiers came nearer, but they did not know that David was in the cave. They were tired. They had come a long way, and the sun was shining so hot. Now they could rest. The soldiers stuck their spears into the ground, then lay down in the tall grass. They laughed carelessly, and said, "Tomorrow we'll catch him." But they did not know that David was close by.

Angry King Saul was tired, too. He wanted to rest by himself, all alone. He did not laugh, he was not happy, he was sullen and angry. His scowling eyes searched the distance. He was looking for David everywhere, but he did not know that David was very close by. Saul wanted to sleep, but not near the soldiers. They were making so much noise; they were so rowdy. He searched for a place where he could be by himself.

Oh, no! Saul was climbing a little way up the mountain, right up to where the dark cave was! It was quiet and lonely there; it was a good place to sleep. He did not know that David was inside. He came near the cave; he looked inside, but did not see anything. That cave was so dark and so deep. Yes, here it would be quiet. Here he would be able to sleep. He walked just a little way into the cave. What would happen if he went any farther, if he would go deep inside that cave? No, he did not do that. He lay down at the entrance of the cave. He lay down with his head on his arms, and he thought, "Tomorrow I will catch David. Tomorrow I will kill him. He is God's friend. Maybe he will become king. I do not want that to happen. I will kill him! Tomorrow!" Wicked King Saul fell asleep.

David and his men saw him. They were terribly afraid, but stayed very quiet. They whispered, "The king is sleeping. He does not know that we are here. What should we do? What if he wakes up and sees us?"

But David was not afraid. He crept near the king. Just a few more steps . . . he came very close.

David's men whispered, "Kill him! Kill that wicked king, then he can never hurt you anymore. Strike him, kill him! Do you not dare? Shall we kill him?"

But David became angry. "No," he said quietly. "No, that is not allowed. We may not hurt the king. That would be very wicked." And David went nearer still. Very carefully he picked up the king's robe. Saul did not feel it — he was asleep. With his knife, David cut a piece off the king's robe. Then he quietly went back to the men farther back in the cave, taking the piece of robe along. Quietly they sat together and waited. Soon the king would wake up.

King Saul stirred. He awoke. He got up. Would he see David and his men now? No, he didn't! He did not see anything. It was so dark far back in the cave. He walked outside and went back to his soldiers. Now they would go and search for David again. Oh, if only they knew where he was! There they went, Saul marching in the lead.

All of a sudden they heard someone calling. They looked around. Who was that? Listen, there it was again. Someone was calling, "My lord the king! My lord the king!"

Saul heard it, too. He was startled. He knew that voice. There, on top of the mountain — stood a man. He was calling. And behind him were many more men. That man was David.

Quietly they had left the cave. Very quietly they had followed the king. Then David had climbed a hill, and now he was calling, "My lord the king! My lord the king!" He bowed respectfully to Saul. Then he said, "O my lord, why are you so angry with me? I have never hurt you. You are chasing me, and you want to kill me. Why, O king? You were sleeping in the cave. I was very near you, but I did not hurt you. Look, I cut a piece off your robe. It is in my hand."

When wicked King Saul saw it, he was ashamed. He had wanted to hurt David, yet David had been good to him. "My son David, you are a good man. I am a bad man. God in heaven is taking care of you. David, I am sorry that I was so wicked. Let us be friends again. I will not try to hurt you anymore."

Saul went back home, but David did not go along with him. David thought, "The king is friendly toward me now, but what if he becomes angry again? I will be very careful." And with his men David journeyed over the mountains. He did not trust wicked King Saul at all.

THE SPEAR AND THE WATER JUG

King Saul had said, "My son David, let us be friends again. I will not hurt you." But the wicked king soon forgot that. He became angry at David again anyway. Once again he said, "I will kill him!" He took his soldiers to search for David. What if he found him!

Look, there went King Saul with a large army through the lonely land. It was quiet and wild there. Everywhere there were large areas of sand, jagged rocks, and here and there a little tree. Saul and his soldiers went farther and farther. They searched everywhere, but could not find David. Evening came, so they could not search any longer. They were allowed to sleep now. But not everyone could sleep. A few soldiers had to stay awake to stand guard.

The soldiers lay on the ground, but a tent was set up for the king. Saul went inside. He was tired and angry. He lay down. He stuck his spear in the ground, close to his head. It was the same spear he had thrown at David when he played on his harp for him in the palace a long time ago. Beside the king was a water jug, too. If he got thirsty in the night, he could drink.

Saul fell asleep. His soldiers fell asleep, too. But the watchers who were supposed to stay awake fell asleep, too. How strange! Now they were all asleep. Who would guard the king?

Look! Who was coming there in the dark night? He was walking very quietly and very carefully. He looked and he listened. He came near the sleeping soldiers. Who was it? Was he going to hurt them? Oh, no, it was David and one of his men. They would not hurt the sleeping soldiers. They were searching for the king. David had hidden himself when it was daytime, but he had seen where the king and his soldiers had gone. He had seen them go to sleep, too. And now in the middle of the dark night, he quietly came to look. His friend, Abishai, followed him quietly. They were very near the soldiers. Yet — how strange! Not one of them woke up. The watchmen were all sleeping, too. There was the king's tent. It stood in the centre of all the sleeping soldiers.

"Come," David whispered. "Let us go near the king. Do you dare?"

Abishai whispered, "Yes."

"Quietly, we do not want to wake the soldiers up."

Again Abishai whispered, "Yes."

Together they walked on. It was a very dangerous thing to do. It was dark and quiet. They stepped right over the sleeping soldiers. Carefully, very carefully. What if one of them woke up? They came to the tent and crawled inside. There lay wicked King Saul. His fists were clenched. Beside him stood a water jug. Beside his head, his sharp spear was stuck into the ground.

THE SPEAR AND THE WATER JUG

"Oh," Abishai said, "now we can kill wicked Saul. Take the spear and kill him with it! If you do not dare, I will do it for you, and then the wicked king can never hurt you again." Abishai was ready to grab the spear, but David pushed him back quickly.

"That is not allowed — we may not do that! He is the king, anointed by God. We may not do that. Come, we'll quietly take his water jug and spear. When the king wakes up, he will wonder who was here, and who took his water jug and spear away. Come."

Quickly they left.

Once again they stepped over all those sleeping soldiers. Not one woke up. It was God in heaven who made them sleep so deeply. He was taking care of David. David and Abishai returned to their friends in the dark night. They brought the spear and water jug along.

The next morning King Saul woke up. He wanted to have a drink, but his water jug was gone. He turned to grab his spear, but it was not there anymore. It frightened him. Who had been so near him during the night? He asked the soldiers, but no one knew. So on they went, along the mountainous rocks to search for David.

Suddenly they heard someone calling from high on the rocks. Startled, the soldiers looked up. There stood David. In one hand he had a spear, in the other a water jug. He cried, "O my lord the king, see, I do not hate you. I will never hurt you. I came very near you last night. Here is your water jug and your spear. We took them along while you were asleep. I could have killed you, but I did not do it. My lord the king, why are you so angry with me? Why do you always chase after me? Why do you want to kill me? Two times I came near you while you were asleep. First in the dark cave, and now in your tent. I did not hurt you. Let me go and do not be angry with me anymore."

King Saul bowed his head. He was ashamed, and hardly dared to look at David. He said, "My son David, you are much better than I am. I acted wickedly. God is taking care of you. I know that."

One of his soldiers went to get the spear and water jug, and Saul went home with his men. David and his men went back into the desert. Wicked King Saul and God's servant David never met again.

Once again there was war in the land. Saul and his soldiers went to fight the enemies. Saul never returned. He died in the battle. Who became king then? David. God Himself had said that long ago, when David was only a shepherd boy. Then Samuel had come, and he had poured a little bottle of oil on David's head and said, "One day you shall become king." And now it had come about. Whatever God says always happens. No one can change that.

David became a good king. He was God's servant. He loved God. He reigned many, many years, and the people loved him very much. And God always took care of him. God takes care of everyone who loves Him.

ELIJAH, THE GREAT PROPHET

Once a wicked king ruled in the land. He did not love God. He mocked God. Do you know what he did? He made an image, an image of wood. He said, "That image is my god. I will pray to that wooden image." But that was wrong. It was very wicked of that king. He was sinning against God who lives in heaven and can see everything. That king did many more wicked things, but his wife, the queen, was even more wicked than him. Do you know what was even worse? The men and the women who lived in the land went to worship the image, too. They did wicked things, too, just like the king and just like the queen. That was terrible. But God, who lives in heaven, saw that wicked king and queen and all those wicked people. He sees everything. He knows everything. Why were they so wicked? God had been so good to them.

The king sat on his throne in his beautiful palace. He laughed and was carefree because he was so rich. He was so merry. He did everything he wanted to do. Around him stood his merry friends. They laughed, too, and they mocked. They also were rich. They wore beautiful clothes, and whatever the king said, they did right away. Everything was festive and so lovely in that beautiful palace.

But look, a man was coming to the palace. Who was he? He did not belong there, and he was not allowed to come, but he came anyway. He walked right into that beautiful palace. He wore very poor clothes. His robe was roughly made of coarse camel's hair. He had a leather belt around his waist, and he was not merry at all. Oh, no. His piercing eyes gazed dark and fierce at the king and his merry friends.

That man did not belong in the beautiful palace. Everything was so splendid and rich there, but he looked so gloomy and poor. He should not have gone to that rich king and his merry friends. Yes, but he had gone anyway, and he was not afraid. Why not? Because God Himself had commanded him to go to the king. That man was Elijah the prophet. He had to tell the people whatever God commanded him to. He spoke to poor people and rich people, and even to the king. There he stood. He looked at the king, pointed his finger and him, and said, "It shall not rain in the land anymore, and at night, no dew shall fall on the grass. This drought will last until I pray for rain again. Thus the LORD has spoken to me, and it shall surely happen."

The king and his friends stared at Elijah. They were a little frightened, but they laughed anyway. They laughed at that prophet of God. They said, "Will there be no rain? And will there be no dew on the grass at night? Oh, what a fool that man is! How can he know? He is just saying something. Come on, let us be cheerful."

Elijah left. He had brought God's message. It was a punishment for the wicked king and his wicked people. Then what Elijah said happened. It was terrible! Not a drop of rain fell out of the sky. And in the night, not a drop of dew hung on the flowers. Everything dried up. The sun burned on the dry land, and the grass and the flowers and the grain all died. The leaves fell off the trees. They were dead, too. And it did not rain. It never rained. Then the people had no grain to bake bread anymore. The animals had no grass to eat. Famine came. It was terrible. That was the punishment for the wicked king and the wicked people. It was their own fault.

That wicked king's name was Ahab. His wicked queen was called Jezebel. Now Ahab no longer laughed. His merry friends no longer laughed either. They were angry, terribly angry at Elijah.

"It is all his fault," they said. But that was not true — it was their own fault. They also said, "We shall catch that bad prophet and kill him! We will do whatever we want to do."

They searched everywhere. Soldiers were sent throughout the whole land to find Elijah. But they did not find Elijah anywhere. Where was he?

Elijah was sitting all alone beside a brook, a little stream high up in the mountains. It was a very lonely place. No one ever came there. The soldiers of wicked King Ahab were not able to find him there. God Himself had shown Elijah that beautiful quiet place. God Himself would take care of Elijah. Now the wicked king and his wicked servants could not harm him. The water of the brook was fresh and cool. Elijah drank as much as he needed. But food, who would give Elijah food? Who would give him bread? Who would give him meat? No one ever came to this quiet place.

Look! Big black birds were coming, flying through the sky. They were ravens. In their beaks they had pieces of bread and pieces of meat, which they had found somewhere. Were they going to eat them? No, they dropped those pieces of food right at Elijah's feet, and then those black birds flew away, far into the sky, until Elijah could not see them any longer. But he could keep the bread and the meat to eat. God Himself had sent the ravens to Elijah. Animals always do what God tells them. Every day the ravens came. Elijah was no longer hungry. He drank from the brook and ate whatever the ravens brought him. That was how God took care of his servant. God takes care of everyone who loves Him.

ELIJAH AND THE POOR WOMAN

There went Elijah. He was leaving the quiet, beautiful spot high in the mountains. Why? Where was he going? Was he not afraid that the soldiers of the wicked king might catch him? Would the ravens bring him meat and bread somewhere else? Elijah went along quietly and contentedly. He wore his robe of camel's hair and the leather belt around his waist. A tall staff was in his hand. He had to journey far, far away. No, he was not afraid of the wicked king's soldiers. Elijah knew that God would take care of him. The brook in the mountains had dried up. The sun had shone so hot and it had never rained. Now Elijah could not drink of that cool water anymore. Now he had to leave that beautiful, quiet place, otherwise he would die of thirst. God had said to Elijah, "Go to another land far away. There a woman will give you food to eat and water to drink. I shall always take care of you."

It was a long way, and the sun was burning hot. That other land was so far away. But Elijah did what God had told him. What God says is always good. The journey took many long days. But one day, Elijah saw a woman walking nearby. She stooped often to pick up dead twigs off the ground. Her arms were full. She must have been wanting to make a fire at home with that wood. Likely she was baking bread, or cooking a meal. She bent over again and again. But why did she look so sad?

Elijah saw the woman. He thought, "Is that the woman who is to give me food to eat and water to drink? I do not know. I shall ask her."

Elijah said to her, "I am very thirsty. Do you have some water for me?"

The woman looked up. She saw the strange man and noticed how tired he was. His feet were covered with the dust of the road. She forgot her own grief. A bit of water? Oh, yes, he could have some. She would fetch it for him. She said, "I will go to my house. I will fetch water for you right away. Are you very thirsty?"

She turned to go, but then Elijah called her back. He said, "I am so hungry. Please get me a piece of bread, too."

The woman was afraid. Sorrow filled her eyes. Bread! She had no bread. No bread at all. She only had a tiny bit of flour left in her house.

"Oh, no, my lord — I cannot give you bread. There is a famine in the land. The hot sun has dried out the grain because it never rains. I am only a poor widow. My husband has died. I have no more food. I have only a tiny little bit of flour in my house, and a tiny little bit of oil in the jar. See, I have gathered wood, and I am going to bake some bread for me and my dear son. We shall share it together. It will be the last food. And then — oh, my lord, then we will have nothing left. Nothing at all. Then my dear son and I will die of hunger. No, I cannot give you anything to eat."

She was so sad, the poor woman.

Elijah saw it. But Elijah was not sad at all. He thought, "God in heaven will take care of us. He will take care of me, and of that poor woman and her dear son, too."

Elijah said, "Do not be sad. Go to your house and bake that bread for me. Do not be afraid. The flour will not run out, nor the oil in the jar. God in heaven will take care of us. Just go to your house and bake some bread for me first. Then bake a loaf for yourself, and one for your son. There will be flour in the pot and oil in the jar until the rain comes. God has told me. Go and do it."

ELIJAH AND THE POOR WOMAN

The poor woman looked at Elijah. Was he deceiving her? Would the flour in the pot and the oil in the bottle run out? Would she and her son have nothing to eat? No, she could see that this man was not deceiving her. He was a prophet. He was a servant of God. God would take care of them all. She made a fire with the dead wood and baked a delicious loaf of bread. Not for her son, not for herself, but for the strange man who was so hungry. Then Elijah ate it.

What about the poor woman and her son? Would they have anything to eat? There, the pan was on the fire again. There was just as much flour in the pot, and just as much oil in the jar! The woman was baking another loaf. This one was for her son. It smelled so good, and it tasted delicious, and he could eat it all by himself! Then she baked another one all for herself. And then — how strange it was! How wonderful! There was just as much flour and oil left. It was wonderful. Only God could do that. He takes care of everyone who loves him.

So Elijah stayed with the widow. He was no longer hungry or thirsty. The poor woman and her son did not lack anything, either. That was a wonderful, happy time. But one day, something terrible happened. The little boy became very sick. He lay quietly on his bed. His cheeks were pale and his hands were cold. Then the dear boy became so sick that he died. His poor mother sat by his side but he could not see her. She cried, and called him by name, but he could not hear her. She took him in her arms, but he could not feel it. He was dead.

Oh, that poor mother! She cried and wept with grief. She called Elijah and said, "O my lord, my dear son has died. Now I am left all alone. I have done many wicked things in my life, and now God is punishing me." She wept with grief. It was so sad, so terribly sad!

Elijah was sad, too. That poor mother! Now she had lost her dear son. He felt so sorry for her. What should he do? Kindly he said to her, "Give me your son." Then he took the dead child upstairs to his own room, and laid him on his own bed. The dead boy looked so quiet, so cold, and so white! No one could help him. No doctor could heal him. Elijah could not either. Only

God in heaven could. He can do everything. Elijah thought, "I shall tell God about it. I shall ask, 'O Lord, make this boy alive again. His poor mother is so bitterly grieved.'"

Then Elijah began to pray. He prayed for a long time. He prayed again and again. He told God everything, and he asked and he pleaded, "O Lord, make this dear boy alive again." God in heaven heard what Elijah asked.

Oh, look! Look! The little boy was opening his eyes. His white cheeks were flushing. He looked at Elijah and put his arms up to him. He was living — he was alive again! Elijah took him up in his arms, he was so happy. The boy was alive again! The Lord had heard his prayer. The Lord was so good! Elijah carried the boy downstairs.

"Mother! Mother!" the boy called.

His mother saw him and heard him. She rushed up to him and took him in her arms. She pressed him tightly to herself and kissed him over and over. Her eyes filled with tears, but now they were not tears of sorrow; they were tears of happiness.

"Oh, my dear, dear son. I have you back! You are alive again. God has done that. God is so good!"

Elijah looked at the happy mother. His eyes shone with happiness, too. Everything had been so terrible before. Now everything was so wonderful. Yes, God does take care of all who love Him.

Did Elijah stay with the woman? No, he could not. He was God's servant, and he had to go to the king and the people again. He had to tell them what God had said.

Elijah went to the king, but wicked King Ahab did not harm him — he did not dare to. For three years no rain had fallen on the land. King Ahab realized that God had done that. God punishes the people who are wicked and do bad things. Elijah prayed for rain, and dark clouds came drifting through the sky. Then wonderful rain fell down on the dry earth. The grass became green, the grain could grow again, and the people did not die of thirst anymore. The Lord felt sorry for them. The Lord was so good to them. Why did they always do such wicked things?

Elijah was God's faithful servant. He always did what God told him to. He loved God with his whole heart. Elijah became very old, and then God took him up to His beautiful heaven. On earth there is much sorrow, but not with God in heaven. Never. There Elijah is happy forever.

A POOR MOTHER AND HER POOR BOYS

Once there was a poor woman who was deeply sorrowful. Who could help her? Who could she tell about her fear? She went to Elisha. Elisha was God's faithful servant, as Elijah had been God's servant before.

The poor woman said, "O my lord Elisha, I have such a great sorrow. I am so sad and afraid."

Elisha kindly asked, "Why are you so sad?"

"My lord Elisha, I have two children, two dear boys. But I may not keep them. That makes me so sorrowful and afraid. My husband has died, so my sons do not have a father anymore. Now we have become very poor. We have no money and no goods, and we have to pay a large sum of money to our creditor. He wants to have the money. That is fair, but we have no money. My lord Elisha, now the creditor is going to take my two sons away from me. He will sell them as slaves so that he gets his money. That is why I am so sad, and that is why my sons are so afraid. They hold on to me tightly. They do not want to leave me, but they will have to when the creditor comes!"

Elisha felt sorry for the poor woman and her sons. He wanted to help her, but he could not. He had no money or goods to give to the creditor. Elisha said, "I cannot help you, but God in heaven, He can help you. I know that. What do you have in your house that you can sell?"

"I have only a jar of oil in my house, my lord."

"Good," Elisha said, "Go and fill every jug, every jar, and every container with oil out of that little jar."

But that was impossible! Fill every jug, every jar, and every container with oil out of that one little jar? But the woman did it anyway. She believed. She knew that Elisha was the servant of God. She also knew that with God all things are possible. She hastened to her house and to her sons. She said, "Close the door, quickly, then we will be alone. Bring me every jug, jar, and container that is in the house."

The boys hurried and brought their mother everything they could find that she could fill with oil. And their mother poured and poured. All the big and little jars were filled. But still the little jar was not empty.

"Bring me some more," she said. On and on she poured. It was a miracle, a great miracle of God. That poor woman and those poor boys were so happy and so thankful.

The woman went on pouring reverently and her sons brought her everything that they could find to fill with oil. Every jug, every jar, and every container was filled. But the little jar was still not empty.

"Bring me some more containers," the mother told her boys.

"Mother, there are no more," the boys replied.

"Then go and ask our neighbours," the mother said. "They will lend us jugs and jars and containers."

Eagerly the boys went to the neighbours and got more containers. Soon they were also filled from the little jar.

"Bring me more containers," the mother asked again.

Her boys answered, "Mother, there are no more, not at our neighbours either."

All of a sudden the little jug was empty. It was enough. It was more than enough. The whole house was filled with jugs and jars and containers of oil. It was a wonderful miracle!

Then Elisha the prophet, God's servant, came. His eyes shone with happiness when he saw all that costly oil. With this miracle, the LORD in heaven had wonderfully helped the poor woman and her poor sons. Poor woman? Poor sons? Not anymore. Elisha said, "Go and sell all this oil. It is worth a lot of money in our land."

"Yes, my lord Elisha. Now all my grief and my fear is gone," the woman answered.

She sold the oil and received a lot of money for it. Now she could pay the creditor. He would not get her sons, her two dear sons. They would be free men when they grew up, not slaves. There was a lot of money left over, too. The woman could buy clothes and food for her sons, everything that they needed. Their hearts were so thankful to God. It was the LORD who had helped them in their great need. He can do everything.

THE RICH MAN WHO WAS A LEPER

Poor Captain Naaman! He was very rich. He lived in a beautiful house. He was able to have everything he wanted. He was the king's friend. He had manservants and maidservants, as if he was the king himself. He rode in a beautiful chariot. He wore beautiful clothes. His servants prepared the most delicious foods for him every day. But rich Captain Naaman was very miserable. Naaman was very sick. Couldn't a doctor come to make him better? Oh, yes, doctors came. But not one of the doctors in the whole land could heal him. No one could. Naaman was a leper. His hands were white and covered with white sores. So were his feet and his face. He would never get better; it would only get worse, much worse. More and more sores would cover his body. In a little while he would die. Oh, he would give away all his money and all his beautiful things if only he could get better! But he did not get better. He never would. Poor Captain Naaman!

There sat Naaman's wife. She was rich, too. She was able to have everything she wanted, too. She sat in a lovely room on a beautiful couch. A little fire was burning in a golden container.

On the fire dark grains of expensive incense burned, making the room smell lovely. Yet that rich woman was sad. She was always thinking about her husband. She was not able to help him, either. No, no one was able to help him.

The door opened and a girl came in. She bowed respectfully to the rich woman. She was a slave. Her father and mother lived far away in the land of Israel. But she could not go to them. She had to stay here, in a strange house, in a strange land with strange people. Why was that?

Some time ago Naaman had been a brave and strong officer. He had gone to war along with the soldiers for his king. He had come to the land of Israel, too, where the girl had lived. Some rough soldiers had stolen her away from her father and mother. They had taken her to that strange land. Now she had to serve Naaman's wife. She had become a slave. Poor girl. Was she not angry with Naaman? Was she not angry with the strange woman? No, not at all! She came into the room of the rich woman who was so sad. She became sad herself. She was sorry for the poor woman, and she was sorry for her poor master Naaman who would never get better. Listen to what she said.

She said, "O my lady, no one can heal my lord Naaman. But in the land of my father and mother lives a prophet whose name is Elisha. He is the servant of God. O my lady, God in heaven can heal Captain Naaman. Maybe Elisha will pray for him. Let my lord Naaman go to Elisha. He is the servant of God."

The rich woman listened. She thought, "This girl is good and loving. She is not angry with Naaman, she loves him."

And she answered the girl, "Yes, I shall tell him about it. He should go to the prophet. How wonderful it would be if he were healed!"

The girl left the beautiful room. Her heart was so happy. She thought, "Yes, if Captain Naaman could be healed, how wonderful that would be!"

Naaman listened to his wife and travelled to Israel. He rode in his beautiful chariot. But he was so very sick. His servants suffered along with him. They looked at their poor master and thought, "Now we are making such a long journey. We are going to that faraway land of the Israelites, where a prophet is living. Maybe he can help our poor master Naaman. How wonderful it would be if he could be healed!" The servants felt sorry for their poor, sick master. They rode on the long, hot road, and they were always thinking of the prophet in the faraway land. Was it true? Could he help Naaman?

There was Elisha's house. The journey had been very long, but now they had arrived. Naaman sat in his beautiful chariot, but he was so sick, so very sick. He looked at Elisha's house. It was only a very poor house. Naaman thought, "The prophet will come outside quickly. He will probably bow low to me. I am such a rich man, and he is such a poor prophet. And then surely he will pray for me to his God. Perhaps he will touch my sore hands and my sore feet, and maybe he will give me some strange medicine. Yes, I shall allow it all to be done. I will do anything he tells me, if only I will be healed."

Some of the servants jumped out of the chariots. They knocked on the door. Surely the prophet would come out right away. He would be impressed by all those beautiful chariots, horses, and servants. And when he saw the rich Captain Naaman, he would bow respectfully.

They knocked again. What was this? The prophet was not even coming to the door himself! He sent his servant, who said, "Captain Naaman, you must go to the River Jordan. You must wash yourself in the water seven times. Then you will be better. My master Elisha said so."

Naaman became very angry. The prophet would not even come himself to help? And did Naaman have to wash himself? He had done that so often, and it had not helped. In his own land the rivers were much more beautiful than in Israel, and the water was much clearer. Was he supposed to wash here? No, that would not help! He would not do it.

Naaman said to his servants, "Turn around. We are going back to our own land."

The servants obeyed, but they were so sorry. Going back to their own land? But then their good master would not be healed. They felt so sorry for him. They drove away very sadly and they said, "O my lord, do what the prophet said. It will be so easy. Let us go to the water and you shall wash yourself seven times. What if it heals you? It would be so wonderful."

Naaman looked angry, but he said, "All right, let us go to the river."

The servants led the horses hastily to the Jordan River. They were so happy. What if their good master was healed?

Soon they reached the river. Naaman took off his beautiful clothes. He walked into the water all the way. He washed himself once, and again, and another time. He washed himself seven times.

And then? Oh, how wonderful! The white sores were gone, all gone. Naaman's hands and feet were beautiful and healthy again. He was better, completely better. Then Naaman said, "Now I know. The water did not heal me, God in heaven did. The prophet prayed for me."

Naaman was happy, so very happy.

"Forward!" he said. "Forward! Back to the prophet."

His joyful servants urged the horses on, and they went fast, very fast.

THE RICH MAN WHO WAS A LEPER

When they reached Elisha's poor house, the servant did not come to the door. Elisha came himself. He was happy, too. God in heaven had helped Naaman. Naaman jumped off the wagon. He walked up to Elisha and said, "Now I know that your God, who lives in heaven, has healed me. In our land we pray to images, but they were not able to help me. Now I shall always pray to your God. He is so mighty. He is so big. He can do everything. But you have prayed for me. I am so happy. What would you like to have from me? You are so poor, and I am so rich. I will give you anything you ask. Would you like to have money, a lot of money? Would you like to have clothes, very beautiful clothes? Would you like to have gold or silver or other beautiful things?"

Elisha answered, "No, I do not wish to have anything from you. I did not heal you. God did. You must love God and be thankful to Him as long as you live."

"I shall do that!" Naaman said. "God has been so good to me."

Then Naaman drove away with his servants. All his money and his gold and his beautiful things he took along back home. The prophet did not want anything, nothing at all. But Elisha's servant thought, "Too bad, my master could have become rich, but he did not want to. Too bad!"

The servant's name was Gehazi. And what did Gehazi do? Quietly he went after Naaman. He thought, "My master Elisha will not know." He called and he shouted and he swung his arms. Naaman saw him coming. They stopped the horses right away. Then what did Gehazi say? He lied. That was wicked of him. He said, "My lord Naaman, give me money and clothes. Visitors have come to my master, and He wants to feed them. He wants to be good to them, but he does not have money himself. So he said to me, 'Run, quickly! Ask Captain Naaman for money and clothes.'"

Yes, that was what Gehazi said, but it was not true at all. Naaman did not know that. So he gave money and clothes to Gehazi. A few of the servants came along to carry the money and the beautiful clothes. Gehazi was so glad. He thought, "I'm smart. Now I am rich. And my master Elisha does not know it." He hid everything.

But when he came back to Elisha, Elisha asked, "Where have you been, Gehazi?"

Gehazi lied again. "Nowhere!"

But Elisha knew everything. Elisha said, "I know what you have done, Gehazi, you have done something very wicked. You knew you were not supposed to do that. You know that God in heaven sees everything. You have lied. You got that money dishonestly. It does not belong to you."

Gehazi was startled. And then the punishment came. Gehazi became very white. He got those terrible white sores, on his hands, on his face, all over his body. Now he was a leper. That was dreadful! But it was his own fault.

Naaman arrived home. He was all better. How wonderful, how very wonderful it was! God had done it.

IN THE FARAWAY LAND

In a faraway land lived a mighty king. His name was Nebuchadnezzar. He was very rich. Thousands and thousands of people had to obey him. He was also very proud and wanted to become even richer. He wanted to become the strongest king in the whole world. He and his soldiers went to war against other countries where his wicked soldiers burned the cities, and took the kings captive. They carried off everything that was beautiful. Mighty King Nebuchadnezzar took it all back to his own land, to Babylon. Everyone feared mighty King Nebuchadnezzar.

One day Nebuchadnezzar and his soldiers came to the beautiful land of Canaan where the Israelites lived. The Israelites were God's people. God had given the beautiful land of Canaan to His people. He had promised it long, long ago to Abraham, Isaac, and Jacob. The Israelites had lived there for many, many years. God always took care of them. But now? Now this great King Nebuchadnezzar and his rough soldiers had come. If only the LORD in heaven would help His people, Nebuchadnezzar would not be able to do anything. God is mightier than all the kings and all the soldiers in the whole world. God is Lord of heaven and earth. Oh, if only the LORD would help His people!

IN THE FARAWAY LAND

Yes, but God would no longer help His people. Why not? Because the Israelites deserved to be punished. They were disobedient. They did not love God, but did bad and wicked deeds. They prayed to images, and forgot God in heaven again and again. Their heavenly Father had forgiven them their wrong, again and again, but now they had become very wicked. Now the punishment would come. They deserved that. It was their own fault.

Mighty King Nebuchadnezzar and his rough soldiers had come. They burned the houses of the people, they trampled over the beautiful grain on the land, and they took the women and children captive. The Israelites wanted to fight with those strange soldiers, but they were all killed or taken prisoner, because God in heaven was not helping His people anymore. The great city of Jerusalem was burned, too. All the beautiful houses were destroyed, and the beautiful temple, too. That was the place where the Israelites were supposed to pray to God, but they did not do that anymore. They had forgotten God. Now that great king was allowed to be boss. Mighty King Nebuchadnezzar could do whatever he wanted with the Israelites. And what did he do? He tied up the men and the women and the children with iron chains, and those rough soldiers took them away, far away to that strange land, to Babylon. It was so terrible, but it was their own fault.

Now the Israelites were living in that faraway land, in Babylon. The men, women, and children had all become slaves of great King Nebuchadnezzar. Now they had to do whatever he commanded. They were very sorry. They thought, "Oh, if only we had not been disobedient! God in heaven is our Father, but we did not love Him. We did wicked and bad deeds. We are so sorry." Yes, but now it was too late. Poor people!

Were they not God's people anymore? Had God in heaven forgotten them altogether? No, their heavenly Father saw them. Their heavenly Father did not forget about them.

One night mighty King Nebuchadnezzar had a dream, but in the morning he could not remember it. That made him angry. All the learned men of the land were called before the king to tell him what he had dreamed in the night. But they could not do that! No one was able to do that. The mighty king became even more angry and was about to kill all those wise men. That was how angry he was.

But then a young man came to the king. He said, "O King, tomorrow I will tell you what you dreamed. I shall pray to my God. He will tell me. He knows everything. He knows what you have dreamed, too."

That young man was Daniel. He was an Israelite who had been taken prisoner from the land of Canaan. There he had been a prince, but now he was a slave of the mighty king. Now he had to live in the strange land of Babylon.

The next morning Daniel went to the king and told him everything. He even told him what the dream meant. The king did not understand how Daniel could do this, because he did not know who God in heaven was. None of the learned men understood either. But Daniel said, "I could not help you myself. But I prayed to God, and the LORD told me everything."

The great King Nebuchadnezzar was very glad. He said to Daniel, "Your God is a great and mighty God." And he gave Daniel beautiful gifts. Now Daniel was no longer a servant, but became a rich ruler in Babylon. That was how God took care of Daniel. No, the heavenly Father does not forget His children.

Another time, King Nebuchadnezzar had a beautiful image made. It was very big and very heavy. It was made of gold. The king said, "When the music plays, and the trumpets sound, everyone must kneel down and pray to my golden image. There shall be a big celebration."

Then came the day of the great feast. Mighty King Nebuchadnezzar and all his servants came before the image. The people came from all parts of the land and also came before the image.

They had to obey the king because . . . look over there. An enormous brick furnace had been built. A great and terrible fire was burning in it. Flames shot up out of it. Whoever did not do what the king commanded, whoever did not pray to the golden image, would be thrown into the fiery furnace, in the midst of the fire.

The trumpeters were ready. Then great King Nebuchadnezzar raised his hands. The music began to play. The trumpets sounded. All those thousands and thousands of people fell on their knees and prayed to the golden image. But three young men were still standing! They were not kneeling, they were not praying. How did they dare to be so disobedient? What if the king saw it? Oh, yes, he had seen it already. They had to come to him right away. He looked very angry. He said, "Why did you not kneel? Why did you not pray? Did I not command it?"

The three young men were not frightened. They were three friends of Daniel, three Israelites. Oh, no, they were not frightened at all. They looked at the king and said, "O King, we may not pray to your golden image. That would be very wicked. We must only pray to God, who lives in heaven. We love God. We want to be obedient to Him. We are not afraid of that fiery furnace."

Then the king became very angry. He cried, "You must obey!" But the three young men did not do it. Then the servants of the king seized them and in his anger, the king said, "Heat the furnace up seven times hotter, and throw them in the midst of the fire. All three off them!"

There they went. They were not afraid at all. They thought, "God sees us. We may not pray to an image. We will not do what the king has commanded. That would be very sinful."

The king's rough soldiers threw them into that terrible furnace, into the middle of the fire. The fire was so hot that those servants themselves fell down dead. Then the great celebration of the golden image continued. The trumpets sounded and the music played, and no one thought of the three young men in that terrible furnace. They must have been burned up long ago.

Suddenly, a servant came up to the king. He cried, "O my lord the king, you have thrown three men in the furnace, but now there are four, and they are walking in the fire."

That terrified the king. He thought, "That is impossible! I shall go have a look right away." He came near the furnace. What was that? How could that be? Yes, there were four men walking in the fire. One was wearing beautiful clothes, which looked as if they were made of sunbeams, so lovely and so bright. The king called to the men, "Come here! Oh, come here quickly!" He was very afraid.

The three young men came out of the furnace right away. They had not been harmed. Not a hair on their head was burnt. Not a thread of their clothes smelled like fire. How could that be? They told the king, "My lord the king, God in heaven sent His angel to keep us safe. The fire did not harm us."

The king bowed his head. He thought, "God in heaven is much mightier than I am. He is much mightier than that image of gold."

The three young men became friends of the great King Nebuchadnezzar. The angel returned to heaven where he lived with God.

That was how God took care of His people, even in Babylon, in that faraway strange land. No, God never forgets His people.

DANIEL IN THE LIONS' DEN

Daniel had became a very old man. Long ago, Daniel had told the king about the dream he had dreamed and what that strange dream meant. But that had been long, long ago. That great king had died many years ago.

Now another king was sitting on the throne. He was a good king. He was very rich and very mighty. Everyone had to obey him. There were also many rich and important rulers living in the land; they were the king's friends. But one of those rulers was the most important, and the king loved him most of all. Who was that? It was Daniel. Yes, he was the king's very best friend. He was the most important man in the land. How had that come about? God had done that. God took care of Daniel, and Daniel was a good servant to the king, the very best. Yes, the king loved Daniel most of all.

But those other rulers were jealous of Daniel. They whispered to each other, "Why is Daniel the king's best friend? Why? He comes from a faraway land. Actually he is a prisoner! And now the king loves him most of all. He is richer and more important than we are. That should not happen. No, it should not be allowed. Daniel must go! Daniel must be killed, and then we will be the richest and most important, and the king will love us most of all."

That was how those scheming men whispered secretly. Daniel did not know about it, and neither did the king.

One day as the king was sitting on his throne, those important rulers came to him. They looked very friendly. They bowed deeply, but their hearts were wicked and cruel. The king did not know that. They said, "O king, we have a wonderful plan. You are the most important king of the world. Whatever you command must happen, all the people must obey you. O my lord the king, we have thought of a wonderful plan. You should tell all the people in your land that they may not ask anything of any god or person than you alone for thirty days. O my lord the king, then it will be as if you are a god. Yes, and if anyone disobeys, he will be punished. He will be thrown into a den where wild lions live. Into the lions' den. Then those wild animals will devour him because he did not do what you said."

The king laughed. He liked it. He thought it was a good plan. He said, "Yes, let's do that."

How happy those important rulers were! But their hearts were wicked and cruel. The king did not know that. The wicked men left, laughing to each other quietly. They whispered, "Oh, if only Daniel is disobedient. Then he will be punished, then he will be thrown into the lions' den! Those wild animals will tear him to pieces. Yes, maybe Daniel will disobey. We will watch him carefully. We will watch to see if Daniel does what the king decrees, and if he does not do it, we will tell the king immediately." Those wicked men laughed about their own evil plan. Daniel did not know it, but God in heaven knew about it. He knows everything.

Everyone in the land heard the king's command, and the people thought, "We will make sure not to ask anything of any god or person for thirty days, or else we will be punished."

Daniel heard it, too. But Daniel thought, "I still want to pray to God every day. I must. God is King of heaven and earth. He takes care of me and gives me everything I need. I may not forget God. No, not even for one day." And every day Daniel went to pray to God in his quiet room.

There went the wicked men. Very carefully they went up to Daniel's house. They looked and they listened close to the open window, very carefully. They whispered, "Look! Look! Daniel is on his knees in front of the window and he is looking up to heaven! Listen! Oh, listen! Daniel is praying. Daniel is asking something of his God. He is not allowed to do that."

And then those evil men hurried away. They laughed wickedly. They said, "We'll go and tell the king right away that Daniel has done something wrong."

They came to the king. The king was frightened. Had Daniel done something wrong? Had Daniel been disobedient? Would he have to be thrown into the lions' den?

"Oh, and I love him the most. It is terrible!" cried the king

"But it must be done. It must be done," those wicked men said. "You have decreed it yourself, and what you say must always happen."

They laughed and whispered to each other, "Now Daniel must go. Now Daniel must die, and we will be the richest and most important."

The king was very sad. Yes, now he could see the evil in the eyes of those men. They were thinking about that wonderful idea to have Daniel killed. They were bad people. But now it was too late. Now that horrible thing had to happen. Poor Daniel!

There he went. Rough soldiers brought him away. They shoved the old man into the dark den where the wild beasts roared. Poor Daniel! Who would help him? The den was so dark and so deep. The wild animals were so fierce, and they were so hungry. Poor Daniel! But God knows everything. He knew how wicked those men were. He could even see Daniel in that dark den.

Night had come, but the good king could not sleep. He kept thinking about Daniel. "Have the wild lions jumped on Daniel already? Have they grabbed him with their sharp claws? Have they ripped him with their sharp teeth? Poor Daniel! He has not done anything wrong." That was how the king's thoughts went. He was so sorry.

DANIEL IN THE LIONS' DEN

Early in the morning he arose and went to look. He went to that terrible den where those wild animals were. He leaned over the edge and called, "Daniel, Daniel! I could not help you! Was your God in heaven able to help you? Daniel! Daniel!"

Were the lions roaring? No, everything was very quiet. But wait! There was a voice. It was the voice of a man. It was Daniel himself. How wonderful! Daniel was not dead! He was alive, he was speaking. The king leaned over farther, he looked and he listened, and his eyes shone joyfully. "Oh, Daniel! Are you alive? Did those savage animals not tear you to pieces? Oh, how is that possible, Daniel?" he asked.

There stood Daniel, quiet and content. He was not afraid at all, even though the lions were walking around looking at him. Their eyes glowed like fire in the dark, but not one of them touched him. Not one. Daniel looked up. He saw the king and said, "O my lord the king, God in heaven sent His angel to save me. Not one of those wild animals has hurt me."

Then the king called to his servants, "Take Daniel out of the den. Take him out of there right away!"

Soon Daniel was standing next to the king. He did not even have one rip in his clothes. He went along with the king to his palace. And the king loved him even more than before. But those wicked men who had deceived the king so wickedly were now thrown into the lions' den themselves. And then, yes, then those wild animals roared and jumped on them and tore them all to pieces. That was their punishment.

The good king was so happy. Daniel, his friend, was still alive! God had taken care of him. And the king said, "Your God is a wonderful God. Everyone in my land must speak with awe about your God, who has saved you from the claws of the lion. No one else but God can do that."

Daniel remained the king's faithful servant, and the king loved him most of all.

The Israelites had already lived for many years in that faraway land, but the heavenly Father had not forgotten His people. God's punishment made them live there for many long years, but then came the day that they were allowed to return to their own beautiful land, to Canaan. There they rebuilt the great city of Jerusalem, and God's beautiful temple, too. The people said, "Now we will not be disobedient again, now we will not pray to images again. We want to love God always. He is our heavenly Father. He always sees us, and He never forgets us."

The New Testament

ZACHARIAS AND THE ANGEL

Long, long ago, Adam and Eve had lived in the beautiful Paradise. But they had sinned. They ate from that one tree which God had told them not to eat from. They had been disobedient. Then they had to leave and go into the wide world, away from that lovely Paradise. It was too bad. Yes, but it was their own fault. But God in heaven had promised them something very wonderful, and what God promises always happens. What was it?

It took very, very long! Adam and Eve had died long ago, and Abraham, too. Moses, who had lain in the reed basket had also died, and all the good kings, and the wicked kings, too. Oh, it took so long, so very long. But the Lord in heaven did not forget His promise. God never forgets what He promises.

One day the beautiful heavens opened and an angel of God came to earth. He came to bring a wonderful message. But the people on earth did not see him. They did not even know that he was coming. Was he going to the king in his beautiful palace? No. Would he cry out in the streets? No. No one saw him, no one knew about it. The angel of God was quietly bringing his message to an old man, even though the old man did not know it yet either.

He was in the quiet room of the temple. Everything in it was made of gold. Seven golden lamp-stands that were never allowed to go out were burning there. The golden table and the golden altar stood there, too. That old man was a priest, a servant of God. His name was Zacharias. He walked to the golden altar, where a small fire was burning, and sprinkled some grains on it. When they burned they made a wonderful smell. Fine blue smoke rose up. It was as if that fine blue smoke was ascending up to heaven, as if it came up to God to tell Him the reverence the people had for Him. Zacharias put more grains on the fire burning on the golden altar.

Suddenly, Zacharias was frightened. What was that? All of a sudden it was so bright, so terribly bright in that golden room, and when Zacharias looked up, an angel of God was standing there. His white robes shone with light as if they were made of sunbeams. Zacharias was even more terrified. He covered his eyes with his hands and did not dare to look anymore.

But the angel said kindly to him, "Do not be afraid, Zacharias, I bring you a good message. You have often prayed to God for a son. Your wife Elizabeth has, too. Now you will receive a son, and his name shall be John."

Zacharias listened. How beautiful, how wonderful that was! But how could it be? He was so old, and his wife was very old, too. Usually children were not born to old people like themselves. How could it be? No, Zacharias could not believe it.

But the angel told Zacharias more news. Something very wonderful. He said, "When your son has grown up to be a man, he shall be a prophet, a servant of God. He will tell the people something wonderful. He will tell the people a wonderful message, a message of God."

Zacharias listened. Oh, it was so wonderful, so wonderful! It made Zacharias so happy. But how could it be? What if it did not happen? No, Zacharias could not believe it.

Then the angel said, "You do not believe me. Because you do not believe me you will not be able to speak until your son is born. This shall be a sign to you that what I have said shall surely happen."

Then, suddenly, the angel was gone. All the beautiful light was gone, too. Zacharias was alone. But he could not speak. Now Zacharias had to believe the message, the message of God.

Zacharias went home to Elizabeth, his wife. He wanted to tell the wonderful message right away, but he could not. He was unable to speak. He had to write it down, and Elizabeth had to read it. How happy the old people were together. Now they would have a little son. He would become God's servant, a prophet, and he would tell the people the wonderful, joyful message of God.

The little boy was born. Friends and relatives of Zacharias came to look at the little one. God had been so good to these old people! The visitors exclaimed, "The little boy must be called Zacharias just like his father."

But Elizabeth said, "No, his name is John." She knew what the angel had said. The people did not. Then they asked Zacharias. But Zacharias still could not speak, so he wrote it down. The friends and the relatives thought, "John? Yes, it is a nice name, but it is such a strange name. Why do they not name the little boy after his father?"

Then suddenly Zacharias felt he was able to speak again. He said, "The Lord in heaven has been so good to us. He has thought of us, all of us. This little boy shall be God's servant, and he shall tell wonderful things to the people."

Zacharias told the people everything that had happened in the quiet golden room of the temple. Reverently the people listened. Oh, yes, that was beautiful, wonderfully beautiful.

Yet the birth of John was not the most wonderful thing. That was still to come. The most wonderful, the most beautiful message was not brought to Zacharias and Elizabeth.

What was that most beautiful message? To whom was it brought?

One day the beautiful heavens opened and an angel of God came down to earth again. Now he came to bring the most wonderful message of all. But the people did not see him. They did not know that he was coming. Would he go to the king this time? Or to the emperor in his palace? No, the angel was quietly bringing his message to a poor young maiden who lived in a small village. The poor young maiden did not know it either.

She was sitting in her little house, in her quiet room. Suddenly, there was a light, a wonderful, beautiful light. In the centre of that light stood an angel of God. Kindly the angel said to her, "Greetings, Mary."

Mary was frightened. She did not dare to look up. Why was this angel coming to her? She was only a poor young girl. And her house was so small.

But the angel said kindly to her, "Do not be afraid, Mary. There are many, many women in the world. God in heaven knows them all — the rich and the poor. But the Lord has chosen you. I bring you the most beautiful and wonderful message. You shall have a Child, a son, and you shall give Him the name Jesus. That Child will be the Son of God. He will come to earth to make the people happy. You, Mary, will be the mother of that Child. Of all the women of the world, the rich and the poor, God has chosen you."

How wonderful that was! God's own Son was coming to the world as a little Child, and Mary was allowed to be the mother of that Child. The angel of God had come to tell her. Mary bowed her head in reverence. How good God was to her!

Then the angel went back to heaven. First he had brought a beautiful message to the old priest in the golden room in the temple. Now he had brought an even more beautiful message. The most beautiful, wonderful message to Mary. Zacharias would have a son, and his name would be John. Mary would have a son, too, but He would be the Lord Jesus, God's own Son. And John would tell the people that the Lord Jesus was coming to earth to make them happy. But the people on earth did not know about it yet.

Long, long ago, Adam and Eve had lived in Paradise. They had been disobedient and they had to leave paradise to go into the wide world. But that was their own fault. They had sinned and become afraid of God. But the Lord in heaven had promised them something wonderful, and what God promises always happens. What was that promise? The angel of God had now told it to Mary: The Lord Jesus was going to come. He wanted to make the people happy again. He wanted to take the fear out of their hearts. Yes, that was the most beautiful, the most wonderful thing that could happen on earth.
No one knew about it yet. But it would surely happen.

JOSEPH AND MARY

Two people were walking along the road, a woman and a man. The man said, "Come along, Mary. Just a little way yet, then we will be in the city."
Mary was so tired. It had been such a long journey and it was so warm. Now evening was coming, and darkness was setting in. But look, there in the distance lay the white city among the green hills. That was where they were going.
"Come, Mary, only a little way farther."

Who were they? And where were they going? The young woman was Mary. The other person was Joseph, her husband. Joseph took good care of Mary. He knew what the angel had told her. Now they knew it together, and they were so happy about it. But they did not tell anyone. They only spoke about it together, quietly and reverently. It was a wonderful secret that filled their hearts with joy. They had come from their own little village far away. The journey had been long and warm, but ahead lay the city of Bethlehem, to which they were travelling. The emperor of the land, Caesar Augustus, had demanded it, and what the emperor commanded, had to be done. There were many other people travelling along the road; they were going to Bethlehem, too. Their names had to be written down in a big book there. Then they would be allowed to go home again. Caesar Augustus wanted to know the names of all the people, and how many were living in his land.

"Only a little way, Mary, and then you may rest."

She was tired, so very tired.

Ahead of them in the town, there would be an inn where they could sleep for the night. All the people journeying along the road would go there. In that big inn would be room for their camels, their donkeys, and their horses, too. Mary and Joseph did not have a camel, a donkey, or a horse. They were too poor. Joseph was only a carpenter, so they were travelling by foot. The other people did not even look at them, they just rode past. But Mary and Joseph were very happy. They knew the most beautiful of all things that would ever happen in the world. And only they knew it, no one else did.

"Come, Mary, just a little farther."

Darkness was coming. They had come near the big inn where all the people were going to stay. Mary was so glad because she could barely take another step. She was so tired. Joseph was glad, too. Now he could find a good place for Mary.

Oh, no! The whole inn was full. There was no room for Mary or Joseph in the inn. The other people had taken every place. But Mary and Joseph could not stay out on the street in the dark night. Would no one say, "Take my place?" No, no one. No one even looked at poor Mary and Joseph. The people were only concerned about themselves. And yet, Mary and Joseph knew the most beautiful thing that would happen in the world, and they were happy together.

"Come, Mary, I will find another place for you. Are you very tired?"

There they went through the dark street again. Poor Mary! Poor Joseph! Then they found another place. It was a dark stable. It was not a house for people, it was a house for animals. It was quiet in there, and cold and dark. But Mary could not stay out on the street in the night, so they went inside. It was allowed.

"Here, Mary, I will make a bed for you in the straw. Are you very tired?"

They searched for a spot in that cold, dark stable, and yet they were happy, because they knew something no one else knew. How beautiful it was! It was the most beautiful thing in the world.

Then it was night. Everything became very still and dark.

THE BABY IN THE STABLE

It was a very quiet and very dark night. But outside in the dark fields some men were wide awake. They were sitting close together. They were shepherds. Their sheep slept contentedly. Sometimes a wolf might come, or a lion, but the shepherds kept watch. They did not sleep. Faithfully they took care of their animals in the quiet, dark night.

Suddenly . . . oh, how terrible! What was that? It was light! Brilliant light in the darkness! And someone was standing in the centre of that light. He was made of light, too. It was an angel from heaven, an angel of God. The poor shepherds! They were terribly frightened. But the angel said, "Do not be afraid. Rejoice, for I bring you beautiful tidings. The Saviour is born. The Son of God has come to the people on earth as a little Child. Go and see. He is over there in the stable, wrapped in cloths and lying in a manger."

The shepherds listened. They did not dare to look. They covered their eyes with their hands, but they listened to the most beautiful message of all from God. Oh, yes, they knew what the Lord in heaven had promised: that some day the Son of God would come to earth. But when that would be they did not know. And suddenly, there in that dark night He had come, there in the stable. The shepherds listened with awe.

Suddenly, more angels came from heaven where God was living. Many, many more angels. It was a host of angels. The sky was full of those beautiful angels. They sang and sang. They sang so beautifully. Never had anyone on earth sung as beautifully as those angels. They sang about God who loved the people so much. They sang, "Glory to God in the highest heaven, peace on earth, and good will to men."

The shepherds listened, it was so wonderful, so very wonderful. Then the angels ascended back to heaven. They had brought the glad tidings to the shepherds. Now they returned to heaven to the throne of God.

Again, it was very dark on earth and very quiet. The people were sleeping. Only the shepherds had heard the wonderful message. They got up quickly and said to each other, "Come, let us go to Bethlehem, to the stable where the Child is. We want to see the Child." They hurried through the dark night and came to the stable. There they knocked reverently. Quietly they entered. Yes, there lay the little one, a very poor baby. He was wrapped in swaddling cloths, just as the angel had said, and lying in a manger, from which the animals would eat. The shepherds came near, quietly and reverently. They fell on their knees and worshipped that Child in the manger. That Child was so poor, so small, and He lay in a dark stable. But the shepherds knew that Child had come from heaven to earth to make the people happy. That Child in the stable was *God's very own Son*.

Mary was sitting on her bed of straw. She looked at her dear Child, and Joseph stood beside her. They were so happy, so very happy together. In that dark night, in the dark stable, when all the people were sleeping, the Lord Jesus had been born. Mary had wrapped His small body in cloths to keep away the cold. There was no cradle, only a wooden manger out of which the animals ate. Joseph had taken it and filled it with straw, and they put the Child in it. Everything was so poor, so very poor. Yet, it was so beautiful. The most beautiful, the most wonderful thing had now happened, on that dark night. Nobody except the shepherds knew about it.

The shepherds were on their knees worshipping the Child. Joseph and Mary wondered, "How did the shepherds find out?" Then the shepherds told them everything. They told about the message of the one angel. They told about the singing of the many, many angels. Mary listened, and she looked. She looked at her Child. Her heart was filled with joy.

A while later the shepherds left, quietly and reverently. Morning had come and it was light again. The people awoke. But no one knew what had happened. Only Mary and Joseph and the shepherds knew. But the shepherds went and told it everywhere. It was so beautiful, so wonderful. They could not return to their sheep quietly. They had to talk about it, and tell the people. They told everyone they met about what had happened in that dark night, in that dark stable. They told about the angel and his message. The Lord in heaven is so mighty and holy, yet the Lord in heaven loved the people greatly. Now the most beautiful, the most wonderful thing that could ever happen on earth, had happened: *The Lord Jesus had been born.*

IN THE TEMPLE

Who were those people walking through the busy streets of the great city of Jerusalem? They were Joseph and Mary, with the Baby Jesus. He was still very small, asleep in his mother's arms. Mother Mary carried her little one very carefully through those busy streets. The people in the busy streets did not know that the little baby was the Lord Jesus; they just looked past them. They did not take notice of Mary and Joseph, nor of the little Child in His mother's arms.

Joseph said, "Come, Mary, we must climb those high steps."

Where were they going? What were they going to do? They were going to the temple, the house of God. All fathers and mothers had to do that when a little boy was born. Joseph and Mary were doing it as well. Already they were climbing the steps of the temple. The temple was very big and beautiful and there were many people who went there to pray to God. But none of the people looked at Joseph and Mary, and they did not look at that little Child at all. They did not know that the Child was the Lord Jesus.

Joseph and Mary were going to the priest. Mary was holding the Child Jesus in her arms. She had received him from God, and now it was as if she wanted to give her Child back to God. All mothers had to do that. Mary did, too. The priest laid his hand gently on the head of the baby. He blessed him. He said, "God shall take care of Thee." But the priest did not know that the little Child was the Lord Jesus, God's very own Son. Only Mary and Joseph knew that.

Then an old man came up to Joseph and Mary. His name was Simeon. His eyes shone with happiness. Carefully he took the Child Jesus in his arms. He looked at Him so joyfully and yet so reverently. Yes, old Simeon knew who that Child was. God Himself had told him. Simeon was very old. He had known that someday the Lord Jesus would be born, but he did not know when. Once God had told Simeon, "You will see the Child before you die." And now suddenly, Simeon saw that poor man and that poor woman coming into the temple — and Simeon knew. That Child was the Son of God who had come into the world to make people happy. Right away Simeon went to that Child. He took Him in his arms, and his old eyes shone brightly. Simeon said, "Now let me die, Lord God, for now I have seen Thy salvation. Now the Son of God has come from heaven to earth. Now the most wonderful thing has happened. This Child will become great. He shall speak to the people of God, and whoever

IN THE TEMPLE

listens to Him and loves Him shall be blessed. But whoever does not listen and will not love Him shall be unhappy."

An old woman also came. She was a good, friendly woman, and her name was Anna. She was always in the temple because she loved God with her whole heart. She also knew that the Lord Jesus would be born someday, but she had waited so long already. Now she suddenly saw that Child, and she knew that He was the Saviour. Immediately she went up to Him. She was so happy, and she looked at Him with kind eyes, and yet so very reverently too.

Mary watched and listened. Joseph did, too. They were so joyful, so very happy. Those old people, Simeon and Anna, were being so kind to their Child, and they spoke such beautiful words. But the Baby Jesus did not know it yet. He was too small, much too small.

Simeon gave the Lord Jesus back to His mother very carefully. Joseph and Mary, with their little one, went back to Bethlehem.

THE WISE MEN FROM THE EAST

It was night and it was very quiet. Up in the dark heavens the little stars shone and twinkled everywhere. But one star was the most beautiful of all.

What was that? A soft sound came through the stillness of the night. Camels were coming. They walked very slowly and quietly, continuing on farther and farther through the quiet land in the dark of night. Their masters rode on slowly. They looked at the beautiful dark blue sky. They kept on looking at that one star, the most beautiful one. They were rich men, who wore beautiful robes of red, yellow, and green. Their camels had beautiful rugs on their backs, and golden jewellery on their heads. Ahead of them rode a servant carrying a long spear. He looked around to see if there were any wild animals or robbers along the dark road. And behind the rich men came more servants riding on camels. They carried large packs of beautiful expensive things with them. Those rich people kept travelling on through the dark land. They kept on looking at that star, the largest one of all, which moved ahead of them all the time. That star was showing them the way.

Where were those rich men going? They looked so happy. They knew something wonderful. Those men were going to visit a King, a newborn King, and they were going to bring him rich treasures. But where did that little King live? They did not know. The rich men looked at that lovely star to show them the way. Wherever the star went, they also went.

Those men came from a faraway land. They were wise men. They had read many books, and many times they had looked at the stars at night. Suddenly they had seen that beautiful, large star. It had amazed them, that was how beautiful it was. And they had said, "A new king has been born somewhere in this big world, but we do not know where. This little young King must be the best and greatest king of the world, because we have never seen such a beautiful star." And those learned men had also said, "Come, let us find that King. Let us kneel before him in worship. Let us bring him beautiful gifts. The star will show us the way."

Now there they went. It was a long way. They went through deserts where the sun burned hot, and the wind blew dry. They travelled over mountains and through forests. Everywhere in those lonely lands there might be wild animals or wicked men who would steal their treasure. But they continued on. They wanted to see that little King and worship Him. Every night the star, that most beautiful one, was in the dark sky again. It made the men so happy.

"Come. We will surely find this little King. He must be the greatest, most wonderful King of the whole world."

In the distance lay a beautiful white city. It was the city of Jerusalem. Had the King been born there? The wise men came near the gate and rode through it. Inside the city they asked the people, "Has a new king been born here?"

But the people looked at them and shook their heads, and said, "We do not know. There is the palace of King Herod. Go and ask there. Maybe King Herod knows."

Then the wise men travelled on. They rode through the busy streets, and all the people looked at them. They looked so wonderful and rich. They had come from such a faraway land. And they were searching for a young King. But there was no young king in the city. The wise men came to King Herod's palace. They were allowed to come inside. They could inquire of the king himself.

But King Herod did not know about a new king, not at all. He was frightened. He was a wicked man. He thought, "A young king has been born? Where, and who is He? Will that young King grow up and chase me off the throne and sit on it himself? Oh, no, I don't want that to happen. It must not happen." King Herod was afraid. But he was clever. He did not say that he was afraid and angry. He called the oldest and most learned men in the city to the palace, the priests of the temple. He asked them, "Do you know if a young King has been born?"

They answered, "No, my lord the king, we do not know. But it will happen someday. We have read that in our books. The prophets foretold it long ago."

"Where? Where will that King be born?" asked King Herod.

The priests answered, "In Bethlehem. We have read that in our books, too."

King Herod was even more afraid. Oh, what if it was true? What if a young King had been born? No, that must never happen! What should Herod do?

Quickly he told the wise men from the faraway land, "Go to Bethlehem. Go and search for the young King there, and if you find him, you must come and tell me immediately. I want to kneel down to Him and worship Him and bring Him beautiful gifts, too."

But wicked Herod did not mean it at all. He was thinking other evil things in his heart. He wanted to kill that young King.

The wise men travelled on again to Bethlehem. And in the dark night, the most beautiful star could be seen again in the heavens. Slowly it moved on through the dark blue sky. Those wise men were so happy. The King must be in Bethlehem. The beautiful star guided them on, until it stopped above a little house. Was this where the King was, in this little house? It was not even a palace. There were no soldiers standing guard at the door. But those wise men looked at the star, which had stopped.

Then they came down from their camels. They gently knocked on the little door, then went inside.

A young woman sat inside. She had a little boy on her lap. The eyes of the rich wise men filled with joy when they saw that little boy. Quietly and reverently they came near. They knelt together in that little house in front of the little boy, that poor little boy on his mother's lap. Yes, this was the young King foretold by the beautiful star in that faraway land. Their servants brought in the beautiful treasures: gold and frankincense and myrrh. Respectfully the wise men laid their treasures before that little Child. It was all for Him. That poor Child was the greatest, most wonderful King in the whole world.

Who was that poor Child in that little house? Who was it? It was the Lord Jesus. He was the Son of God. He was the King of heaven and earth. But the people in Jerusalem did not believe it. They did not come to worship Him. The rich wise men from a faraway land believed it. They had come to worship the Lord Jesus and to bring Him beautiful gifts. Their hearts were filled with happiness.

And then? Did they quickly go back to the wicked King Herod to tell him everything? No, they did not. That night they had a dream. In that dream God told them not to go back to King Herod. They listened to the voice of God. They did not go back to the king. They journeyed back to their own faraway land a different way. They did not go through the big city of Jerusalem again.

WICKED KING HEROD

Wicked King Herod waited and waited. But the wise men from the faraway land did not come. He waited for days. He waited for weeks. They did not come. They never came. Then he became so angry and so afraid, he clenched his fists in anger. He said, "I shall kill that young King anyway."

He called his soldiers. They were wicked, cruel men. They were just as wicked as their evil king. He said, "Go to the city of

Bethlehem. Go into the houses and take all the little boys and kill them. I do not know who the young King is. I do not know where he lives. But take all the little boys and kill them. Then the little King will be dead, too. He must be killed."

Those rough, cruel soldiers went away. They rode to Bethlehem, and they did everything the king had told them to. They went into the big houses and the small houses. They grabbed the little boys out of their mother's arms, and they killed them all, every little boy. Poor little ones. The poor mothers cried and wailed with grief. But those rough, cruel soldiers were not sorry. Then all the little boys in Bethlehem were dead, and wicked King Herod thought, "Now that little King must be dead, too." And he laughed cruelly.

Along a lonely road walked a man leading a donkey. The man was holding onto the donkey by the reins. Carefully they went on over the bumpy road covered with rocks and stones. On the donkey sat a young woman. She was holding a Child in her arms. Who was that man? Who was that young woman? Who was that Child in His mother's arms? They were Joseph and Mary with the little Child, Jesus. Joseph led the way. Carefully the donkey stepped over the big stones that lay on that lonely road.

"Come along, Mary, do not be afraid."

No, the Child Jesus was not dead. The soldiers of the wicked king thought that they had killed all the little boys in Bethlehem. They thought the young King was dead, too. But that was not true. He was still alive. He could not be dead. The Lord Jesus had come to earth to make the people happy. Did that wicked king think he could kill Him? No, that could never be. God in heaven had not allowed that, and what God does not allow, will not happen.

One night Joseph had a dream. In the dream an angel of the Lord stood near him. The angel had said, "Joseph, you must not stay in Bethlehem. You must quickly go to the faraway land of Egypt. You must take the Child and His mother, because King Herod wants to kill the Child." The Lord in heaven knew what the wicked king wanted to do. The Lord knows everything. He knows what sinful people secretly think in their hearts. Obediently Joseph went away in the middle of the night.

"Come along, Mary, do not be afraid. God will take care of the Child."

There they went. The land was lonely, the road was difficult, and Egypt was far away. But that did not matter. Not at all. From heaven, God Himself looked down on them. He would take care of them. Would the soldiers of the wicked king hear of Joseph's flight? Would they chase him? No! Would the wild animals of the desert come and hurt them? No!

Quietly they travelled on over the hills and the hot sand. Joseph held onto the donkey, and Mary held the Child in her arms. The donkey walked on and on, gently rocking the Child to sleep. In the dark cold nights Joseph would make a fire so that the Child would not be cold. During the day, when the hot sun burned, Mary held the little One under her robe. Then the hot sunshine would not be able to hurt Him. Far, far in the distance was Egypt.

"Come along, Mary. We must not be afraid. God will take care of the Child."

King Herod was so happy. He thought, "Now that young King is dead." But it was not true. The Lord Jesus was safe in Egypt. Then King Herod became very, very sick and died.

Joseph and Mary and the Lord Jesus lived in Egypt. One night Joseph had another dream. He saw the angel of the Lord. The angel said, "Joseph, you may return to your own land. The king who wanted to kill the Child Jesus has died and cannot hurt Him anymore."

Then Joseph and Mary with the Lord Jesus went back the long, difficult way through the desert. Oh, how happy they were! They would much rather live in their own land. But they did not return to Bethlehem. They went back to their own village, where they used to live, back to Nazareth. The Lord Jesus was not a very small Boy anymore. He had become a big Boy. The people of the small town loved Him very much. But they did not know that He was the Son of God.

WHEN THE LORD JESUS WAS TWELVE YEARS OLD

How wonderful it was! The Lord Jesus was allowed to come along with Joseph and Mary to the big city of Jerusalem. That was the beautiful city where the temple, God's house, stood. Every year there was a celebration in the temple. Then people would come from all different cities and places to Jerusalem. It was very busy in the city. That celebration was called the Passover. Joseph and Mary went to Jerusalem every year, too. And when the Lord Jesus turned twelve years old, He was allowed to come along for the first time. The Lord Jesus wanted to see the beautiful temple so much. It was the house of God, His Father. The Lord Jesus thought about God very much. He liked to hear people speak about His Father who lived in heaven. And now He was allowed to come along to that great celebration in honour of God. Oh, it was wonderful!

There they went, the many men and women, and also the many children, who played along the way. Nearer and nearer they came to Jerusalem. One more hill to go over. When they were on top of that hill, they could see the big, beautiful city. The houses were white. They shone in the sunshine. But the white temple with its golden towers was the most beautiful. Then those

WHEN THE LORD JESUS WAS TWELVE YEARS OLD

people fell on their knees. The children did, too. They prayed to God very reverently. They sang Psalms together in praise to God. Then they entered Jerusalem. Joseph and Mary and the Lord Jesus also entered. Now the Lord Jesus could see the beautiful temple, the house of God. He was also allowed to go inside.

Oh, yes, He had been in there once before, when He was only a baby. Then His mother had carried Him in her arms. But He did not remember that. The people went into the temple to thank God. God had been very good to them, and the Lord Jesus thanked His Father in heaven, too. He sang along with the beautiful songs, and listened to the priests speaking about God. What a wonderful Passover it was for Him!

That feast lasted seven days. But then the people went home again. They were cheerful and happy. Together they left the city through the gate. Together they walked the road to their villages and cities. Joseph and Mary did, too. Mary looked around. She did not see the Lord Jesus. But she went on. She thought, "He must be playing with the children somewhere. He will come to us soon."

But the Lord Jesus did not come. Then Mary became concerned. She talked to Joseph about it, but he said, "Do not be worried. Jesus has never been disobedient. He must be walking with the other children over there. He will come to us soon." And on they went with the other people.

But the Lord Jesus did not come at all. Mary kept turning around to look for him. How anxious and afraid she was becoming! Where was Jesus?

Then Joseph became anxious, too. He said, "Let us go and search for Him."

He was not with the other children. Where could He be then? "Come, Mary, we will go back."

They searched along the way. They searched over the hills. They searched among the bushes. But the Lord Jesus could not be found. Was He lost?

It grew dark. How afraid Joseph and Mary were! Jesus had never been disobedient. Maybe He was still in the city of Jerusalem. Maybe He did not know that Joseph and Mary had left with the other people. They hurried back to Jerusalem and went through the gate. They searched everywhere in the streets. They asked people if they knew where Jesus was. No one knew. He looked just like any other ordinary boy. No one had seen Him. Mary cried from fear. Oh, it was their own fault! They had not taken care of Jesus. It was not His fault. He was always obedient. They searched for a long time.

Then they came near the temple. Could He be in the temple? No, He would not be in there. But they went inside anyway. Suddenly — there they saw Him. There He was! He sat near the old, learned men, who were teaching the people about God. He sat there listening, and those wise old men asked Him questions. He always knew the answers. Those wise old men thought, "What an intelligent boy he is. He is so young, yet He knows so much and He listens so well to us. We have never seen a Child like that." But they did not know that He was the Lord Jesus, the Son of God.

Mary saw Him sitting there. She ran up to Him and put her arms around Him, holding Him close. She said, "Oh, Son, here Thou art! Why didst Thou worry us so? We did not know where Thou wert, and we were very anxious."

But the Lord Jesus said, "Mother, I must be in the temple, in the house of My Father. I must listen when the wise men speak to Me about My Father. Did you not know that?"

No, Joseph and Mary had not thought about that. Yet it was true. God in heaven was the Father of the Lord Jesus. Then together they went back home. The Lord Jesus went obediently. They were all very happy.

Joseph was a carpenter. He had to go back to work. Mary had to go back to work too and the Lord Jesus helped them faithfully. He never did wrong and everyone loved Him. Many years passed by. The Lord Jesus grew up and became a man.

JOHN THE BAPTIST

Many people were standing close together, listening quietly. They were listening to someone speaking to them. He was standing on a big rock. He was very poorly dressed. His robe

JOHN THE BAPTIST

was made of camel's hair and he had a leather belt around his waist. Yet all the people listened to him very earnestly. Who was that man?

His name was John. He was the son of Zacharias, the old priest. Zacharias had been in that quiet golden room in the temple, when the angel of God had come to him. The angel had said, "You shall have a son, and his name shall be John."

That had been a very long time ago. Now little John had become a man. Now he stood there speaking to the people, and they listened closely. John told them something wonderful. He told them that the Lord Jesus had come to earth to make them happy. He also told the people that they were not allowed to do wicked things.

That frightened them. They asked John, "We have sinned so much. What must we do?"

John said, "You must love God. You must be obedient, and always do God's will."

John could see that the people were sorry about their sins. He told them, "I shall baptize you, and God in heaven will forgive your sins."

Then they went to the river together, and the people waded into the water. John scooped up the water with his hands and poured it over them. That water made them clean. John said,

"That is how the Lord wants to make you clean of your sins. He wants to take away all your sins."

One day they saw a Man coming. The people did not know who He was. He asked John to baptize Him, too. John was shocked. He looked reverently at the Man. He said, "No, no, there is no need for that. Should I baptize Thee? Thou art much greater than I am. I am only an ordinary man. I have done wrong myself. But Thou, Thou hast never sinned. Thou art the Master, I am Thy servant."

But the Man said, "I want to be baptized anyway." Then He walked into the water, and John baptized Him. Suddenly, something wonderful happened. Heaven opened above them. A white dove descended on the head of the Man and God Himself said from heaven, "This is My Son, My Beloved." Who was that Man standing in the water? It was the Lord Jesus Himself. No, the people did not know yet who He was, but John the Baptist knew Him.

The Lord Jesus had become a man. Now He had come to the people to tell them about God, His Father, who lives in heaven. Now He had come to the people to make them happy. He was their Redeemer. He was their Saviour.

THE DISCIPLES

The Lord Jesus did not live in the village of Nazareth anymore. He journeyed through the land to tell the people about God, His Father, who lives in heaven, who knows everything and sees everything. Now the people would know that He, the Lord Jesus, was the Son of God. From heaven He had come to earth. He wanted to do everything that His heavenly Father commanded. The people loved the Lord Jesus.

One day the Lord Jesus was walking along the seashore. Two men were fishing there. They tossed their net into the water, and dragged it out again to catch the fish. They were brothers. One was called Peter and the other Andrew.

The Lord Jesus saw them. He said to them, "Follow me."

The two men did so right away. They put away their nets and went along with the Lord Jesus. That was wonderful! They were allowed to be His friends. They could go with Him wherever He went. He would be their master, and they would be His disciples. Oh, yes, they did what He said right away.

A little farther on were two more men. They were fishermen as well. They sat in their boats mending their nets. They were brothers, too. One was called John and the other James.

The Lord Jesus saw them. He called them, too.

They came right away. Their father, who was in the boat with them, took care of the nets. They went with the Lord Jesus and were allowed to be His disciples too.

That was how the Lord Jesus found His friends. They were poor, common people. The Lord Jesus did not go to the emperor or the king. He did not go to the priests or the very rich, important Jews in the big city of Jerusalem. No, He went to poor fishermen along the seashore. The Lord Jesus did not look to see if they had beautiful clothes, or whether they lived in beautiful houses. He did not look to see whether they were very smart or learned. Oh, no, the Lord Jesus looked at something very different. He looked at their hearts.

He did not want to travel through the land by Himself. He wanted friends along. They would see and they would listen, and He could tell them and teach them many things. He would be the Master, they would be His followers. The Lord Jesus knew everything. He knew what people thought deep down inside their hearts. He saw that these simple men wanted to serve God honestly and faithfully, and that is why they could become His disciples. The Lord Jesus chose more disciples, twelve men all together. Later, when the Lord Jesus would return to heaven, these men would have to go to faraway countries to tell about God. But the disciples did not know that yet.

THE WEDDING AT CANA

What happy people were in that house! And what delicious food and drink was on the table. Music and singing could be heard. It was a wedding. In the little village of Cana a young man and a young woman were getting married. Their fathers and mothers, their brothers and sisters, their friends and neighbours, were all coming to celebrate this happy occasion with them. Mary, the mother of the Lord Jesus, had come to the wedding, too. The Lord Jesus was also there with His disciples. Servants were busy bringing the food to the people. Everyone could have as much as he wanted. The servants were taking care of everything. That wedding in Cana was a very happy celebration.

    Suddenly, Mary went quietly to the Lord Jesus. She told Him something. She asked Him something. She whispered, and did not look very happy at all. What had happened? Did Mary not like the celebration? Oh, yes, she did like it, but she had seen something. She had heard something. The wine, that delicious drink, was all gone. Now the servants did not have wine to bring to the people when they were thirsty. The servants were sorry about that, and the bridegroom was much more sorry. He was the bridegroom, the host. All those people had come to his celebration, and it was his duty to see that they had enough food and drink. But all the wine had been used up. That was too bad! What would they do now?

    Mary had heard it, and she had noticed how sad the bridegroom and his servants were. So quietly she went to the Lord Jesus and whispered, "They have no wine." She thought the Lord Jesus would be able to help. He could do anything.

    But the Lord Jesus said, "Not yet."

    Still, Mary was very glad. She walked up to the servants and said, "When Jesus tells you something, you must do it right away."

    In the house stood six large stone pots to keep water in. The water would stay cool and fresh in those stone pots. But now they were empty. Look, the Lord Jesus was calling the servants. They came right away. They remembered what Mary had told them. Then the Lord Jesus told them, "Fill those pots with water."

Right away they did that. They went to the well, and filled the pots to the brim. Then they brought them back to the Lord Jesus. They wondered, "What does the Lord Jesus want to do with all this water?"

Oh, how strange! He told them, "Take some and bring it to the master of the feast."

The master of the feast was the most important of the servants. He had to take care of everything. He had to take care of the food and drink, too. The servants gave him the water which they had taken out of the pots. He tasted it. He tasted it again, and he looked at them with big, wondering eyes.

"This is wine!" he said. "This is delicious wine!" Quickly he went to the bridegroom and said, "What delicious wine we have here! This is better wine than we had before."

But the bridegroom looked surprised, too. Wine? Delicious wine? How could that be? Was not the wine all gone? The bridegroom did not understand it. The master of the feast did not understand it either. But the servants did. They pointed to the Lord Jesus among the people, and they whispered reverently, "He told us to fill the pots full of water. And now suddenly it is not water anymore. The Lord Jesus made that water into wine!"

The celebration could continue. Oh, how happy that bridegroom and his servants were! How happy Mary was. The Lord Jesus had helped them so wonderfully, but so quietly. The people had not even noticed. And yet it was a big miracle. No one could do such a thing! But the people heard about what the Lord Jesus had done anyway. The one told it to the other.

In awe and reverence the people looked at the Lord Jesus. Only He could do something wonderful like that. The disciples whispered, "How mighty and wonderful our Master is. Yes, He must be God's Son." As the days went by they would see many more wonderful things.

A NET FULL OF FISH

The Lord Jesus could tell wonderful stories. No one could do it as well as He could. When the Lord Jesus spoke, the people just had to listen. Everything would become very quiet. The Lord Jesus told about God in heaven again and again. But He also told about wicked things that the people did. He knew everything. How gladly the people listened! They wanted to hear more and more. That was how beautiful it was.

One day the Lord was near the sea speaking to the people. But they were crowding Him so close. Everyone wanted to be up front, close to the Lord Jesus. What He said was so wonderful. But there was hardly any room for the Lord Jesus to stand.

Near the shore two fishermen were working. They had been fishing all night, but had not caught anything. Now they had come home with an empty boat. They were rinsing their nets. The nets had to be very clean, and then they had to be dried. After that they would fold them up and put them back in their boats. The two fishermen were Peter and Andrew. They were two disciples of the Lord Jesus.

He called to them and asked them something. Oh, yes, that was fine. They would do that right away. Anything their Master asked they would do. They loved Him so very much. They went to their boat and the Lord Jesus came along. He entered their little boat. The people thought the Lord Jesus was going away. That would be too bad! But He was not. No, that was not what the Lord Jesus was doing. Peter and Andrew pushed their boat just a little way into the water and then tied their boat down. Now the Lord Jesus could speak to the people. They could hear Him well, but they could not crowd Him any longer. Now the Lord Jesus had a good spot Himself. Yes, that was good. Some of the people sat down in the sand close to the sea, and others climbed on the rocks lying there. Now they could all listen well. Some even climbed in other boats lying there on the shore. They wanted to listen well to what the Lord Jesus was telling them. No one was able to tell it as good as He could. It became very quiet again. Listen, only the Lord Jesus' voice, quiet but clear, could be heard.

He told them that He had come from heaven to earth to make the people happy. One day He would return to heaven, to His heavenly Father. And everyone who loved Him and obeyed Him would one day come to heaven to live with God, too. The people listened, and many thought, "Oh, yes, we want to love the Lord Jesus. We want to do what He says."

When the Lord Jesus was finished speaking, the people left one by one. Then suddenly the Lord Jesus said to Peter and Andrew, "Take your boat farther into the sea, to the deep water. Then cast your nets out again."

Cast them out in the deep water? In the middle of the day? The two fishermen looked very surprised at the Lord Jesus. It was so strange! They always went fishing in the middle of the night. When the sun was shining they could not catch anything. Were they supposed to fish now, in the middle of the day?

Peter said, "Lord, we have been fishing all night, and have not caught anything." But Peter thought, "If the Lord tells us to, we should obey." He also said, "Master, when Thou sayest it, we shall cast out the nets immediately."

The boat glided over the quiet water, farther and farther from the shore to the deep sea. The Lord Jesus came along.

Then Peter and Andrew cast the nets in the water. They left them there a little while, and then they said, "Now we must pull them up again." They pulled. But they could not get them up! They pulled and pulled. They were so heavy. They were full of fish! They pulled harder. The nets were so full that they tore. Peter and Andrew could not pull them up. But in the distance near the shore was another boat. Other fishermen were in it, John and James. They were also disciples of the Lord Jesus. Peter and Andrew called, "Come! Come and help us!" They waved their arms, and they shouted louder, "Come! We cannot pull up the nets by ourselves!" They were glad, so very glad. Never had they caught this many fish.

John and James quickly came to help. Together they pulled, together they worked. All those fish were gathered in their boats.

But then the two boats were so full, it almost made them sink. No, never had they caught this many fish. How could this be?

The men looked at the Lord Jesus with awe and wonder. He had worked this miracle. Peter became a little afraid of his Master. He fell down on his knees before the Lord Jesus and said, "O Lord, why hast Thou come to me? I have done so much wrong. Thou knowest everything. Thou canst do anything. Thou art the Son of God, and we are poor, sinful people."

But the Lord Jesus said kindly to him, "Do not be afraid of Me, Peter. From now on you shall be a fisher of men."

A fisher of men? How strange! Oh, but the Lord did not mean catching men in a net from the sea. He meant something else. Peter was the Lord Jesus' disciple. He could tell the people about God. And when the people listened and loved God, and obeyed God's will, then it would be as if Peter had caught them. That was what the Lord Jesus meant. Peter understood. That was a wonderful, beautiful day for those men. They would always follow the Lord Jesus. From then on they always stayed with Him.

A SICK MAN HEALED

How strange! Four men were walking through the street carrying a bed. Yes, a bed! And on that bed lay a sick man. They were very, very careful. They told the sick man, "Only a little farther. See, there is the house where we have to be." They looked very happy and the sick man looked happy, too. His eyes shone with happiness. There, in that house was where they had to go. These good friends were carrying him there on his bed. No, he could not walk at all. He could not even move his legs or his arms. He was paralysed. He always had to lie quietly on his bed. And he would never get better. Poor man! How sad.

Where were they bringing him? Were they bringing him to a doctor? Oh, no; no doctor could help him. Were they bringing him to a hospital? No, that would not help him either. Where then? They were bringing him to the Lord Jesus.

The friends had heard that the Lord Jesus had come to their city. He was staying at a friend's house. Then right away

A SICK MAN HEALED

those men went to their sick friend and said, "Come, the Lord Jesus is in the city. The Lord Jesus, who helps the poor, and heals the sick! Come quickly."

The Lord Jesus! Oh, yes, the people were talking about how He healed the sick, and made the blind to see and the deaf to hear. Yes, the poor sick man had heard about the Lord Jesus, too, but he had never seen Him. And now the Lord Jesus was here in the city. Here, near him! But it made the sick man sad, too. He was not able to go to the Lord Jesus. Then his friends said, "We will bring you to the Lord Jesus. Come quickly!" And those good men each took a corner of the bed. Oh, if only the Lord Jesus would heal this poor lame man. How wonderful that would be!

There they went through the streets. They walked as carefully as possible. Soon they reached the house where the Lord Jesus was staying. The sick man's eyes shone. They were so near the Saviour! They wanted to go inside the gate to the house. But what a crowd of people! They all wanted to go inside. They all wanted to be near the Lord Jesus. They wanted to see Him and listen to Him. The whole house was full of people. So were the hallways. And more people were pushing near the gate to get inside. And now those four men with their sick friend wanted to go inside, too, but they could not. It was impossible. Yes, they asked the people, "Please let us through." But the people did not want to give up their own places. They did not even listen to those men. They did not even look at the sick man.

How sad! How very sad. Now the Lord Jesus was so very close, and the poor sick man was not able to get near Him. What now? The friends looked so sad. "Shall we wait? But later the people will crowd even more. Maybe the Lord Jesus will leave." No, waiting would not help. Should they bring their poor friend back home? Should they put him back on his old spot? Then he would never, never get better. No, not back home. They had to get to the Lord Jesus. Oh, if only they could bring their poor friend to Him, he could be healed. But they were not able to come near Him. Or could they?

What were those strong men doing? They were climbing the outside stairs, carrying their sick friend on their shoulders. But what were they going to do on the roof? That was not where the Lord Jesus was. Their eyes were shining again. They had thought of something wonderful. Soon they were on the flat roof, and they laid their sick friend down. Then they said to each other, "Yes, this is about where we have to be. Maybe a little farther." Then they went on their knees and took some of the flat tiles off the roof. They took off more and more tiles. They were making a big hole in the roof. But it had to be made even bigger. They looked down. Yes, they could see the Lord Jesus. He was standing right underneath the hole.

Quickly they tied four ropes to the four corners of the bed. The poor sick man looked happily at his friends. Everything they did was fine with him, if only he could get near the Lord Jesus.

Slowly the men lowered the bed through the hole. They held onto the ropes tightly, and lowered the bed farther. It came down in front of the Lord Jesus, who was speaking to the people in the house. Now at last the sick man was near the Lord Jesus.

But wouldn't the Lord Jesus be angry at those bold men who had made a hole in the roof? And wouldn't He be angry at the sick man, too? No, the Lord Jesus is never angry at anyone

A SICK MAN HEALED

who asks for His help. He looked kindly at the poor man. He noticed how the sick man's eyes pleaded, "O Lord, Thou canst do anything. Thou canst heal me. Do not send me away. Help me!"

Then the Lord Jesus said, "Do not be afraid. I forgive you your sins." How strange! The Lord Jesus did not say, "I will heal your sick arms and sick legs so you can walk and work again." But He said, "Your sins are forgiven."

Yes, that was strange. But the Lord Jesus knows everyone. He knew the sick man, too. He knew everything about him. He knew that the man had done much wrong. The poor, sick man heard the Lord Jesus saying, "Your sins are forgiven." How wonderful that was! Doing wrong makes you afraid. But now he would not have to be afraid any longer. The Lord Jesus had forgiven him his sins. The Lord Jesus was not angry with him anymore. Yes, that was wonderful, wonderful!

But then the Lord Jesus said more. He said, "I say to you, get up, take up your bed, and go to your house."

Get up? Go to his house? But the sick man could not stand. He could not walk! But when the Lord Jesus said those words he suddenly was able to.

The poor sick man got up. He jumped up! Just like that, he stood on his legs. And he rolled up his bed with his hands. His legs and arms were not paralysed anymore. Suddenly he was strong and healthy. He had been so miserable and pitiful. But not anymore. The Lord Jesus had done this miracle. He had spoken only a few words and then that poor man had been totally healed. How wonderful. How wonderful!

The man went back to his house. He carried his bed on his shoulders. Yes, now the people made way for him. Those people looked at him amazed. How could this be? They looked at the Lord Jesus with awe. Softly they whispered to each other, "How wonderful this is! How great and mighty the Lord Jesus is. Now we have seen His mighty works ourselves."

UNCLEAN! UNCLEAN!

A poor, sick man was walking along the road. He was a pitiful man. His clothes were dirty and torn. He was so tired and weak, he could hardly walk. But that was not the worst. Something much more terrible was wrong. He was a leper. He had ugly sores on his face and on his hands. There were loathsome white sores on his whole body. That poor man was very sick. He walked along the quiet country road because he was not allowed to come into the city. He had to live by himself in a little house outside the city. People were afraid of him. If he touched them with his sick hand, they could become sick, too. That would be terrible. No, he was never allowed to come into the city again. He always had to stay in the lonely country, all by himself. And when people came by on the country road, he had to immediately call out, "Unclean! Unclean!" Then people would stay far away from him. The people were afraid of getting that sickness. The poor man! He would never become better again. The sores would only get worse and worse. He would become sicker and sicker, and then he would die, all by himself.

Slowly he walked along the quiet road. Where was he going? He gazed into the distance. Every so often he stopped and listened. What did he hear? Oh, his eyes were filled with gladness, and he tried to move faster. His sore legs shuffled along, but still he tried to go faster. What did he see, and what did he hear? A crowd of people was coming in the distance, and in the centre of that crowd walked the Lord Jesus. That poor leper did not look at all the people. He only looked at the Lord Jesus. He had heard that the Lord Jesus healed sick people and helped them. If only the Lord Jesus would heal him, too! On he walked. He wanted to ask the Lord Jesus himself. He wanted to plead with Him. He came closer and closer.

But he was not allowed to be close to people. He was supposed to go to the side of the road; that was the law in this land. And he was supposed to cry, "Unclean! Unclean!" The poor man forgot all about it. He forgot all about that law and the people. He only thought about the Lord Jesus. He came right up to the Lord and fell on the ground in front of the Lord Jesus' feet. He stretched out his hands, those dirty, sore-covered hands, to the Lord Jesus, and he asked, he pleaded, "If Thou wantest, Thou canst make me better. Help me! Help me, Lord!"

The people saw the man. They became frightened and quickly stepped backward. They were so afraid. What if he touched them? "How awful! A leper! So dirty and sick! He may not come near us," they said to each other very loudly.

The poor man did not even hear it. He only looked at the Lord Jesus and prayed, "Help me! Help me, Lord!"

Did the Lord Jesus become alarmed? Oh, no, the Lord Jesus was sorry for the poor man. He did not say, "Go away!" He looked at the pitiful man with love. Yes, He even took the leper's dirty, sick hand in His own.

The people saw it. It horrified them. The Lord Jesus dared to touch that sick man! How could He? But the Lord did not look at the fearful people. He only looked at that sick man, and He said, "I want you to be better."

Suddenly, that very minute, the poor man was better. The sores were gone! His tired, weak legs became strong. He was completely healthy! The man was so happy, so very, very happy. He had been so terribly sick. But not anymore! The Lord Jesus was so very good, He was so mighty, He was so great! He loved the poor and sick people.

The happy, healed man went his way to the city. Now he did not have to live alone in a little house way out in the country any longer. He was allowed to live with his family and other people again. No one was afraid of him anymore. And he told everyone about what the Lord Jesus had done for him. He could not keep quiet about it. He had to tell. It was so amazing! It was so wonderful!

A POOR MOTHER AND HER POOR DEAD SON

Out of the city gate came a sad procession. All those men and women were grieving. They walked very quietly. In the centre of the crowd, a dead person was being carried to his grave on a bier. It was a funeral.

Underneath a white cloth lay the body of a young man. He had died. Now the men were carrying him to his grave. Off in the mountains was a tomb. That was where they would lay him, and then they would roll a big stone in front of the opening. Then they would go home and forget about him. Slowly they walked on.

Behind the bier walked his mother. That poor mother! She was so very sorrowful. She was weeping with grief. She had loved her son so much, but now he was dead. Now he was not aware of anything anymore. Now the men were bringing him away, forever.

The poor mother! Now she did not have anyone anymore. First her husband had died. Only one child had been left to her. Now she had lost him, too, for always. She was left all alone. They had loved each other so much. The boy had loved his mother, and his mother had loved him. No, she would never, never forget him. The poor mother! She walked along, her head bowed, and her hands in front of her tear-filled eyes. She was so very, very sad, no one could comfort her. No one could take her grief away. No, no one.

Farther down the road, another procession was coming. It was full of happy people. They were talking loudly and

A POOR MOTHER AND HER POOR DEAD SON

energetically. They were coming to the city. Who was walking in the centre? It was the Lord Jesus with His disciples. Those happy people were about to pass the sad people on the road. The happy people saw the sad procession. They saw the dead young man and his mother. It made them stop talking.

The Lord Jesus saw the funeral, too. He saw the poor woman. He heard her weeping with grief. Then the Lord Jesus was filled with compassion. That poor mother! She had lost everything. He walked up to her, and said to her, "Do not weep."

The poor woman did not understand. Should she not weep? Should she not cry because her dear son was dead? She had loved him so much, and now this strange man was telling her, "Do not weep." She did not know who this strange man was. She could only think of her son, who lay there, white and cold, and that they were bringing him away to lie behind that stone.

But the Lord Jesus said more. He told the men who were carrying the dead man to stop. When the bier was put down the

Lord Jesus took away the white cloth lying over the dead man, and said, "Young man, I tell you, get up!"

Suddenly, the dead man opened his eyes. He sat up. He was alive! Yes, he was alive again! He had been dead, but the Lord Jesus had made him alive. The people saw it, and they were astounded. The young man's mother saw it, too. She went to her son. She had him back! The Lord Jesus had given him back to her. Now he could come home with her. He was not sick anymore; he could walk, too. He would work for her and take care of her. Now she would not be alone, and they would love each other even more than before. Oh, what a happy mother she was now! She took him in her arms. She held him to her heart. She was so happy, so very happy! And the Lord Jesus had done it all.

Then all the people travelled back to the city. Together they went through the gate. No one was sad. Everyone was happy, the mother and her son, and the people, and the disciples. They looked reverently and thankfully at the Lord Jesus. He had done that wonderful miracle. No one in the world was as mighty as He. And everywhere the people told what the Lord Jesus had done.

THE DAUGHTER OF JAIRUS

It was very quiet in the house. People spoke only in whispers. Mother was crying. Father was looking at his poor child lying on the bed. There was deep sadness in Father's eyes. Oh, his dear girl! There she lay. Her cheeks were white, her hands were cold, and she lay so quietly. She did not speak, not one word. Poor child! She was very sick, deathly sick, and no one could help her. Father could not. Neither could Mother. Not even the doctor could help her. In the house everything was quiet and fearful and sad.

But outside in the city it was very busy. More and more people were coming past, a big multitude. In the centre walked the Lord Jesus. Everyone looked at Him, everyone listened to Him. No one knew about that very sick little girl until a man came pushing his way through the crowd. His eyes were very sad. He pushed himself through that crowd of people until he came very close to the Lord Jesus. Then he said, "O Lord, my daughter is sick, deathly sick. She will die! Please help her! Help my poor child. Come with me to my house, Lord. Lay Thy hand on her head, then she will be healed. Then she will be better again."

That man was the father of the sick girl. His name was Jairus. Someone had come to tell him that the Lord Jesus was in the

THE DAUGHTER OF JAIRUS

city. Immediately he had run out to find him. Not one of the doctors could help his child. But the Lord Jesus could. He can do everything. And the Lord Jesus felt sorry for that father and his poor child. He went along with Jairus.

But it took so long, so very long. The people were crowding them and the house was so far away.

Then a sick woman came quietly near the Lord Jesus and softly touched His clothes. She was very shy. She thought, "Now the Lord Jesus will not notice anything, and yet I will get better." And that is exactly what happened, the sick woman was healed. But the Lord Jesus had noticed it. He spoke very gently with her. He was not angry about it. Oh, but it took so long, so long! Jairus waited and waited, and all the time he thought of his poor child at home.

Suddenly a servant came walking up to Jairus. He looked very sad.

Jairus was frightened. "What is wrong? What is wrong?" He thought something very dreadful must have happened.

It was dreadful. The servant said, "Your daughter is dead."

"Dead?"

Then it was too late, too late! There was no need for the Lord to come anymore. Jairus could not speak. He wept with grief. Now no one could help. His little girl was dead. Now he might as well go home alone.

But the Lord Jesus had heard what the servant said. It did not worry Him. He said to Jairus, "Do not be afraid. Only believe."

Jairus did not understand that very well, but he stayed very close to the Lord Jesus.

Finally they came to Jairus' house. It was not quiet there now. The neighbours and friends had come. They were crying and wailing loudly because the little girl had died.

But the Lord Jesus said, "The child is not dead. She is asleep."

The people mocked and laughed. "Asleep?" they said to the Lord Jesus. "If only that was true." They knew better. The poor little girl had died, and had to be buried, and then the father and mother would not have their little girl anymore.

But the Lord Jesus went into the room where the little girl lay on her bed. All the people had to stay outside. Only the father and mother and some of the disciples could come inside. There the little girl lay, white, cold, and silent. The Lord Jesus went up to her. He took her cold, white hand in His, and He said, "Daughter, I tell you, get up!"

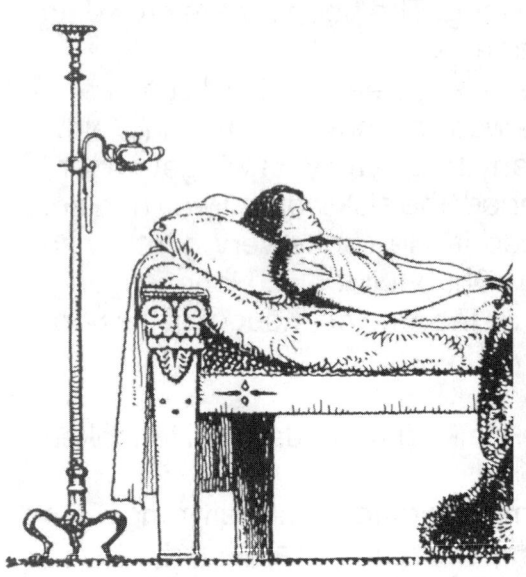

Then a wonderful miracle happened. The dead girl opened her eyes, she sat upright. She saw the Lord Jesus. She saw her mother and her father. She reached out her arms to them. She was so happy. She had been dead, now she was alive again. And she was better, completely better. She was able to get up and eat and play.

Her father and mother were so happy and thankful. The people outside had laughed. They had said, "It cannot happen. Never!" But the father and mother had not laughed. They knew that the Lord Jesus can do everything. They had believed in Him. Now this great miracle had happened. They had received their girl back. She was not deathly sick anymore either. Now everything was wonderful and happy. The Lord Jesus had done that. He can do everything.

SICK AND FORGOTTEN

What a poor man! Was there no one, no one who would come to help him? Was there no one who thought about him?

He was lying in a hospital. But it was a very strange hospital. There were no doctors in this hospital. There were also no nurses to take care of the sick. The poor man was lying on a thin mattress on the floor, and he waited. No one looked at him. No

SICK AND FORGOTTEN

one asked him anything. He had lain there and waited a long, long time. He had waited for many years, thirty-eight long years. He had become old in that hospital. His legs were sick. They were lame, so that he could not walk. All those long years he had not been able to walk. And no one ever thought about him. He would likely die in that strange hospital. He was forgotten. Completely forgotten. Poor man!

It was very busy in that hospital. New patients came there all the time. When they were better, they went away again. That poor man on his bed in the corner was never healed. He never left.

But how did sick people get better in that strange hospital? Look, in the centre of the five rooms of the hospital was a pool. It was a still pool, as smooth as glass. But sometimes, suddenly, the quiet water in the pool started to bubble and move. And then, oh, then there was such fear among the sick people. And yet they became happy, so wonderfully happy. They knew that an angel had come from heaven. He had quietly touched that water, and whoever entered the water first was healed.

The first! Everyone wanted to be the first. They crawled or they walked quickly to the water. The sick who could not walk were carried there. Everyone had a father, or a strong son, or friends. Everyone except for the poor man on the bed in the corner. He had no one. Every time the angel came, one sick person was healed. Then that sick person happily left for home. The poor man could never reach the water, and when he tried, someone else was always first. That person would be healed. But he had never been the first. He had waited in his sorrow for thirty-eight long years. He would surely die there.

One day there was a celebration in Jerusalem. It was the Passover feast. The hospital, which was called Bethesda, was close to the city gate of Jerusalem. During that celebration it was very busy in Bethesda hospital. Many people came to visit the sick, and talk to them, and take care of them. No one came to talk to or take care of the poor man on the bed in the corner. He was forgotten. He saw it, and it made him so very sad and lonesome.

Suddenly a man came near. A stranger. The sick man saw Him, but he did not know who the stranger was. Surely He would pass by, too. Everyone passed him by.

But no! That strange man stopped beside him, and He looked at him with gentle eyes. He asked, "Do you want to be healed?"

Be healed? Become healthy? But that was impossible. He could not get near the water. And there was no one who wanted to carry him. Would this strange man maybe want to carry him when the angel came? If only that was true! Of course, he had to be the first in the water. No doubt, someone else would be first anyway.

The sick man said, "Sir, I have no one to bring me to the water. And if I try, someone else gets there first." He said it so sadly.

The stranger heard that. He noticed the sadness in the poor man's eyes.

He said, "Stand up, take up your bed, and walk!"

What was that? How strange, yet, how wonderful! The poor, sick man looked at the stranger. He did not know who He was. He had never seen Him before. But the stranger looked so compassionately at the poor man. And something wonderful was happening to his body. He felt it. Stand up? Take up his bed? Walk? Yes! Yes! He wanted to, and he could, too! He could feel it. He did not think any longer of the angel who had to come and touch the water to make it bubble. He heard those wonderful words from the stranger and he believed. And he stood up, just like that. For thirty-eight long years he had not been able to stand up. Now he could! It was a miracle, a wonderful miracle.

He rolled up his bed. He wanted to thank that kind, friendly man who had so unexpectedly made him very happy. His eyes shone with happy thankfulness. He wanted to say . . . but the strange man was gone! Quietly He had disappeared in the crowd.

That was too bad. Who was that kind, friendly stranger?

The sick man, who was not sick anymore, took his bed and went into the city, to the temple, to thank God for the wonderful thing that had happened. And in the temple he saw the stranger again. It made his heart so happy. He heard that it was the Lord Jesus, the Son of God, who had so amazingly saved him. The Saviour!

The Lord Jesus knows all people. The grown-ups, and the little children, the healthy ones and the sick. He knows who is alone and forgotten. His heart is filled with compassion.

THE STORM AT SEA

It was dark. Evening had come. The Lord Jesus was tired. All day long a great crowd of people had surrounded Him. He had told them many things. He had taught them much. He had healed many sick people. He had made many sad people happy. But now it was evening, and the Lord Jesus was tired. Yet the people did not go home. They wanted to listen to Him some more. But the Lord Jesus said to His disciples, "Let us go in a boat to the other side of the sea."

Whatever the Master said they would do right away. Quickly they prepared a little fishing boat, and went with the Lord Jesus on the dark sea. When the people could not see the Lord Jesus anymore, they went home.

It was very quiet on the sea. The water was calm and peaceful. The disciples rowed on slowly. But the Lord Jesus lay down in the back of the boat, His head on a pillow, and fell asleep. Gently the boat glided over the quiet, dark water. The disciples talked in whispers, not wanting to awaken their Master, who was so tired.

Suddenly across from the mountains came the wind. It came down on the smooth, dark water. It drove the waves high, and the little boat rocked up and down, up and down. The disciples became afraid, and said, "A storm is coming. Do you hear the wind howling from around the mountains? Come, let us row harder, then we will be on the other side sooner. Then that fierce wind cannot hurt us. Hurry!"

Swiftly they moved their oars through the water, pulling as hard as they could. They were brave, strong men, those disciples. Hurry!

The Lord Jesus did not hear how it howled over the water. The Lord Jesus was sleeping very contentedly.

But the wind became rougher. It hit the water and swept it up into big waves. The waves foamed and the little boat swung wildly back and forth, back and forth. The fierce wind threw water over the boat and over the disciples. It screamed and howled! It seemed as if it wanted to push that little boat away and all the people in it down into the deep, dark water.

The Lord Jesus lay in the back of the boat. He slept peacefully. But the disciples were afraid, very afraid. Oh, yes, often they had been in a storm with their little boats. They knew the fierce wind that could come around the mountains. But never had it been as wild as this night. No, it had never been this way before. It grabbed the boat and nearly turned it over. The boat groaned and creaked. The water splashed into the boat. They were sinking! Soon they would sink down into the dark deep sea. Who would help those poor people in that fierce storm? The sea was so wide and wild, the boat was so small and weak, and the dark water was very deep. But the Lord Jesus slept peacefully.

The disciples hung onto the edge of their boat. They trembled with fear. How could the Lord Jesus sleep? Did He not know that this terrible storm was drowning them all? Oh, that awful wind! There it came again. It grabbed the little boat.

"Master, oh, Master!" shouted the disciples. "Master, wake up! The storm will drown us all. O Lord, help us, save us. We shall perish!" They were so terribly afraid.

Then the Lord Jesus woke up. He stood up. That dreadful wind howled around Him. Those wild waves threw their foam up against Him. But it did not frighten the Lord Jesus. He was not afraid of that fierce storm at all. Quietly He stood there in the back of the boat. He stretched His hand out over the water. He said to those wild waves and that fierce wind, "Peace, be still!"

Immediately those fierce waves ceased and the wild wind blew away into the dark distance. Immediately it was quiet, very quiet on the dark sea. The wind and the waves had to obey what the Lord Jesus told them. He was also Master of the great sea and the fierce storm. They listened to His voice.

The disciples watched it in fear. They bowed their heads. They did not dare to look at their Master. He was so mighty and so strong. Could He even command the sea and the wind to be still?

The Lord Jesus said to them, "Why were you so afraid? I am with you. Did you not believe that I would help you?"

They did not dare to say a word, they were so ashamed. The Master was able to do anything. He could heal the sick and bring the dead back to life. He was the Son of God. Why had they been so afraid? There was no need for them to be afraid. He would not have let them drown. They looked at the Lord Jesus with reverence. Now they loved Him even more.

Then the boat went on over the quiet sea. The water glistened smoothly and beautifully. The bright stars twinkled in the heavens. Now all was well.

FIVE LOAVES AND TWO FISH

One beautiful day, the Lord Jesus sailed across the sea with His disciples to a quiet spot between the mountains. He wanted to be alone with them. But when they got to that quiet spot, the people were there already. They had noticed that the Lord Jesus had gone to that quiet place between the mountains. Quickly they had walked all the way around the sea to be there, too. Now the Lord Jesus was not alone. More and more people came. They brought their sick and their weak, their deaf and their blind. They came with all their griefs to the Lord Jesus.

Didn't those troublesome people anger the Lord Jesus? He wanted to be alone so much. No, the Lord Jesus never becomes angry at anyone who comes to Him with his grief. Never. He saw them coming from between the mountains and He was filled with compassion. All those sick, all those weak, the deaf and the blind, He healed them all. And He told them about God, His Father in heaven. He told the people that they should love God and each other, too.

But it was getting late in the day. Soon the evening would come. The disciples thought, "The Master is forgetting that evening is coming. The people must have something to eat."

They went to the Lord Jesus and said, "Master, it is late. The people must have something to eat, and they did not bring anything. Send them away to the distant villages to buy some bread before darkness comes."

The Lord Jesus heard what they asked, and what was His answer? Did He say, "Oh, yes, let the people quickly go because they are so hungry?" No, the Lord Jesus said something entirely different, something strange: "You give those people something to eat."

The disciples looked at their Master in amazement. They thought, "We? Must we feed the people? That is impossible! We have no bread. And if we tried to buy bread, which would cost a lot of money, we still would not have enough. Look! There are so many people, hundreds, thousands of men, women, and children. No, that is impossible."

The disciples did not know what to do. But the Lord Jesus knew. He is always able to help, always!

He asked, "How many loaves do you have?"

Andrew said, "Master, here is a little boy. He has five loaves and two fish. But that is not nearly enough for so many people." Andrew thought, "Five little round loaves and two fish! If all those men and women and children had to share those loaves and fish, they would not even receive a crumb. No, five loaves and two fish won't help."

But the Lord Jesus said, "Let all the people sit in the grass and bring me the loaves and the fish."

What was the Lord going to do? The disciples did not understand. But immediately they obeyed their Master. The men and women and children all sat down in the grass. There was a group here, and another group there. A little farther was yet another group. The large meadow between the mountains was filled with people. The little boy gave his loaves and fish to the Lord Jesus. And then?

The Lord Jesus stood up on a little hill. Everyone could see Him. He folded His hands, and He looked up to God in heaven. The Lord Jesus prayed before they began. It would be a huge meal. The people had never been at such an enormous gathering to eat before. But where was the food? There was no food. Only five loaves and two fish, for all those thousands of people?

The Lord Jesus broke the loaves and the fish into pieces. The disciples put the pieces in a basket. They would serve the people. The Lord Jesus kept on breaking the food. Another basket was filled, and another, and another. Each disciple walked around with a basket, filled to the brim with bread and fish.

Every man, every woman, every boy, and every girl could take as much as they wanted. The Lord Jesus kept on breaking the food, and the little loaves and the little fish were not finished. What a great and wonderful miracle! All the people received food from the Lord Jesus. The disciples thought the Master had forgotten those people. No, the Lord Jesus knew they were hungry. He never forgot the people, never.

The disciples came back to the Lord Jesus. There was even bread left over, and everyone had had enough. But all the pieces had to be gathered together. Not one piece of bread should be lost or wasted.

And when the disciples gathered it all in, there were twelve full baskets left over. There was even more than when they had started. What a great and wonderful miracle the Lord Jesus had performed!

The people and the disciples, all the hundreds and thousands of them, came to the Lord Jesus. Their eyes were filled with reverence and gladness. They lifted up their hands high and they shouted and cheered. They said, "The Lord Jesus must be our King. Yes, He must drive the enemies out of our land. He must be King. He can do anything. He must sit on the beautiful throne of the king, and we will be His servants."

The Lord Jesus heard what the people cried, but it made Him sad. He did not want to be rich. He did not wish to sit on a king's throne. He did not want to fight the enemies. No, He wanted something very different. He wanted to make the people happy. He wanted to forgive the wrong they did, the wrong that brought such fear to their hearts. He wanted to bring them to heaven one day, to God His Father. That was much better and much more glorious than being a king.

Then the Lord Jesus told the people to go home. Evening had come, and it was getting dark. He told the disciples to go away in their boats across the sea. But He Himself went all alone up the mountains. He went to a quiet place to pray. Praying is speaking reverently to God. That was what the Lord Jesus wanted to do that night. He wanted to be close to His Father. He wanted to tell Him everything. That was why He wanted to pray all alone.

WALKING ON THE SEA

The night was dark. The wind blew wildly about. The Lord Jesus had prayed all alone in the mountains to His Father in heaven. Now He went back to the sea. But the water was so dark. The waves were splashing wildly. The wind howled over the water. The Lord Jesus remembered His poor disciples. They were in their little boat on the sea. But now with the storm it would be very dangerous, and they would be very afraid. They would be far away in the dark, no one would be able to see or hear them. But the Lord Jesus could see them. He can see everything. He could hear them, too, even though they were far away. He was able to hear everything. He was thinking about them. But the poor disciples did not know that.

How they struggled. They were not able to get their little boat any farther. Again and again the wind pushed them back. It blew them this way and that. Oh, what if that wild wind blew their boat over? What if they fell into that dark water? The men were

WALKING ON THE SEA

very frightened. They talked together. "Do you remember a while ago when there was a storm at sea? Then we were afraid, too. But then the Lord Jesus was with us. He was asleep. Do you remember? We woke Him up and then He told the wind and the waves, 'Peace, be still!' But now we are all alone."

They struggled on. The wind blew their boat around and around. It went up on a high wave, then it slid into a deep trough. Oh, what if it blew over? The poor disciples said, "If only the Lord Jesus was with us, then we would not be afraid. And if He was sleeping, we would not even wake Him up. We would not be afraid anymore. Oh, if only He was with us! But now we are so alone. Who will help us? The Lord Jesus does not know that we are here, and the danger is so great. He cannot see us, and if we call He cannot hear us. Oh, who will help us?"

Foolish men! Why were they so afraid? Couldn't the Lord Jesus see them? Couldn't He hear them? He knows everything. He knew the fear and the need of the people.

The disciples tried to get ahead with their boat, but they could not. They did not know what to do. Then suddenly — What was that? Over there! Who was walking there? Who could walk on water? Right on top of the water? They were terrified. They screamed with fear. Yes, someone was walking on the water, right over those wild waves. But that was impossible! It could not be! That could not be a human being! But what was it then? It had to be a ghost! Again they shouted in fright.

Suddenly they heard a voice. That voice came to them from over the water. That voice said, "Do not be afraid. It is I."

And then they knew who was walking there, walking to them on the waves. It was the Lord Jesus. They recognized His voice. Their fright was gone, and their fear was gone, too. How wonderful! It was the Master Himself. And one of the disciples could hardly stay in the boat. He wanted to go to the Master. That was Peter. Peter called, "Lord, let me come to Thee on the water."

The Lord Jesus said only one word: "Come."

Peter dared to go. He climbed over the edge of the boat and stepped onto the dark water. He did not even sink. That was because the Lord Jesus had said, "Come." And then Peter walked toward his Master. He was not even afraid at all. He walked right over the waves. The Lord Jesus was so mighty. If the Lord Jesus had said it, then Peter was not allowed to be afraid. He came very close to His Master.

But then, just for a second Peter looked down at that dark water under his feet. Just for a moment. That water was splashing back and forth. It splashed and foamed against Peter, and then he thought, "What if I sink into that deep water?" Peter became terribly afraid. He forgot the Lord Jesus. For just a moment Peter forgot Him, and he started to sink into the water. With a frightened scream, he cried, "Lord, save me! Help me, I am drowning!"

But the Lord Jesus did not let Peter drown. He reached out His hand and grasped Peter's hand and set him on top of the water again. Then He reprimanded Peter, "Why did you become afraid? Do you not believe?"

Peter was ashamed. He should not have been afraid. The Lord Jesus had said so Himself.

Together they went to the boat, walking over the water. Then the water quieted. The little boat sailed over the smooth water to the other side.

The other disciples were ashamed, too. The Lord had known all along that they were in need. He had seen them all along, even though they were far away. He had heard them, and had come walking to them on the waves of the sea. They had been so afraid. But they should not have been. They had known the Lord Jesus would always help, even if He was far away. But they had not believed it. Now they did. They fell down at the Lord Jesus' feet, and they worshipped Him. And they said quietly, "Yes, truly, Master, Thou art the Son of God."

THE UNFORGIVING SERVANT

One day the Lord Jesus told a story to His disciples. It was a parable. He wanted to teach them something. The story started beautifully.

Once there was a king, a rich and mighty man. Everything he commanded had to be done. One day he said, "Everyone who owes me money must come to me and pay the money back."

One of his servants was terribly afraid when he heard that. Pay back all the money he owed to his master? But he could not do that. He owed him so much money, but he had none to pay him back with. But he had to go anyway. His heart trembled with fear.

There sat his mighty master, high on his throne. And he said, "Pay me what you owe me."

That poor servant! He could not do that! He did not have any money. There was no one to help him. He could not earn all that money either. Even if he worked hard his whole life long, it would not be enough money to pay back his master. Poor man! What was he to do?

"I cannot pay my debt," he said with a trembling voice. "I can never pay you my debt. It is so big! It is too big!"

Then that strict master became very angry. He looked at his servant and said, "You cannot pay me? Then I will sell you as a slave."

He said to his servants standing nearby, "Take this man and sell him. He shall never be a free man again. Sell his wife, too, and his children. Sell all his possessions. He may not keep anything. And give me the money that it brings."

In his terrible grief, the man fell at the feet of his angry master. Lifting his hands he pleaded and begged, "O master, have mercy on me! Have patience, do not punish me."

And then, did the king drive his servant away from his throne? No, that king listened to his poor servant. His kind heart was filled with compassion. He said, "Go home, you do not have to pay me anything. I shall not punish you." That stern king was a good master.

And the servant? All his fear, all his sadness left him. He cried with joy. Now he was free, totally free. He would not be sold as a slave, and he would never have to repay all that money!

What a good king! The servant should have been very thankful to his master, all his life.

But when that servant turned to go to his house, a great sin came into his heart. As he was going home he met another servant. He said to him, "You still owe me some money. Give it to me. Give it to me right away."

It was only a little bit, but that other servant did not have anything. He could not repay even that little bit. He was frightened, and he begged, "Have mercy on me — have patience! Do not punish me. I shall repay you later. Have mercy on me!"

But the man who had himself pleaded and begged his king not to punish him for his big debt — that wicked man did not have mercy. He wanted to punish this other servant for a very small debt. He grabbed him by the throat. He said, "You will pay, now! Right away! If you cannot, I will have you imprisoned."

How cruel, how unmerciful was the man who himself had been afraid and sad first and then had been made so happy.

Did he not remember his good master? Did he not think about his own big debt?

The other servants of the king saw it all. It made them sad. They felt so sorry for the man who was put in prison for that small debt. They said to each other, "Let us tell our master about it."

How angry the good king was when he heard it!

"Bring the man who had a big debt to me," he said angrily.

The man came.

Now there was no mercy in the king's heart anymore, only stern rebuke.

The king said, "You owed me such a great debt. I did not punish you. That other servant owed you a very small debt, but you punished him severely. Was your heart not joyful? Did you not have any mercy? Now I shall punish you, too.

"Take him! Throw him into prison and keep him there until he has paid me everything, everything! That is just!"

The servants grabbed the wicked man with the merciless heart. He would have to pay everything back. But he was not able to. Yet it was his own fault.

The story about the unforgiving servant had started so wonderfully. Now it had ended so terribly. It was a parable. The Lord Jesus wanted to teach something to His disciples, and also to us. All of us, grown-ups and children alike, are often like that wicked man. We do many wrong things, but the Lord in heaven will forgive us our sins, if we reverently pray to Him asking for forgiveness. When someone else hurts us, we become angry and do not want to forgive. Then we are like the unforgiving servant. That should not to be. We must forgive others when they hurt us because God has forgiven us all of our many, many sins.

JESUS, THE FRIEND OF LITTLE CHILDREN

Where were all those children going? The big ones were walking ahead, and the little ones were carried by their mothers.

And what made them look so happy? They were going to the Lord Jesus.

"Come!" their mothers said. "See? There is the Master in the distance." Yes, the little ones wanted to come, and the mothers wanted it very much, too.

The Lord Jesus was sitting there. And now the mothers were coming to Him with their children, from all sides. But what did they want?

Were those children sick? Were their mothers going to ask the Lord Jesus to heal them?

No.

Were those children poor? Were they going to ask the Lord Jesus to give them clothes and beautiful things?

No.

Were those children hungry? Were they going to ask for bread?

No.

But what then?

The mothers knew that the Lord Jesus loved people very much. He always wanted to help them and make them happy. It would be so wonderful if the children could come to Him, too! The mothers loved their children so much, and they wanted to bring them to the Lord Jesus. If He would look at them with His kind eyes, lay His hands on their heads, and bless them, oh, that would make them so happy!

Now they could come. All the grown-ups were going away and the Lord Jesus was left alone with His disciples.

"Come," the mothers said. "Come, the Master will not send you away."

But when the disciples saw all those children coming, it made them upset. They said, "Go back, do not bother the Master. You are too little." The disciples wanted to send the mothers with their children away.

JESUS, THE FRIEND OF LITTLE CHILDREN

They thought, "Adults, big people — they can come to the Lord Jesus. But not children. They are so little, still so foolish. The Master is much too busy. He cannot look at and listen to children. And they are not sick. No, children should not come to disturb the Lord Jesus. He is so great and mighty. He is so wonderful and holy. He is the Son of God! He cannot be bothered with those foolish little children. No, no, go away! You cannot come to the Master."

That was too bad!

But the Lord Jesus heard it. He saw the disciples drive the children away. They were not allowed to do that. They should not stop the children. The Lord Jesus wanted to be the Friend of children. He loved the little ones. He said, "Let the children come to Me. Do not forbid them."

And then they came. Just like that, they came to the Lord Jesus. They looked at Him with joyful eyes. Then they dared to reach out their little hands to Him. They were not at all afraid. That made the Lord Jesus happy. He looked kindly at them, and He let them come near Him. They laid their hands on His lap and their heads against His arms.

He loved them. He laid His hands on their heads and He blessed them. He gave them a promise of something beautiful. It was not toys, or good food, or beautiful clothes. Oh, no, it was something much more wonderful. The Lord Jesus promised them that one day, if they loved Him, they could live with Him in heaven, in the beautiful heaven with God.

Then the Lord Jesus talked some more to the disciples and the mothers. They were difficult words. The children did not understand what the words meant, but they did realize that the Lord Jesus was their Friend, and that He loved them very much. Then they went home with their mothers, very happy.

No, the Lord Jesus did not want children to be afraid of Him. He wanted them to come to Him and love Him. He wanted to be their Friend and Saviour. He wanted to bless them, no matter how little they were. He wanted to help them, and make them happy. And the most wonderful thing of all — the Lord Jesus wanted to bring the children to heaven if they loved Him and obeyed Him.

THE LOST SON

The Lord Jesus was a good story-teller. No one could tell stories the way He did. It was so beautiful, the people just had to listen when He spoke. And He wanted to teach them something with each story He told. One day the Lord Jesus told a beautiful story called "The Lost Son."

A father had two sons. He loved them both very much. That father was very rich. He gave his sons everything they needed. But the one son, the youngest, was not satisfied. He did not want to stay with his father in their beautiful, rich house. He wanted to go travelling, far, far away, into the wide world.

"The world is so wide, so big, so beautiful, and so wonderful. In those faraway, strange countries of the world it will be pleasant. I want to go away from my father's house," he thought.

THE LOST SON

The younger son said to his father, "Father, you are rich, but you are very old. You will soon die. Then we, my brother and I, will get all your treasures, your money, and your goods. Father, give me my money now, right now. I want to go far away into the wide world, which is so big and beautiful and wonderful."

That made his good father very sad. He thought, "I love my son, but my son does not love me very much." Yet that good father took his money and divided it equally. The one portion he gave to his youngest son. The other portion he kept for his eldest son.

Then the youngest son went away into the wide, wide world. He was so jubilant he did not think about his father at all anymore. Like a rich man, he travelled on a beautiful camel. For a long time his father sadly watched him go. But the rich son did not even turn around to wave.

His brother also watched him go. He thought, "Let him go. He is bad, I am much better than he is."

But the father softly whispered, "Poor boy! Now you are going away, far away. You are forgetting your father, but your father will not forget you. Never!"

Those faraway, strange lands were wonderful, and the rich son was so happy. He held banquets every day. He had many merry friends. They ate and they drank and they had wild, frolicsome times. The rich son never thought about home or his good father. The wide world was so wonderful, so joyful, and so rich. But the parties and celebrations were very expensive. All that delicious food and drink was very expensive, too. The rich son had to pay for all of it.

One day his money bag was empty. All the way empty! He sold his camel, but soon that money was gone, too. Then he was not a rich son anymore. He was a poor son, and that was his own fault.

It became much worse. A famine came in the land where he lived. There was very little bread for the people. No one gave him any either. He had no money to buy any and he did not dare to ask. Poor man! He was so hungry, so very hungry! And he was very sad, but it was all his own fault.

Then he went to work for a farmer. As a very poor servant, he had to do the dirtiest work. He took care of the pigs, dirty animals that were always rooting around in the mud.

When the pigs were fed with the food the farmer prepared for them, the poor son wanted to eat along with the pigs. He was that hungry. But he was not allowed to eat the pig food. Poor man!

Once he had been very rich and happy. Now he was very poor and wretched, and so very alone. No one helped him. All his friends had forgotten him, because he no longer had money for feasts. He sat there among the pigs, with all that grief in his heart.

Then he thought, "It is my own fault. I forgot my father. I left. Oh, if only I were back at my father's house! If I only could be a servant for my father at home. But my father must be very angry with me, because I was such a wicked son. I will go back to my father anyway. I shall kneel before him. I shall say, 'Father, I am so wicked, I am not worthy to be your son. But let me be a servant, the least of servants. If only I can live with you again, my father.'"

That was what he thought in his great misery. And he got up and went the long way back to his father's house.

He was coming near, but no one recognized him on the road. He looked like a beggar. His body was so thin. His clothes were torn. His feet were very dirty. No one said, "That is the rich man's son who went away into the world." No one knew him or thought about him anymore.

Was there no one who thought about him?

In the distance an old man was coming along. It was the father. His head was bowed with sorrow. He looked and he searched. Every day he searched. He was always thinking about his son who went away.

Then he saw that poor dirty beggar coming. He recognized him right away. Oh, yes, that good father knew his son. It did not matter how poor or how dirty he was. He hurried up to him. He took him in his arms. He pressed him to his heart. He kissed him. He was so happy, so very happy that his son was back home!

THE LOST SON

"Oh, Father! I have been so wicked! I am not worthy to be your son anymore. Let me be the least of your servants."

But his father said, "Come along! Come along! You are not a servant! You are my son. You will remain my son. Come along!"

Ahead on the hill was the beautiful old house. There they went together.

The father called his servants. He said, "This is my son. I thought that he was dead. But look, he is alive. He was lost, but has been found again. Come! Give him beautiful clothes, give him new sandals. Give him a golden ring on his finger. He is my son, whom I love very much. Come let us have a big, wonderful celebration!"

And that was what they did. That was how the lost son came back to his father's house.

But the other son, the older one, was angry. He did not want to be happy. His father called him, but he said, "No! My brother was wicked. I am better than he is. I am angry! I shall not come to the celebration."

Then the oldest son stayed outside alone. Inside was the big celebration. Everyone there was happy and cheerful. That good father loved his son who had come home so very much. He was not angry at him, only glad, very, very glad.

That was the beautiful story of the lost son which the Lord Jesus told the people. He wanted to teach them something. God in heaven is the Father of everyone. But people often do wrong. They forget God. They go their own way, and do what they want just like the lost son. But doing wicked deeds makes you afraid. And then people become unhappy. They become afraid of God. When the lost son realized he had been wicked, he was afraid of his father. He hardly dared to come home.

But when people are sorry for their sins, when they pray to God in heaven, and ask the Lord to forgive their sins, then those people can be God's children again. Then their fear will go away and they will become happy again.

That was what happened with the lost son. His father was not angry with him. When he came home to his father, there was a celebration.

When people come to God with their wrongs and ask Him for forgiveness, the angels have a celebration in heaven.

That was what the Lord wanted to teach the people with the beautiful story of the lost son.

THE GOOD SHEPHERD

The good shepherd took care of his sheep. He knew them all, the big and little ones. He gave them each a name. His sheep knew the good shepherd, too. They would not follow a stranger. They would only follow the good shepherd. He took care of them. He gave them food and drink. And when wild animals came to steal a sheep to tear it apart and eat it, the good shepherd would fight for his animals. He never forgot one of his sheep.

There went the sheep. The shepherd walked ahead and the sheep followed him. He knew the good spots where grass grew and fresh water flowed. He showed them the way. They ate the delicious grass and drank the clear water. And the little lambs played in the beautiful meadow. They were not afraid at all.

The good shepherd watched continuously. If one of the sheep strayed too far the shepherd would throw a stone at it. That did not hurt the sheep. It only frightened it and it would quickly come back. If a wild animal came, a wolf or a bear or a lion, then the good shepherd would take his big cudgel. That was a heavy stick which shepherds used to hit the wild animals. And he would fight that wild animal. That was very dangerous. But the good shepherd was brave. What if that fierce animal tore the good shepherd apart? But he was courageous and always did it anyway. He loved his sheep.

In the evening they all went back to the fold. Then the shepherd stood at the door, and all the sheep walked in underneath his staff, one by one. He counted them one by one.

There came a sheep with a bloody head. What had happened to it? Perhaps the poor animal had walked into the thorn-bushes to eat some of the tender buds. But then the thorns had scratched its head, and now it was bleeding. The good shepherd noticed it right away. He put some oil on the poor animal's wound. That would stop the bleeding. Then he continued counting them one by one. They all went inside.

The shepherd did not see any left outside. Were they all inside?

No. There was one sheep missing. The good shepherd could not see it anywhere. He had one hundred sheep, but now one was lost. All were in the fold except that one.

Now what did the good shepherd do? Did he close the door? Was he angry at that one sheep? Did he say, "It is your own fault?" Did he say, "Now you must stay outside, alone in the dark night?" Did he say, "Now the wild animals may as well eat you up. You went too far away?"

Oh, no, no! The good shepherd did not do that. He did not say that. He had compassion on that poor lonesome sheep in the dark. Where could it be? What if the wild animals came and found his sheep? The good shepherd was very tired. He wanted to go to sleep. But he would not go to sleep. He loved that poor animal too much. He was going to look for his lost sheep.

He searched everywhere. He looked along the quiet road, but he did not see it. He searched in the dark forest, but he did not find it. He pushed through the thorn-bushes. He climbed over the steep rocks. He lowered himself in deep holes, which might have had wild beasts living in them. Had those wild animals eaten his sheep already? The good shepherd searched everywhere.

Suddenly, he heard something. He heard the bleating of a sheep, so sad and afraid. Quickly the good shepherd went there. Oh, yes, there was the poor sheep! He picked it up in his arms.

The sheep was so tired of wandering and it was so afraid in the dark. It could not walk anymore. But it did not have to. The good shepherd took the poor animal in his strong arms. Quickly he brought it back home, to the other sheep in the fold.

Now he had them all together again. All one hundred. He was so happy! Would he go to sleep now? Oh, no. He called all the other shepherds. He called his friends and his neighbours. And then he had a celebration because he was so happy that the one lost sheep was found.

He said, "Let us be joyful. Rejoice with me because I have found my sheep which was lost."

Yes, that was how much the good shepherd loved his sheep.

That was a beautiful story. The Lord Jesus told it to the people. He said, "I am the Good Shepherd."

But where were His sheep? The Lord Jesus did not have any sheep. No, but the Lord Jesus wanted to teach the people something. He is the Good Shepherd, and the people, the children who listen to Him, are His sheep. He loves them so much. He takes care of them so well. And if one forgets the Lord Jesus, if one goes his own way, if one is disobedient to God, does the Lord Jesus forget him then, too? No. The Lord Jesus wants to make him obedient again. He wants to make him happy again. That was what the good shepherd did with his lost sheep.

The good shepherd loved his sheep very much. But the Lord Jesus loves the people and the children who listen to Him, much, much more.

THE GOOD SAMARITAN

The Lord Jesus told this beautiful story to the people.

One day a man was travelling along the lonely road. He was journeying from the big city of Jerusalem to another city, all alone. Quietly he walked along. He did not see anyone on the road.

But suddenly — oh, that poor man! Suddenly, wicked men jumped out on him. They were robbers. They had hidden themselves among the bushes and behind the big rocks. He had not seen them. But now they were suddenly in the middle of the road. They grabbed him with their rough hands. They took all his money away from him. They pulled the clothes off his body and hit him. They hit him so hard that he fell down beside the road. There he lay, almost dead. The robbers laughed. They took his money and his clothes, and went away, far away into the hills and the forest. They didn't even look back.

There he lay without clothes in the burning sun. He could not stand up. He was bleeding, and he was hurt so terribly. The poor man! Who would help him? Would he die of pain?

Footsteps! Someone was coming. Was it the robbers again? Oh, no, it was a priest. That was wonderful! The priest was a servant of God. He came from the temple in Jerusalem. When he saw that poor man, he would surely help him.

He was coming closer. Yes, he saw the poor naked man. He saw the blood. Did he immediately go and help him? No! He looked the other way, and walked quickly by on the other side of the road. He did not even look back.

That priest thought, "Just let him lie there. It would be so difficult to help him. I will just go by. He does not see me anyway." He was not a good priest. He was not a good servant of God.

The poor man just lay there. The sun was burning on his naked body. His bloody wounds hurt so badly. And he was so thirsty. But no one came to help him. Would he die of pain?

Footsteps again! They were quiet footsteps. Someone was coming. Who was that? It was a Levite. That was good! That was wonderful. The Levite was a servant in the temple. He always had to help the priests. He was a servant of God, too. He was coming closer. Surely he would soon see that poor man. Maybe he would help him. He should.

There he was. Did he hurry to the poor man? Did he go to him? No, he turned his face the other way. Swiftly he passed by on the other side of the road. He did not look back even once. The Levite thought, "Just let him lie there. It would be so difficult to help him. I will quietly walk by. He does not see me anyway." He was not a good Levite. He was not a good servant of God.

The poor, poor man! Would he die of pain? The priest had not helped him. The Levite had not either. They had just left him lying there. Now, surely no one would help him. Poor man!

Again, there were footsteps on the road. Different footsteps. Who was coming? It was a donkey. On the donkey was a man. But that man came from another land. He was a Samaritan. Surely he would not help the poor man. The men from that land were always angry at the Jews, and the Jews were always angry at the Samaritans. He came very close. Surely he would see the poor man. Maybe he would laugh at him. Maybe he would say, "Serves you right!"

There he was. Did he ride by on his donkey? Did he laugh at him? Did he say, "Too bad for you?" Did he say that?

No, he jumped off his donkey right away. He walked up to the poor man and he asked, "What happened? Are you in great pain? Are you thirsty? Are you afraid? Do not be afraid of me. I will not hurt you."

The good Samaritan gave him something to drink and he washed his bloody wounds with wine. Then he gently poured oil on them. That would ease the pain a little.

The donkey quietly waited nearby. But the good Samaritan did not climb back on his donkey. He did not go on. He did something else. He lifted the hurt man up in his strong arms and he carried him to his donkey. That poor, hurt man would ride the donkey. The Samaritan would walk beside it himself.

There they went along the lonely road. Gently the donkey went ahead, step by step. The good Samaritan walked beside him, and he held onto the hurt man. The man could not ride alone. He was hurt too much. He leaned his sore head on the Samaritan's shoulders. That was all right. Oh, yes, he could do that. Slowly they went on step by step.

That good Samaritan said, "Do not be afraid. I will take good care of you."

Soon they came to an inn. The donkey stopped and the good Samaritan carried the poor man inside very carefully. He was afraid to hurt him. Then the poor man got a bed to sleep on. He had food and drink, and clothes to wear. The good Samaritan took good care of everything, like a good father takes care of a child. He stayed with the sick man that night in the inn. The donkey slept in the stable.

But when it was morning, the Samaritan had to travel on. The poor man could not come along. He was still too sick. But the good Samaritan called the innkeeper. That was the man who lived in the inn. He said, "I must journey on. Will you take good care of that poor man? Here is some money. Give him food to eat and something to drink, and take good care of him.

Will you do that? I will return after a while and then I shall give you more money. But you must be very good to the poor man, so he will quickly recover."

Then the good Samaritan went away, and the poor hurt man could slowly get better.

That was the beautiful story the Lord Jesus told to the people. And the Lord Jesus asked, "Who was most kind to the poor man? The priest? The Levite? Or the Samaritan?"

The people knew. They should not be like the priest or the Levite. They all had to be like the good Samaritan. They should always help each other when there was need for it, even if it was very difficult.

LAZARUS

Once, a long time ago, a good man lived in a little white house. His name was Lazarus. But he did not live there alone.

LAZARUS

His two sisters lived with him in the same house. The one was called Mary, the other one Martha. The brother and sisters loved each other very much. Do you know who often visited them? The Lord Jesus. He loved Lazarus, Mary, and Martha very much. He enjoyed coming to their house.

But one day something terrible happened. Lazarus became sick. He became sicker and sicker. The doctor could not help Lazarus. Would Lazarus die? Oh, how sad Martha and Mary were! They stood beside Lazarus' bed and cried quietly. They whispered to each other, "If only the Lord Jesus was with us. He could help Lazarus. He could heal him. Oh, if only the Lord Jesus was here!"

But the Lord Jesus was not there. He had gone far away with His disciples.

"The Lord Jesus does not even know Lazarus is so sick," Mary and Martha told each other. "If only He knew, then He would come swiftly to help Lazarus. If only He knew!"

But then Mary and Martha sent a messenger to the Lord Jesus. He would have to go quickly and find out where the Lord Jesus was. He should say, "Lord, Lazarus is very ill, and Thou dost love him so much." If the Lord Jesus heard that, He would surely come immediately to His sick friend and heal him. That was what Mary and Martha thought.

"Go quickly, hurry!" they told the man. "Lazarus is very sick. If the Lord Jesus does not come right away, Lazarus will die. Run! Quick, hurry!"

And the man went away. He ran as fast as he was able. He loved Lazarus, too. All the people in the village loved Lazarus and his two sisters. They were such kind, friendly people.

But it did not help. It did not help at all. Lazarus became more sick. Martha and Mary cried, but Lazarus could not hear it anymore. Lazarus was dead! Even if the Lord Jesus would come now, it would be too late.

Now Lazarus was dead. His friends from the village came and folded white cloths around him, and then carried him to his grave. There in the mountain was a dark cave. That was where they carried Lazarus, and they rolled a big round stone in front of the opening.

Poor Martha and Mary. Now they were alone. Now it was so very quiet and sad in the house. Oh, if only the Lord Jesus had come! But now it was too late. Now Lazarus had died. Now Lazarus was gone.

The messenger had run very fast. He came to the Lord Jesus and said, "O Lord, Lazarus is so sick, and Thou dost love him so much."

The man did not know that Lazarus had died already. The disciples did not know it either. But the Lord Jesus did. He knows everything. He saw everything, even though He was very far away. What did the Lord Jesus do? Did He go quickly with the man? No. Was He very sad? He loved Lazarus so much. But the Lord Jesus remained there for two more days.

Then He said to His disciples, "Let us go. Lazarus, our friend, is asleep. But I am going to wake him up."

The disciples thought, "Do we have to take that long journey for that?" They said, "Master, if Lazarus is asleep, he will get better. Sleeping is good for sick people. Let us stay here." They did not know that Lazarus was dead.

But then the Lord Jesus told them. "Lazarus has died. But I am glad because now you will see wonderful things. Come, let us go to Lazarus."

Now? It was too late now. And the Lord Jesus was not even sad. How strange!

Together they went on their journey. It was a long journey. The village was far away. But finally they saw the little white houses there in the distance.

Who was that running toward them? It was a poor woman crying very hard. Her eyes were red from crying. It was Martha. Some people had told her that the Lord Jesus was coming down the road. Now she was quickly going to Him. Mary did not come. She was too sad. She had stayed at home. She sat and cried there.

Martha came up to the Lord Jesus. She reached her hands out to the Lord. She said, "O Lord, if Thou hadst been here, Lazarus would not have died! But now it is too late."

Yet Martha was happy because the Lord Jesus was near her.

The Lord Jesus answered Martha, "Your brother will arise. Where is Mary?"

Quickly she went to tell Mary. She had to come right away. Oh, yes, she should come, too. Martha walked home and she said, "Mary, come. Do come, the Master is here and He calls you."

Mary came along, and the people of the village came, too. They loved the sisters so much.

Mary saw the Lord Jesus. How she wept with grief! She fell on her knees before the Lord Jesus and she said just like Martha, "O Lord, if Thou hadst been with us, Lazarus would not have died."

Then the Lord Jesus asked, "Where is Lazarus now? Show me the place where he lies."

Together they went to Lazarus' grave. There in the mountains was a cave, but the big round stone lay in front of the opening. Mary and Martha were crying and the other people cried, too. Their grief was so great. Lazarus was dead, Lazarus was gone.

The Lord Jesus was sorrowful for all these people. He was so deeply sorry about their grief. And the Lord Jesus wept.

The people whispered, "Look, the Master is weeping. That is how much He loved Lazarus. Oh, if only He had been here, He would have healed Lazarus!"

Then suddenly the Lord Jesus commanded, "Take away the stone."

Martha was frightened. "O Lord, Lazarus has been dead for four days already."

But the Lord Jesus looked up. He prayed to His Father in heaven.

And then some men rolled the great stone away. There was the gaping dark hole. In there it was quiet, very quiet. Lazarus was dead.

But the Lord Jesus walked to the grave and He called, "Lazarus, come out!"

Then out came Lazarus! There he came. He was not dead anymore, no, not when the Lord Jesus called him. Now he came back out of that dark cave. Now he was alive again! What the Lord Jesus commands always happens.

Oh, how happy Martha was! How happy Mary was! Now they had received their brother back again. He had been dead, but now he was alive. No, the Lord Jesus had not come too late. The Lord Jesus never comes too late. How happy, how very happy they were! Joyfully they all went home. And the Lord Jesus went with them.

THE BLIND MAN

How busy the road was. What a crowd of people! Where were they going? They were going to a feast. They were making a long journey because in a few days there would be a big celebration in Jerusalem. It was the Passover, and that was where they were all going. They were glad and cheerful.

The Lord Jesus was among the people, too. He was also going to the celebration in Jerusalem. He went every year. When He was only a boy of twelve, He had gone for the first time. Then Joseph and Mary thought He was lost. That was a long time ago. Now the Lord Jesus was going to the feast again.

The people were looking hopefully at the Lord Jesus. They were talking about Him. They were whispering. Softly they were saying to each other, "The Master is going to the feast. Maybe He will become king. Oh, that would be wonderful!"

But the Lord Jesus heard it. No, He did not want to become a king. He did not want to wear a crown of gold. He did not want to sit on a king's throne. He did not want to be rich and mighty. The Lord Jesus wanted something very different. But the people did not know that yet. Joyfully they continued on to Jerusalem. What happy activity on the road!

But alongside the road was a poor, dirty beggar. His clothes were torn, his feet were bare. And he had no money to buy bread. He just sat quietly beside the road. He lifted his thin arms up when someone passed by. Maybe they would give him something to eat, or some money.

Why did he not go to work to earn money? He could not work. He was blind. Yes, his eyes were open. They were wide

THE BLIND MAN

open. But he could not see anything. Everything was dark for him. Everything was black. The sun was shining. But even though he was sitting in the sunshine, everything was dark, black as in the night. Poor blind man! Someone would give him a piece of bread, and he could put it in his mouth. But he could not see it. He could not see anything. Not in the morning, not in the afternoon, not at night when the lamps were burning. Never.

What was that? The poor blind man sitting alongside the road heard something. Listen, there were people coming. It sounded like an excited crowd coming. He could not see them. He could only hear the people. He put his long skinny arms out. Maybe he would receive something from those people. Perhaps they would give him some money to buy bread. Yes, there they came.

But what was going on? Why were there so many people on the road? Why were they so cheerful? He cried, "What is going on? Please tell me. What is it?"

And the people said, "Do you not know? The Lord Jesus is coming by, and we are coming with Him."

"The Lord Jesus?" The blind man was startled. He raised his hands high, and he shouted and called loudly, "O Lord, help me! Help me! Have mercy on me!" He could not see a thing. Everything was so dark. Oh, where was the Lord Jesus? The man could not see him. He did not know where He was. But he called, he shouted! Oh, yes, he could do that. And his hands reached up high as if he wanted to grab the Lord Jesus.

"O Lord, help me!"

"Quiet," the people told him. "Be quiet. Don't shout so loudly!" They thought, "The Lord Jesus is too busy with all the people around Him. They are all happy people. The Lord Jesus has no time to listen to this poor dirty beggar beside the road."

"Be quiet!" they told the blind man. "Don't shout like that!"

Don't shout? What then? What if the Lord Jesus passed by and did not see him?

That poor, blind man called even louder. "O Lord, have mercy. Help me! Help me!"

Would the Lord Jesus not hear him? Would He pass by? Would that poor man always have to sit along the way? And would he then always be in darkness? It was so busy. All those people were talking so loudly. They made so much noise. Had the Lord Jesus not heard the blind man?

Oh, yes. The Lord Jesus heard it all. The Lord Jesus hears everyone who calls to Him. Everyone. No matter how far away, no matter how they call.

The Lord Jesus stopped. He wanted to listen to that beggar, even if he was poor and dirty. He always wants to listen. He said, "Let the man come to me."

Quickly the people did it. They went to the blind man. "Stand up! Quick!" they said, as they helped him to stand up. "The Master is calling you."

There went the blind man. His old torn robe fell from his back. But he did not notice. He left his stick lying on the ground. He was going to the Lord Jesus. He did not need his stick anymore. He stumbled through those people, his hands in front of him. Everything was so dark, so dark!

Suddenly he heard a kind voice asking, "What would you like Me to do for you?" That was the Lord Jesus' voice.

How the blind man trembled with joy! He pleaded, "Lord, I would like to see."

The Lord Jesus said, "See! You believed that I would help you, so now I will help you, too."

Then suddenly that darkness, that terrible darkness, was gone. It became light. Everything was light, and so beautiful! So great and so wide.

But the poor blind man who was not blind anymore, looked first of all at the Lord Jesus, who was so good to him, who had made him so wonderfully happy.

The Lord Jesus walked on. The people walked on, too. And the poor man? He did not go and sit in his old place by the side of the road. He did not put his hands out in front to ask for bread or money anymore. He did not even take his stick to feel carefully along the way. He could see! He could see everything. But he only looked at the Lord Jesus. He loved the Lord, and he went after Him, just like all the others.

All those excited people pressed alongside the Lord Jesus. But who do you think was the happiest of all? Who do you think loved the Lord Jesus most of all?

HOSANNA! HOSANNA!

The Lord Jesus had been in the little village where Lazarus, Mary, and Martha lived. But now He was going with His disciples to Jerusalem. The people crowded around Him. They were going to the big city, to the feast. As they neared a hill, the road climbed up over the hill and went down the other side. And there, on the other side lay the beautiful white city of Jerusalem.

But the Lord Jesus did not climb up the hill yet. He stopped. He called two of His disciples. They had to get something for Him. It was a strange request. They had to get him a donkey.

The Lord Jesus told them, "Go to that distant village. There you will see a donkey. It will be tied, but you must untie it. And when the man who owns the donkey asks, 'Why are you doing that? That is my donkey,' then you must say, 'The Master needs him.' Then he will not be angry. Then he will surely let you take the animal."

The two disciples hurried away. Soon they came near the village. There was the donkey. They untied him. But then the owner came.

"Why are you doing that?" he asked. "That is my donkey!"

The disciples said, "The Master needs him."

Then they were allowed to take the animal right away. "Is it for the Lord Jesus? Then you may take it."

They brought the donkey to their Master.

What did the Lord Jesus do then? He sat on the donkey to ride over the hill and into the city. Quickly the disciples took off their robes. They folded them up and laid them on the donkey's back. They thought it was wonderful that the Lord Jesus was going to ride. He always walked, but now He was going to ride. Now He would be like a king. A king? Oh, yes! Yes! A king! And then the disciples had a wonderful idea. A king may not ride on the dust of the road. Everything must be good and rich and beautiful for a king. Yes, they had a grand idea. And all the people who were thronging around the Lord Jesus knew what to do, too.

They all took off their robes and spread them on the road in front of the donkey's feet. Then they took branches off the trees and laid them on top of the robes.

How beautiful it was! How beautiful! Now the Lord Jesus rode over a soft carpet of robes and branches, just like a king. And the people started to sing and cheer.

"Hosanna! Hosanna!"

The people picked more green branches and waved them high in the air. It was all in honour of the Lord Jesus. How the people sang, "Hosanna! Hosanna! Blessed is He who comes in the name of the Lord! Hosanna! Hosanna!"

All those men and women and children danced and leaped around the Lord Jesus. They sang and they sang and they sang. They were so happy.

The people thought, "Now the Lord Jesus will become King in Jerusalem. Now He will drive the enemies out of our land. He shall sit on the throne, where long ago great King David sat. He shall wear a crown of gold. How wonderful it will be!"

The people were so happy.

But the Lord Jesus Himself? Oh, no, He was not happy. He was sad. Why?

He did not want to become rich and mighty. He did not want to become king here on earth. He wanted to become King in heaven.

Those people thought, "The Lord Jesus will make us rich and important, too."

But the Lord Jesus did not want that. He wanted to give them something better than money and goods. Something wonderful. Something that would last forever and ever. He wanted to bring them to heaven with God. But something sad had to happen to the Lord Jesus first. He knew it. And He wanted it to happen, too. The people did not know it yet. They did not think about sad things at all. They only thought about happy things. They sang and they danced.

Now they were on top of the hill. They could see the beautiful white city, Jerusalem. It shone in the sunshine. And from the city people were coming toward the Lord Jesus. They were happy and singing, too.

"Hosanna! Hosanna! Our king is coming!"

They waved their palm branches and they spread their clothes on the road for their king.

And the Lord Jesus? He wept. He loved those people so much. Yes, now they were singing. Now they were happy. But if He did not want to become their king, they would be angry with Him. They would do terrible things to Him. The Lord Jesus knew what would happen. He knows everything. He wept. But the people did not understand. They just went on singing and pushing each other through the gates.

But, near the gate were important men. They were the most important of the city. Those men did not sing along. Instead, they looked angrily at the Lord Jesus. They did not love Him, and they did not want to believe that He was the Son of God. But all those other people listened to the Lord Jesus. And they sang for Him. That made those dignified, important men even more angry. That should not happen. It was not allowed.

They said to the Lord Jesus, "Make those people keep quiet. Thou art only an ordinary man. Why are they singing like that? Make them be quiet!"

But the Lord Jesus did not command those people to keep quiet.

Oh, how angry and wicked those dignified men looked as they watched the Lord Jesus. They hated Him. They whispered to each other and clenched their fists. Yes, they even planned wicked and bad things against the Lord Jesus.

But the Lord continued to ride among all those singing people. He rode through the gate into the big city of Jerusalem.

And then, did the Lord Jesus become king? Did He drive all those strange enemies out of the city? Did He put on a golden crown, and a beautiful royal robe? Oh, no. No. The Lord Jesus did not want to do that. He did something very different. He healed the sick and the blind and the deaf. He helped the poor and made the sad happy. He loved the people so much. He did not think about a crown of gold. He wanted to do much, much more for the people. But they did not know that. First everything would be very sorrowful, and then it would become wonderful. But they did not know that yet.

The crowds thought it was too bad that the Lord Jesus was healing the sick and helping the poor. They thought it was too bad that He was not going to become a king. They stopped singing and they stopped dancing. They threw away the green branches. Too bad the Lord did not want to become king. Those people did not understand anything about that terribly sad thing that would become so wonderful. They went home and left the Lord Jesus alone with His disciples. If He did not want to become king, they wanted nothing more to do with Him. Those foolish, foolish people!

JUDAS

It was a dark, dark evening and it was very quiet in the streets of the city. But one man stealthily walked along, all by himself. Carefully he looked around. He was afraid. Why? He was going to do something bad, something terribly bad. He knew that, but he was going to do it anyway. And that was why he was so afraid.

Just a little bit farther stood a beautiful rich house. Silently he stood in front of the door. Now he had to knock. Would he do it? Would he go into that rich house? Would he do that terrible thing? Or would he run away fast? No. His eyes were dark and angry. He did not walk away. He knocked. And then he entered that rich house.

Who was that man? At whom was he so angry? And what was he going to do in that rich house?

It was Judas. He was — yes — he was one of the disciples of the Lord Jesus. But he was a wicked disciple. The disciples all loved their Master very much, except Judas. Judas was angry with Him.

Angry? At the Lord Jesus? How could that be? The Lord Jesus never did anything wrong. He only did good. Yes, but even so, Judas was very angry with Him. Why? How could that be?

Judas was thinking, "The Lord Jesus is so mighty. He can do anything. He can make me rich. I want to be rich so very much! The people wanted to make the Lord Jesus king, but He does not want to. Why not? Oh, it is too bad, because then I would become a very important man. I would like to be an important man. The Lord Jesus says He is going to die. Then what about me? Must I always remain a poor disciple? No, I do not want that! I am angry at the Master."

Those were Judas' thoughts, and his dark eyes burned with anger.

Judas was selfish. He was allowed to take care of the money purse. When the Lord Jesus and His disciples needed food, Judas would always buy the bread. When they met a very poor man or a very poor woman, Judas would give them some money from the purse. But Judas loved money. Sometimes he took some of the money from the purse for himself. Judas was a thief. He wanted to be rich so very much. But he had not become rich, and that was why he was so angry with the Lord Jesus.

Then he entered the rich house. He entered a beautiful room where the Pharisees were gathered together. They were the rich and most important Jews and the chief priests of the temple. The rich and proud Jews were angry with the Lord Jesus, too. They said, "All the people listen to Him, and they do not listen to us anymore! He is only an ordinary man, the son of a carpenter. No, that should not be allowed. The people must listen to us. We are the best, the most important of the land."

Thirty silver pieces? Thirty beautiful shining coins? Yes, Judas would do that. Yes, he sure would. He would betray his Master, the Master who was always so good to him.

Judas was going to betray Him. He would make sure that the servants of the priests could catch the Lord Jesus and tie Him up. He received the silver pieces and put them in his pocket. Oh, how nicely they jingled! Judas loved money. Then he left, going into the dark streets again. With a friendly face Judas went back to the Lord Jesus.

Judas, the betrayer. The Master had always been so good to him, so kind. But now? Now Judas was acting so friendly, but he did not mean it. He was saying, "I am your friend," but it was not true. Judas was an enemy. He was a traitor.

And he thought no one knew it. He said to himself, "The other disciples do not know it, and the Master does not know it.

No one knows that I have received money from the priests to help catch the Lord Jesus." That was what he thought, but it was not true. The Lord Jesus knew it anyway. He knew everything, and He was very sad about it. Why, oh why was Judas doing something so wicked?

THE LAST SUPPER

The time for the Passover Feast had come. It was celebrated in every home. The Lord wanted to celebrate with His disciples, too. The disciples were happy. The Lord Jesus was sad. But He still wanted to eat and drink together with His disciples one more time. The very last time.

He called two of them and gave them instructions on what to do. "Go to Jerusalem. When you walk in the streets there, you will see a man. He will be carrying a large water jug on his shoulder. Go with that man, and when he goes inside a house, you must go inside the house, too. Then you must ask the owner of that house, 'Where is the room where the Master can celebrate the Passover with us?' Then that man will show you the room right away. And then you must prepare everything for the celebration."

The two disciples went. They gladly did whatever the Lord Jesus told them. They came into the city. Look! There was a man with a large water jug on his shoulder, just as the Master had said. They followed him, and when he entered a house, they followed him inside. Then they asked the owner of that house, "Where is the room in which the Master can celebrate this evening?"

The man of the house showed them right away where they could go. Yes, it was just as the Lord Jesus had told them. And those two disciples prepared everything for the feast.

The day passed by. Evening came. Then the Lord Jesus went with His disciples to the quiet room where everything was prepared for the feast. The disciples were happy. The Lord Jesus was sad. Yet He wanted to eat and drink with them together just once more, the last time.

And the disciples? They did not know that. Oh, no. They were thinking about very different things. They thought, "Who is the greatest of us all? Who is the most important disciple?" Each one thought, "Maybe I am." Yes, that was what they were thinking.

Then they all began entering the room. All the disciples had leather sandals on their bare feet. Those bare feet had become very dirty because the road was dusty. Would they go to the table with those dirty feet?

Near the door was a large jug of water and a big bowl. But there was no servant to wash their feet. Yet those feet were very dirty. Who would be the servant?

"Not me," Peter thought. "I do not want to be a servant to the others. Perhaps *I* am the greatest, the most important, the best."

"Not me," James thought.

"Not me," they all thought.

And they went to sit around the table with their dirty feet. The disciples only thought about their own importance. They did not notice that their Master was sorrowful.

That made the Lord Jesus even more sad.

They all sat down around the table. The bread and wine stood ready for them. Oh, how strange! The Lord Jesus stood up. He did not say anything, but He walked to the door. He got the jug with water, and the big bowl, and a towel. How strange! What was He going to do? Oh, was the Lord Jesus going to be the servant? Then He went down on His knees by one of the disciples. Carefully he poured some of the water out of the jug. He poured it over the feet of the disciple; the dirty water fell in the big bowl. And then the Lord Jesus dried the disciple's feet with the towel. Now those feet were not dusty anymore. They were clean.

The Lord Jesus stood up and went to the next disciple to wash his feet. How strange! The Lord Jesus was acting like a servant. Yet, He was the Master. He was not a servant. Why was He doing that? The disciples were dismayed. They had been too proud to wash each other's feet. Now the Master was doing it. They were ashamed. They thought, "Oh, if only we had done it."

THE LAST SUPPER

The Lord Jesus did not say anything. He did His work like a poor slave.

He came to Peter, but Peter pulled his feet away. "No, Lord, not me, not me! Thou art the Master. Must Thou wash our feet? A servant should do that. No, Lord, I do not want Thee to do it."

But the Lord Jesus answered, "Then you cannot be my disciple anymore, Peter."

Not be a disciple of the Lord Jesus? Not belong to the Lord Jesus? That frightened Peter. He loved the Lord Jesus so much. He wanted to be the best disciple. He said, "O Lord, wash my feet. And wash my hands and my head. I want to belong to Thee. I love Thee so much."

But that was not necessary. The Lord Jesus only washed Peter's feet. And the feet of all the others.

Then He brought the bowl and the jug away. The disciples watched. They did not dare to say anything. They were very ashamed. The Lord Jesus asked them, "Do you know why I washed your feet? To show you that you must not be proud. You must always help each other. I am the Master. Yet I was willing to wash your feet. I was willing to be your servant. Do you know who is the greatest and most important? The one who is willing to help the other. The one who is willing to be a servant, he is the greatest of all. That is what I taught you. Will you always remember to do that?"

Then they ate together. But the Lord Jesus was sad. He said, "This is the last time. Now I will die."

Frightened, the disciples looked at their Master. Was the Lord Jesus going away from them, for always? Oh, that would be too bad. They became sad, too. But then the Lord Jesus said something else that frightened them even more. He said, "This night the enemy will come and take me prisoner. And one of you will help the enemy. That one will betray me."

"Who? Who, Lord?" all the disciples asked. "Who will betray Thee? Who is the wicked one?"

Judas also heard what the Lord Jesus had said. It upset him terribly. He thought, "The Master knows. Oh, the Master knows!" But Judas, the wicked Judas, still looked very friendly. And he too asked, "Is it me, Lord?"

Quietly the Lord Jesus said, "Yes, Judas, you are the one."

The other disciples did not hear it. They ate and they drank together. But it was not a happy celebration.

Then the Lord Jesus said to Judas, "Go and do what you must do."

Judas got up and quickly left. What was he going to do? The disciples did not know. The disciples thought, "Maybe he still has to go and buy something for the celebration. He has the money pouch. Maybe he has to give some money to the poor." No, the disciples did not know what Judas was going to do. But the Lord Jesus did.

In the dark evening, Judas went to the chief priests and the Pharisees, the proud and important Jews. There were soldiers and servants there, ready to capture the Lord Jesus. Judas would show them the way. Judas, the traitor!

Judas had gone away and now the Lord Jesus was left alone with the other disciples. He told them many things. He told them that He must suffer much and that He was going to die. It was all so sad. But He also told them that He was going to His Father in heaven, to God, and that one day, they would come to the beautiful heaven, too. That was wonderful. They listened, and yet it was a sad celebration. Why was the Master going away? Why was He going to die? Why did He have to suffer? He was the Son of God. It made the disciples so sorrowful.

When night came the Lord Jesus said, "Arise. Let us go." And together they went outside into the darkness.

IN THE DARK NIGHT

There went the Lord Jesus with His disciples into the darkness. The disciples pressed closely against their Master. They wanted to stay close to Him, very close to Him. But then the Lord Jesus said something sad again. He said, "This night, something terrible will happen. The enemy will come. They will bind Me and take Me away, and you will all become afraid of the enemy. You will all run away and leave Me alone."

"Oh, no, Master! We will stay with Thee. We will not be afraid. We will not leave Thee alone," the disciples cried.

IN THE DARK NIGHT

And Peter declared, "Oh, no, Master! I will stay with Thee. I love Thee so much. Maybe the others will go away, but not me. Even if the enemies want to kill me, I will stay close to Thee."

The Lord Jesus looked at Peter in great sadness and said, "Peter, you will be the most scared of all. Very early in the morning, the rooster will crow. By that time you will have denied Me three times. You will say that you do not even know Me. That is how afraid you will be of the enemy, Peter."

That was what the Lord Jesus told him. But Peter could not believe it. He loved His Master so much.

Through the gate they left the city. Outside near a mountain was a dark, quiet garden. It was the Garden of Gethsemane. That was where the Lord Jesus was going with His disciples. It was so dark and quiet there.

The Lord Jesus took three of His disciples into the garden. They were Peter, John, and James. To the others He said, "You stay here."

A little way farther, the Lord also said to Peter, John, and James, "You stay here. But do not go to sleep. You must think about Me. I am so sorrowful."

The disciples sat down on the grass. The Lord Jesus walked farther into the garden alone. What was He going to do? Why was He so very, very sad?

The Lord Jesus went into the garden to pray. In the dark, He fell on His knees. He talked to God, His Father in heaven. "Help Me, help Me!" He said. "O Father, what is going to happen now is so dreadful! But I will do it. I will do everything Thou wantest." The Lord Jesus was so afraid, so afraid of what was going to happen to Him.

He stood up. He walked back to His three disciples. Oh, they were asleep! They were not even thinking about their poor Master. He was so afraid. That made Him sad.

He woke them up. "Can you not stay awake a little while?"

Then the Lord Jesus went back to pray once more. "O Father, help Me! Something terrible is going to happen. I am so afraid, but I will do it. I will do what Thou wantest me to do." Big drops of perspiration formed on the Lord's brow. That was how afraid He was.

Then He walked back to His disciples once more. Again they were asleep. They had forgotten their Master. They were tired, and they went on sleeping. It was so very, very sad for the Lord Jesus.

Again He left them. Again He fell on His knees and prayed. He pleaded, "O Father, help Me! I will do what Thou wantest me to do." And the drops of sweat on His brow became like great drops of blood. That was how afraid and sad He was.

How terrible it was! How very terrible! The Lord Jesus had never done any wrong. He did not deserve any punishment. But the people did. The people had done much wrong. The men and the women and the children, too, all of them. They deserved punishment and were not allowed to go to live with God in His beautiful heaven.

But the Lord Jesus loved the people so much. He wanted to carry the punishment that they deserved. And then the beautiful heaven would open for the people, too. That was the wonderful thing that the Lord wanted to give to the people.

But the punishment! That punishment was so severe. The Lord Jesus had to carry that all by Himself. That punishment made Him so afraid, so very afraid.

"O Father, help Me!" He prayed.

Then an angel came down from heaven. He stood beside the Lord Jesus and spoke quietly to Him. That took the fear away from the Lord Jesus' heart. Oh, yes, He wanted to bear the heavy punishment for the people. He was not afraid of that dreadfulness anymore. The Lord Jesus got up. He went to His disciples who were still asleep. They did not even know how afraid their Master had been.

"Arise, let us go!" he told them. With a start they awoke.

In between the trees they could see a light coming. What was that? Voices were whispering. Footsteps were coming. Who were they? They were the servants of the chief priests. They had come to capture the Lord Jesus.

In front came a man with dark, brooding eyes. He whispered to the soldiers, "Come along. I know which one is Jesus. I will give Him a kiss. And then you must catch Him." That man was the wicked Judas.

There he came. He walked right up to the Lord Jesus. His face was friendly. He pretended to look happy to see his Master again. It was all falsehood. He gave the Lord Jesus a kiss.

But the Lord Jesus knew. He knew everything. He said, "Are you betraying Me with a kiss, Judas?"

Then the soldiers of the chief priests came forward. They had swords and sticks and ropes with them. But the Lord Jesus was not afraid anymore.

He asked them, "Who are you looking for?"

And they answered, "We are looking for Jesus."

The Lord Jesus said, "I am He."

Those rough soldiers were so startled, they fell down to the ground.

But again the Lord Jesus said, "I am He. Take Me along."

The soldiers got up and grabbed the Lord Jesus, binding Him with ropes.

Peter could not bear to see that happening. He became very angry with those men. He took his sword and swung it around. He hit one of the soldiers and cut off his ear with his sharp sword.

But that was not right. The Lord Jesus did not want that to happen. Not at all. He said, "Put your sword away, Peter. That is not good. If I pray to My Father in heaven, thousands of angels will come to help Me. But I will not do that. This terrible thing must happen. I want to carry the punishment."

And then the Lord Jesus healed the ear of that servant. The Lord Jesus loved these rough men, these enemies, too. But the soldiers bound His hands behind His back with ropes and took Him away as if He had committed a great wrong.

The disciples all fled away into the darkness. They left their poor Master alone.

The chief priests and the other important Jews were waiting. They sat together in that beautiful big room. Then the servants brought in the Lord Jesus. Oh, how angrily and wickedly those Pharisees looked at the Lord Jesus, and yet they were glad. In their anger they thought, "Now Jesus has been caught. He will die." They had planned this long ago already.

The Lord Jesus stood there, His hands tied behind His back. Soldiers with sharp spears stood next to Him, and false witnesses came to tell evil things about the Lord Jesus. But it was not true. They were all lies. The Lord Jesus had healed the sick, helped the poor, and raised the dead. That was not doing wrong. He had only done good. Yet, He had to die. That was what those Jews had decided.

The high priest stood up and shouted angrily at the Lord Jesus, "Art Thou the Son of God?"

The Lord answered, "Yes, I am. I am going to heaven, and one day I shall return on the clouds. And all men will see Me."

Then those Jews became even more angry. They cried, "It is not true! Thou art not the Son of God. Thou art the son of a carpenter. Thou art not allowed to say that!"

They shouted and they yelled, "He must die! He must die! We will bring Him to the judge, and then we shall kill Him!"

The soldier standing nearest the Lord Jesus hit Him in the face. That was how angry those men were with Him.

"Come!" they cried. "Night is almost over, soon morning will be here. We will bring Him to the judge. He must die! Come!" They dragged Him along.

But the Lord Jesus had never done any wrong.

PETER

All the disciples had fled. They did not dare to come along. They were afraid of those soldiers with their sticks and swords. They thought, "What if they take us prisoner, too? No, we do not dare to go along with our Master." They left the Lord Jesus alone, all alone.

But who was carefully following the soldiers? It was John. He knew the woman who always had to open the door of that big, rich house where the chief priests and the Pharisees had gathered together. John would ask that woman if he could come inside, too. He felt so sorry for the Lord Jesus. He wanted to see His Master so much.

Peter asked, "May I come, too? Do you think that woman will allow me in, too?"

"Come along," John said. "Maybe she will let you in, too."

And then together they went through the dark night to the high priest's big, rich house. What would those important men do with their Master?

They were allowed in. Peter was, too. Now they could be very close to the Lord Jesus again. Yes, but also close to those dangerous enemies. It made Peter afraid.

Then the woman at the door asked him, "Do you belong to that Jesus, too? Are you not one of His disciples?"

Peter was terrified. That woman knew him! That was dangerous. What if she told the soldiers and the servants that he was a disciple of the Lord Jesus? And what if those men grabbed him and tied him up? Peter became very afraid. He thought, "I am not going to say yes. I will say no. I shall lie."

And Peter told that woman, "Me? A disciple of Jesus? Why, I do not know the Man." Then quickly Peter walked to the inner court of the house.

That was the first lie.

A fire was burning in that inner court. It was a cold night, and the servants and soldiers stood by the fire to warm themselves. They were talking together. They were telling each other about the Lord Jesus, whom they had caught.

Nearby, in a beautiful large room where lamps were burning, the Lord Jesus stood before the high priest. His hands were bound behind His back. They could see Him very clearly when they looked inside.

Peter came to stand near the fire, too. He was shivering with cold.

But then one of those servants said to him, "Aren't you one of Jesus' disciples? Yes, you are one of His disciples."

Peter became afraid. How he trembled with fear. "No!" he said. "Oh, no, I am not one of His disciples. I do not know that Man!" Quickly Peter walked away from the fire.

That was the second lie.

A little while later, another servant said to Peter, "Yes, I can see you are a disciple of Jesus. Did I not see you during the night in the dark garden? For sure, you were with Him, too. I can tell from your speech. You talk just like the other disciples."

Peter became terribly afraid. He did not know what to do. Oh, what if they grabbed him and bound him, and hurt him or killed him?

"No!" he snapped. "I do not know that Man!" And then he said angry words, bad words. "No, I am not a disciple of Him! I do not know the Man."

That was the third lie.

But then, a rooster suddenly crowed. Peter heard it. Oh, how awful! Peter suddenly remembered what the Lord Jesus had told him in the dark garden. Yes, now he remembered. The Master had said, "Peter, you will be most afraid of all. Early in the morning the cock will crow. By then, you will have denied Me three times, saying that you do not know Me. That is how afraid you will be of the enemies."

Yes, now Peter remembered. Now the rooster had crowed. Now it had happened. How terrible!

Peter looked toward the room where the Lord Jesus was standing, and then the Lord turned and looked at Peter. So sorrowfully, so very sorrowfully. The Lord Jesus could not say anything. But His eyes said that He was very sad about Peter. It was as if those eyes were saying, "Do you not know Me, Peter? I know everything. Why have you denied Me three times? Why have you caused Me such great pain, three times?"

Peter did not dare to look any longer. Putting his hands in front of his eyes, he walked away very ashamed. Away from this terrible house. Away into the darkness. Tears came to his eyes and he cried. He cried bitterly. Why? Why had he caused his Master such a great grief? Oh, if only he had not done it! He was a bad, wicked disciple. He thought he was the best, but he was the most sinful of all. He fell on his knees in the darkness. He was so terribly sorry. He prayed and begged, "O Lord, forgive me! Forgive me! I have done such a great wrong."

The Lord Jesus was brought away by the wicked servants to the judge. But He could hear Peter's prayer on that lonely dark spot. The Lord Jesus always hears when someone prays to Him in fear and repentance.

CRUCIFY HIM! CRUCIFY HIM!

Morning had come. Even though it was still very early, it was very busy in the streets of the big city Jerusalem. More and more people came, and the crowd was getting bigger. They were all going to the house where Pilate the judge lived. Why? Why were they pushing like that? Why were they calling and shouting so angrily?

The Lord Jesus was standing there before Pilate, the judge. And that judge Pilate asked the people, "Has this man done a great wrong? Must I punish Him?"

"Yes! Yes!" shouted the chief priests and the Pharisees. "He is a wicked man! He must die!"

And that great crowd of people shouted with them, "He must die!"

Pilate asked, "What has He done?"

The people told many mean, wrong things about the Lord Jesus, but they were all lies. They just kept yelling and shouting, but none of it was true.

The Lord Jesus heard it. He heard everything. But He was not angry at those wicked, faithless people. Quietly He stood there; He did not say a word. But He was so sad. So very sad about those people. He had always helped them. He had healed their sick. He had done them only good. He had always loved them. And now they wanted to kill Him.

Pilate, the judge, looked at the Lord Jesus. He looked so tired and pale and was so silent. Pilate heard what those people were shouting, but he did not believe it. He thought, "It is a lie. This pale, quiet man has not done any wrong. I can see that." Then Pilate, the judge, should have said, "Go. Thou hast not done any wrong. I shall not punish Thee."

Yes, that was what Pilate should have said. But he did not. Pilate was afraid of that screaming crowd. He thought, "If I let Jesus free, those Jews will be so angry with me. No, I do not dare do that."

CRUCIFY HIM! CRUCIFY HIM!

Pilate was a fearful judge. Pilate was a false, dishonest judge. He was just as bad as those wicked, screaming people on the streets there. The Lord Jesus had done no wrong. Yet Pilate was going to punish him. He asked the people, "What should I do with this Jesus? I do not know what wrong He has done."

The people shouted, "Crucify Him! Crucify Him! He must die!"

Then, what did Pilate do? He got an idea. He called his soldiers and told them something. Those rough, wicked men laughed. Oh, sure, they would do that right away. They grabbed the Lord Jesus with their rough hands, they pulled the clothes off His body and tied Him to a pole. And then — oh, how terrible! They hit Him with sticks and whips on His bare back. That hurt horribly. But the Lord Jesus stood quietly. He did not cry. He did not scream. He did not complain. He did not say one word. Silently He bore that cruel pain.

Those rough, wicked soldiers laughed. "Come," they said, "We shall make Him king. A king for fun!"

What were they going to do, those wicked men? They put a dirty old red soldier's robe on the Lord Jesus. "That is His royal robe," they said. Then they wove a wreath of sharp thorn branches. They pressed that on the Lord Jesus' head. How terrible! Those sharp thorns hurt very much. The blood trickled down the Lord Jesus' brow. "That is His royal crown!" those wicked soldiers shouted. Then they pushed a stick into His hand, mocking, "That is His sceptre." The Lord Jesus did not say one word. He bore the pain and the sorrow quietly and patiently. He did not even look angrily at those rough men.

Pilate, the dishonest judge, looked at the Lord Jesus standing there. He was not sorry. He only thought, "Now I will show Jesus to the people. He is so tired, so white with pain. Blood is trickling down His face. When the people see Him, maybe they will feel sorry for Him and cry, 'Let Him go!' Then I will set Him free."

So Pilate brought the Lord Jesus outside onto the high steps in front of the house. He pointed at the Lord Jesus and said, "See, the Man!"

Would the chief priests and the other Jews, would all those screamers be sorry for the Lord Jesus now? Would they cry, "Set Him free!"?

No. They had no pity. Oh, those wicked people! A few days ago the Lord Jesus had come riding into the city of Jerusalem sitting on a donkey. Then they had shouted so joyfully, "A king is coming!" They had spread their robes on the road. They had waved palm branches and spread them before His feet. And now? Now they shouted and screamed, "Away with Him! Crucify Him! Crucify Him!" Now they wanted to hang the Lord Jesus on a cross to die.

They thought, "We wanted to make Him king, but He did not want to be king. We thought that He could do anything. Now He allows Himself to be bound with ropes and whipped by soldiers. No, He is not the Son of God. He is a deceiver. Away with Him! Crucify Him! Crucify Him!"

That was what they shouted and screamed, those people. And the chief priests and the proud Jews shouted the loudest.

Pilate was afraid. Would he have to kill Jesus anyway? He should not. Jesus had no fault. But Pilate, that fearful, dishonest judge, did not dare to let the Lord Jesus go. He told those angry Jews, "You take Him. You do with Him whatever you want."

"Yes, that is good!" they cried.

Pilate handed Jesus over to the soldiers. They took the Lord Jesus and pulled Him along off the steps.

"He must die!" the Jews shouted. "Away with him! Crucify Him! Crucify Him!"

GOLGOTHA

How terribly sad! There went the Lord Jesus. He was the Son of God. He was the King of heaven and earth. And there He went as if He was a criminal. Rough soldiers pushed Him along. In front walked servants with big nails and a heavy hammer. The Lord Jesus had to carry the heavy cross Himself, on His sore shoulders. He could hardly do it. His knees trembled. He was so tired. The pain was so severe. And the big wooden cross was so heavy.

GOLGOTHA

"Come on! Hurry up!" the soldiers said.

So they went through the streets, through the gate, and out of the city. A short distance away was a hill. That was where they were going. There the Lord Jesus would have to die.

The people jostled and shouted behind the soldiers. They were curious. They wanted to see everything. They came near the hill called Golgotha. On the hill the cross was set up. Those rough, cruel soldiers put the Lord Jesus up on that cross. And then — oh, how awful! They drove the long, sharp nails right through the Lord Jesus' hands and feet into the wood. That hurt. It hurt so much! But the Lord Jesus did not look at those cruel men angrily. Willingly and patiently He allowed them to do it, even though it hurt so very much.

Quietly He prayed to His Father in heaven. He asked if God would forgive those wicked men and all those people for the pain and the sorrow they were giving Him. He prayed, "Father, forgive them. They do not know what they are doing."

There the Lord Jesus hung on the cross. The chief priests and important Jews looked at Him. They laughed. They said, "Come off the cross if Thou art the Son of God! Thou hast helped so many people, now help Thyself. Come off the cross, if Thou art able. Thou art not able to do it."

That was how those wicked men mocked. Not one of them thought about the pain and the sorrows of the Lord Jesus.

Could the Lord Jesus not come off the cross? Could He not help Himself? Could He not punish those wicked men for their wickedness? Oh, yes, the Lord Jesus was able to do that. He was able to do anything. But He did not want to. All that pain and grief He wanted to carry because He loved them so much. All the people of the world, all the men, all the women, and all the children, had sinned. They deserved punishment, but the Lord Jesus wanted to bear all that punishment for them, alone.

Let those chief priests and others shout, "Come off the cross! Thou art not able to do it!" Let them hurt Him.

The Lord Jesus bore it all, willingly and patiently. And there was no anger in His eyes.

On each side of the Lord Jesus stood another cross. On each cross hung a man. They were wicked men. One of them was a murderer. Now the Lord Jesus, who had never done anything wrong, hung between criminals.

One of the men mocked Him, too. He said just like the chief priests, "If Thou art the Son of God, come off the cross and help us, too. Thou art not able."

The Lord Jesus did not answer.

But the criminal on the other side did not mock. He was sad. He thought, "I am a wicked man. I am hanging on a cross and bearing great pain, but I deserve it. The Lord Jesus does not deserve this terrible thing. He is God's Son. And when He dies, He will go to heaven. But me? I am so afraid to die."

Then in his fear he cried to the Lord Jesus, "Lord, remember me when Thou comest into heaven. O Lord, I have done so much wrong, but remember me. Do not forget me."

Did the Lord Jesus become angry at that man? Did He say, "It is your own fault?"

No. The Lord is never angry when someone is sorry. He said to that criminal, "Today you shall be with Me in Paradise."

That was wonderful for the man who had done so much wrong. The Lord Jesus forgave him his sin. He would be able to go to heaven when he died, anyway.

Look, who was that slowly climbing up the hill? It was a man and a woman. They were so sorrowful they could hardly walk. It was the disciple John, and Mary, the mother of the Lord Jesus. Poor Mary! How she wept with grief. John held her tight in his strong arms. When she saw the Lord Jesus on that terrible cross, she was so deeply sorry for Him. It was as if she felt that terrible pain with Him. She loved Him so much. And now He would die. Then she would no longer have Him with her. Poor Mary!

The Lord Jesus saw her, and He said to her, "Now John must be your son." And to John He said, "Now Mary must be your mother."

Yes, John would do that. He took poor Mary along to his home. He would take care of her. He would take care of her very well.

It was midday. The sun was shining hot. But suddenly it became dark, terribly dark! The people were frightened. They fled away from the hill of Golgotha. There hung the Lord Jesus, all alone in that deep darkness. That darkness lasted for three long hours. That darkness made the Lord Jesus very afraid. All the people had fled. But it seemed as if His Father in heaven had forgotten Him, too. In His fear He cried, "My God! My God! Why hast Thou forgotten Me?" How sad it was on that hill of Golgotha.

But then the light returned, and the people returned, too. They came to look again, and to mock again. Those wicked people!

The Lord Jesus was thirsty. He wanted to drink. He said, "I thirst." One of the soldiers heard it. He wetted a sponge and put the sponge on a branch of hyssop and lifted it up high. And then the Lord Jesus could drink a little.

Then everything became quiet again. The Lord Jesus' head hung down on His chest. His eyes were closed. He was dying. Then once more He lifted up His weary head. Once more He looked around. And then a great joy filled His eyes, and He cried out with a loud voice, "It is finished!"

He had finished His difficult work. He had borne all the pain and sorrow. Now that terrible event the Lord Jesus had foretold was past. He had carried the severe punishment for the people so that they could come to God again.

Wearily the Lord Jesus bowed his head down again. He spoke a few soft words to His Father in heaven, "Father, into Thy hands I commit My spirit."

Then He died. There hung the Son of God, dead on the cross. That was what the sinful people had done. But the Lord Jesus loved the people very much.

When evening came, a few friends of the Lord Jesus came up the hill. Some women who loved the Lord Jesus came along. Carefully they took His dead body off the cross. He should not remain hanging there. He had to be buried.

How those men and women cried with grief! Now the Master was dead. Now the Master was gone forever. He would never look at them again with His kind eyes. He would never speak to them again with His friendly voice.

They were so terribly sad. They folded a large white cloth around the Lord Jesus. They put spices which smelled lovely inside the cloth. Then those men reverently carried Him away. And the weeping women followed along.

Their poor Master! Now He was dead. He had made other people alive. Now He was dead Himself. Poor Master! They carried Him to His grave. In a garden nearby was a tomb where they carefully laid the Lord Jesus down. Then they rolled the heavy stone in front of the opening. Weeping with grief they went away. Now their Master was gone forever.

The chief priests and the Pharisees were glad that Jesus was gone. He was dead. Now He could not do miracles anymore. Now the people could not listen to Him anymore. Now the people would listen to them again. Now the chief priests and the proud Jews would be the most important in the land again. How happy they were about that!

But they were fearful, too, because the Lord Jesus had once said, "I shall die. But after three days I will rise again." Of course that could never happen. It was impossible. But the Jews were still afraid. And then, what did they do? They commanded soldiers to guard His grave for three days. They were told to keep a good watch. Now the chief priests and Pharisees were content. Now the Lord Jesus was gone forever!

THE HAPPY MORNING

It was still early in the morning and very quiet in the city. But three women were awake. Together they hastily walked through the streets. Swiftly they went through the gate out of the city.

The sun shone so beautifully, but the women did not look at the golden sunshine. They walked along with heads bowed in sorrow.

"Oh, our dear Master!" they said. "Oh, it is so sad. Now the Master is gone forever! Now He will never look at us again with His kind eyes. Now He will never tell us anything again with His friendly voice. Come, let us go to His grave and bring Him dried herbs. We will prepare the poor dead body of our Master with oil that smells beautiful. But how sad it is, how very sad."

That was how they spoke together.

Then suddenly one of the women said, "We cannot get into the grave. What about that heavy stone? We cannot roll it away. What will we do now?"

The women went on anyway. They saw the garden where the Lord Jesus' grave was. It was so quiet there, so lonely. They entered the quiet garden. There was the grave.

But what was that? How could that be? The heavy stone was rolled away and the dark grave was open. The women were frightened. How could that be? Had wicked men come and rolled the stone away? Had they taken the dead body of the Lord Jesus away? How could those women bring their poor Master the fine spices and oil now?

One of the women became so sad, she walked away. That was Mary Magdalene. She went back to the city to tell the disciples. But the other two women continued on.

Where could the Master be? They looked into the dark grave. It was empty. They walked a little way into it.

Then suddenly that dark grave was not dark any longer. It was filled with a beautiful light. Two angels stood by the grave. Their robes were shining white, as beautiful as the sun. In fear the women bowed their heads.

But the angels said, "Do not be afraid. We know who you are looking for. You are searching for the Lord Jesus, but He is not here anymore. He has gone out of the grave. He has risen from the dead. See, there is the place where He lay. But He is alive again. Why do you seek the Master here? Do you not remember what He told you earlier? He said, 'I shall die, but after three days I will arise from the dead.' Do not be grieved and afraid any longer. The Master is alive. Go quickly and tell the disciples, and also Peter. Go quickly and you will see Him, too."

Oh, how happy those women were! The Master was not dead anymore! "He is alive! He is alive!" they kept saying to each other. "Come, let us run fast and tell the disciples. Oh, how wonderful it is! How wonderful!"

With happy hearts the two women walked through the golden sunshine. Their eyes were not full of tears anymore and their heads were no longer bowed.

Suddenly Someone stood in front of them and said, "Greetings!"

Who was it? The women looked at Him. Then they fell on their knees before Him. They took hold of His feet and worshipped Him. It was the Lord Jesus Himself! He was alive. He was looking at them with His kind eyes. He was speaking to them with His friendly voice. He said, "Go and tell all My friends. They shall see Me, too."

And then suddenly, the Lord Jesus was gone! How happy those women were! How quickly they hurried back to the city.

Oh, it was such a happy, wonderful message that they were bringing. The Lord Jesus was alive again!

Yes, the Lord Jesus was alive. He was God's own Son. He could not stay in that dark grave. The soldiers had kept watch well. But in the dark night an angel from heaven had come. The soldiers had been terribly frightened, and they had fled, running away as fast as they could. The angel had rolled the stone away. Then the Lord Jesus had risen from the grave.

The wicked Jews thought the Lord Jesus was dead forever, was gone for always. Oh, no, that could not be. He had borne the heavy punishment because He loved the people so much, but now, now He was the king of heaven and earth. Forevermore!

MARY MAGDALENE

It was very peaceful near the open tomb. The heavy stone stood beside it. The lovely flowers bloomed and the joyful birds sang in the sunshine. A woman came near the open tomb. She cried and cried. She was so sad. She did not see the pretty flowers. She did not hear the happy bird songs. Her eyes were filled with tears. She stepped closer to the tomb.

Who was this woman? Had she not heard about the wonderful happening yet? No. It was Mary Magdalene. A little while ago she had walked away, but the two other women had gone near the grave. They had heard what the angel had said, and they had seen the Lord Jesus. Mary Magdalene did not hear or see anything. She was filled with sorrow; yet she wanted to come to the tomb again. She walked right up to the empty tomb.

"It is empty," she thought. "Surely some men have been here. They must have taken the dead body of the Lord Jesus away. Now I cannot even bring Him my spices and oil." She leaned against the tomb and she wept. Tears streamed down her cheeks. Where had the men brought the Lord Jesus? If only she knew.

She looked inside and saw two men sitting there, wearing shiny white robes. But Mary Magdalene could not see very well. Her eyes were too full of tears.

Those men asked her, "Why do you weep like that?"

Mary Magdalene answered, "Because they have taken my Lord away, and I do not know where they have laid Him." Then she turned around and left. "Oh," she thought, "if I only knew where the Lord Jesus lies."

Suddenly a Man stood before her. He asked, "Why are you weeping? Whom do you seek?"

Mary Magdalene was not able to see very well because her eyes were filled with tears. She did not know who it was, but she thought, "Maybe it is the gardener, the man who takes care of the garden. Has that gardener taken the Lord Jesus from the grave? Maybe he has. Does the gardener know the place where the Lord Jesus lies? Maybe he does."

And then she asked him, "Oh, Sir, if you have taken the Lord Jesus away, tell me where you have laid Him."

What did the Man say then? He spoke only one word. Gently He said, "Mary."

Mary was afraid. She looked up, and then a great joy shone in her eyes. Immediately she knew who the Man was. She heard it in His voice. It was the Lord Jesus Himself. He was alive! He was alive again! He was standing right there.

"Master! Dear Master!" she cried out, and fell on her knees before Him, about to hold His feet. How she wanted to keep Him close, always very close to herself.

But the Lord said, "No, Mary, do not touch Me. I will not always remain here. I shall go to My Father in heaven. But you may tell the disciples and all my friends that I am alive again."

Mary Magdalene returned in haste to Jerusalem. "The Master is not dead anymore! He is alive!" she thought over and over. Oh, how wonderful that was, how very wonderful! Her eyes shone with happiness, and when she came to the disciples, she shouted it out with a loud voice, "The Master is not dead anymore! He is alive again!"

But the disciples still could not believe it. The two women had told them, and now Mary Magdalene was saying it. But still the disciples thought, "Maybe the women are mistaken. Maybe they did not look and listen well. No, we cannot believe it."

Yet it was true. It was very true.

WHO WAS IT?

The day was almost over and soon evening would come. Along the road it was very quiet. Only two men were walking on it. They had come from the big city of Jerusalem and were travelling to the little village in the distance. They were two of the Lord Jesus' friends. They spoke quietly and mournfully with each other. "How sad it is that our Master is dead. He suffered so much pain on the cross, and now He is gone from us forever. Now we do not have a Master anymore." That was what they were unhappily discussing together as they walked home on that quiet country road.

Suddenly there was another Man walking beside them, a Stranger. Kindly He asked, "What are you discussing, and why are you so sad?"

They looked at the strange Man. His words sounded friendly and His eyes looked kind, but the two men did not know Him. They asked, "Do you not know? Have you not heard about the terribly sad thing that has happened in Jerusalem?"

The Stranger asked, "What has happened?"

"Do you not know? Have you never heard about the Lord Jesus? He made the blind to see. He healed the sick. He could speak so wonderfully; everyone had to listen when He spoke. But the chief priests took Him prisoner and they hung Him on a cross. Oh, it is so sad! Now He is dead; now He is gone forever. We thought that the Lord Jesus would become King and drive all our enemies away from our land. But now He is dead. It is so very sad. And this morning some women went to His grave. They said there were angels there and that the Lord Jesus is alive again. But we doubt it. Likely it is not true and that makes us so sad," the friends told the Stranger.

But that strange Man did not look sad at all. He began speaking to the two friends. "The Lord Jesus came to earth to make the people happy. He wanted to carry their punishment. He wanted to suffer pain for them. He wanted to die for them, too. Did you not know that? He is the Son of God."

That strange Man spoke so kindly and wonderfully. The other two listened and listened. It made them glad, but they did not understand why. They did not know that friendly Man. Who was He?

Soon they entered a little village, the home of those two men. The other one, the Stranger, was going to travel on. But He should not do that. The two friends said, "Come with us into our house. Eat with us and sleep with us. You should not go on now. The road is very dark at night. Stay with us."

The Stranger gladly accepted, and together they went inside. They sat down to eat bread. The stranger sat in the middle. He was given the best place.

And then the Stranger took the bread and broke it. He folded His hands and prayed, and then gave each of the men a piece.

Then suddenly those two men were afraid. Suddenly they saw who that Stranger was! Yes, it was the Lord Jesus! It was the Lord Jesus Himself.

"Master! Master!" they cried. But then they were alone again. The Lord Jesus had suddenly disappeared.

They no longer wanted to eat bread. They were not even thinking about bread. They were much, much too happy. Quickly they got up and said to each other, "Come, let us go back to the city immediately, to the disciples. Let us tell them, 'The Master is alive! We have seen Him ourselves! We walked with Him along the way and did not even recognize Him. When He spoke our hearts were so happy, but we did not realize why. We wondered, who is He? But now we know!' Come, let us quickly go and tell the wonderful news."

Hurriedly they walked back along the road, back to the disciples. They must hear that wonderful news, too, all of them!

All of the disciples? No. Not all of them. Judas, the traitor, was not there anymore. He was gone. He had died. He could not hear the wonderful news.

They came into the city and went to the room where the disciples were together. It was a room with locked doors and closed windows. The disciples were afraid of the chief priests. The two men knocked at the door. Immediately they were allowed in.

Then the disciples shouted to them, "We know something wonderful! The Lord has truly risen. Peter has seen Him!"

And the two men called back, "We have, too! We have, too! The Master is not dead anymore."

How happy that evening was. A little while ago everyone had been filled with sorrow — now their sorrow had been turned into gladness.

Suddenly those people became very afraid! The Lord Jesus was standing among them. He had not knocked; no one had opened the door for Him. The door was locked, the windows were sealed. And yet, He was standing there with them.

He looked at them, and He knew they were frightened.

He said, "Do not be afraid. It is I." Then the Lord Jesus showed them the places on His hands and feet where the nails had been hammered through when He hung on the cross. "Come, look!" He said, "Touch Me. It is I."

How very happy the disciples were! They looked at their Master timidly. Was it true? Was it the Lord Jesus Himself?

"Yes, it is Me. Do you have something for Me to eat?" He asked.

Then the Lord ate a piece of fish and a little honey. The disciples watched Him. Yes, yes! It was the Master. He *was* alive! It was true. It was sure. And it was wonderful, so very wonderful.

The Lord Jesus stayed with them that evening and taught them many beautiful things. They listened and they thought, "Why were we so sad? The Master could not stay in the grave. He is the Son of God. He is much stronger than the grave."

BY THE SEA OF TIBERIAS

It was night, a very quiet night on the dark sea. The men in the little boat threw out their nets to catch fish. They pulled it up, but there was not even one fish splashing in the net. They threw their net out again and again, all night long, but they did not catch anything. That was too bad. Far in the distance where the sky met the dark water, the light was dawning. Morning was coming.

Those men were all disciples of the Lord Jesus, and again and again they talked to each other about what had happened in Jerusalem. The Lord Jesus, their Master, had died, but had risen from the dead. They had seen Him two times already in that quiet room. They had listened to Him speak. They longed for Him all the time, but they did not see Him anymore. Then they had gone fishing on the Sea of Tiberias, just as they used to. But in that quiet dark night, not one fish was caught. That was too bad. And now the new day was dawning in the distance.

"Look!" one of them said. "Look, on the shore. There is a Man standing there alone."

But no one could see who it was. The land was still too dark and far away. Slowly the boat neared the shore.

"Listen," one of them said. "Listen, the Man is calling us."

They listened and over the quiet water they could clearly hear what the Man was saying. He asked, "Do you have something for me to eat?"

Food? No, they did not have anything to eat. And they could not give Him any fish to fry. Not even one.

So they called out, "No, we have nothing. We have not caught anything all night."

Then that Stranger on the shore called out, "Cast your nets out on the other side of the boat!"

The disciples said, "Can that Man on the shore see into the water better than we can? Can He see fish we cannot see? Who is that man? What a friendly voice He has."

So they cast out their nets on the other side of the boat. Then they tried to pull them up again, too. Yes, they tried, but they were not able to. It was too heavy with fish. It was filled with beautiful big fish. The net almost tore. They had to pull it along through the water to the shore.

The disciples were afraid. Who was that Man alone there at the edge of the water? Would it be? Could it be? They looked at each other, afraid and yet so wonderfully happy. John was the first to cry out with joy, "It is the Lord!" The others knew it, too. It was the Lord Jesus waiting for them early in the morning on the shore of the lake.

Peter stretched out his arms to his Master. But the little boat was too far from the shore, and it was going so slowly with that net full of fish it was pulling. Peter could not wait. He picked up his cloak, which he had taken off while working in the boat. Hastily he covered himself with the robe and jumped into the water. The water was shallow near the shore. Quickly he waded to the land, where His Master, whom he loved so much, was waiting. He wanted to be near Him first of all the disciples.

When he came to the shore — how strange! There was a fire, and on the fire lay some fish. How could that be? But it was not strange. Had not the Lord Jesus once fed thousands of people with five loaves and two fish? Nothing was too wonderful for the Saviour. He was the Lord of heaven and earth.

Then the other disciples came, too. Together they pulled the heavy net onto the land. One hundred and fifty-three fish were flopping in the net. Big, beautiful fish! The Lord Jesus said they should put some of those fish on the fire, too, then they could sit down and eat together. How wonderful it was to be with the Master, whom they loved so much. To be together, eat together, and speak together. Just as it used to be. To look at Him and listen to Him.

When breakfast was finished, the Lord Jesus said to one of the disciples, "Simon, do you love Me?" Simon was Peter's fisherman name.

Peter looked at His Master and said, "Yes, Lord, Thou knowest that I love Thee."

But a little later the Lord Jesus asked Peter again, "Simon, do you love Me?"

Peter was startled. Did the Master not believe what he had told Him! And again Peter said, "Yes, Lord, Thou knowest everything. Thou knowest I love Thee."

But a little while later the Lord Jesus asked a third time, "Simon, do you love Me?"

That made Peter very sad. Now he knew why the Master had asked him three times if he loved Him. Three times, because Peter had said three times, "Jesus? I do not know that Man." That was on the sad night when his Master stood before the Jewish judges, before He died. John and Peter had quietly come to watch. Peter had stood warming himself by the fire on that cold night and then one of the servants of the judge had asked him, "Are you a disciple of the Lord Jesus?" Three times he had said, "Jesus? I do not know that Man!" That was how he had denied his Master that night, before the rooster crowed three times.

And now on this happy morning, at the Sea of Tiberias, the Lord Jesus wanted to hear three times that Peter loved Him. How sorrowfully Peter looked at his Master. He was truly sorry. Why, oh why had he been so afraid that night? Why had he not honestly said, "Yes, I am a disciple of the Lord Jesus. I belong to Him. I love Him."

But when Peter looked at the Master, he saw in His eyes that the Lord Jesus had forgiven him his sins. And Peter said with a trembling voice, "Yes, Lord, Thou knowest all things. Thou knowest that I love Thee."

Then the Lord Jesus said, "Feed My sheep."

My sheep? But Peter understood. The Lord did not mean animals, He meant people. The Lord Jesus Himself was the Good Shepherd. All the people and children who loved Him were His sheep. Now it was Peter's task to take care of those people and children. There was great thankfulness in Peter's heart. He had never loved His Master as much as now. And never, never again would he say that he did not know the Lord Jesus. Never, no matter how dangerous it was. He was allowed to be a disciple of the Master again. He would remain one, too. No enemy could frighten him again. He would suffer, would even die for His Master if it was necessary. Now he belonged to the Saviour forever.

For the rest of their lives the disciples never forgot that early morning at the Sea of Tiberias. Certainly not Peter. Everything the Lord Jesus had said he remembered deep in his heart.

THE ASCENSION

It was so wonderful that the Lord Jesus came to His disciples and friends again and again. But He could not always stay with them. He had told Mary Magdalene, "I shall go away, I shall return to My Father in heaven." The Lord Jesus only stayed for a little while.

One day the Lord Jesus was gathered with all His disciples and friends in Jerusalem. Then He said, "Let us go."

Together they left the city. They passed the quiet Garden of Gethsemane where the Lord Jesus had been so sad and the disciples had slept. Then everything had been sad. But now everything had become joyful.

The Lord Jesus spoke to His disciples. He said, "When I have gone to heaven to My Father, you must tell the people everything that has happened. You must tell the people in this land and throughout the whole world about Me. Whoever believes in Me and loves Me, I shall some day bring to heaven, where My Father is. All the people must know that I carried the punishment for them."

The disciples listened. Oh, yes, they would be willing to do that, to tell the people about the Lord Jesus. But it was so difficult. They could not speak as beautifully as their Master. Would the people even listen to them?

But the Lord Jesus spoke more words to them. He said, "When I am gone, you must stay together a little while in Jerusalem. I shall always think about you. I will see you when I am in heaven and I will hear you. I know everything about you, and I shall always help you. Then the Holy Spirit shall come to live in your hearts, and you will always know what to tell the people. Then you will remember everything that I taught you, too. Then you will not be afraid of anyone either. From heaven I will always look down on you."

That was how the Lord Jesus spoke to His disciples and friends. When they came to a mountain, the Lord Jesus stood still. All the people, the men and the women, stood around their Master. They looked at Him with great happiness and reverence. They loved Him so very much.

The Lord Jesus stretched out His hands over them all. He blessed them. And then — it was so strange, but it was wonderful, too. The Lord Jesus' feet were not standing on the ground anymore! He went up, higher and higher, to heaven.

The people fell on their knees. They lifted their hands in prayer. They saw the Lord Jesus go. They looked and looked, until a cloud came under His feet, and the Lord Jesus was taken from their sight. Yet, they continued looking and they waited and waited.

Suddenly, two angels stood near them. They asked, "Why are you looking up? The Lord Jesus has ascended to heaven. But He will return again some day, just as you saw Him go up. That day everyone shall see Him."

Then the disciples, Jesus' friends and the women, went back to Jerusalem alone. Were they sad that the Lord Jesus was gone again? No, not anymore. The Lord Jesus was not away. He had gone up to heaven, to God, His Father. But He was looking down on them, and He could hear what they said. And He was thinking about them.

He had told them that they should wait a little while in Jerusalem. And then? Then they could go to the people. That would be so wonderful! But now they had to wait a little while longer.

PENTECOST

There was a big celebration in Jerusalem. A great number of people were on the streets. They had come from their own villages and cities to Jerusalem to celebrate the great feast. Many people had come from strange countries, too. They were going to the temple, the house of God. They were going to worship and thank Him. God took care of the people. He let the grain grow on the earth. He gave them what they needed.

The chief priests and the Pharisees were there, too. They were sitting up front. They were sitting in the most beautiful room of the temple. They thought that they were the best servants of God.

The disciples also came together to celebrate the great feast. But now they no longer argued about who was the greatest and best among them, or who would sit in the best place. Now they truly loved each other, and they talked about their Master who was in heaven with God.

It was already ten days ago that the Lord Jesus had gone up to heaven. He had told them, "You must stay together a little while in Jerusalem. Then the Holy Spirit will come to live in your hearts." The disciples had been waiting for ten days already. But they knew that because the Master had said it, the Holy Spirit would come. Now at this great feast they were together with all the other people. During this great celebration, the Holy Spirit came to live in their hearts. What the Lord Jesus promises always happens.

Peter was standing in the midst of all those happy disciples. He started to speak to all the people there. He began to tell about the Lord Jesus. More and more people came to listen to him. Yes, that was what Peter was doing, fearful Peter, who once had been so afraid of the chief priests. But now he was not afraid anymore. Now he knew what to tell the people. He told them that the Lord Jesus had died on the cross. That He was buried in a dark tomb. But he also told them that the Lord Jesus had risen from the dead and had ascended into heaven. The Lord Jesus was the Son of God, but the people had killed Him.

All those men and women from the cities, villages, and strange countries listened to Peter. He spoke so wonderfully. But they became afraid. They thought, "The people hurt the Lord Jesus so much. They even killed Him. We did that, too. But now He is in heaven with God. He must be terribly angry at the people and at us, too." They became afraid of the Lord Jesus. They asked Peter, "What must we do? What must we do?"

Peter answered, "No, the Lord Jesus is not angry at the people. Not at you either. He will forgive your sins if you are truly sorry and pray to God. And then you must love Him, and you will not be afraid anymore, but become happy. Then some day you, too, may live with the Lord Jesus in heaven."

Many, many people said, "We want to love the Lord Jesus. We want to become His disciples, too. We want to do everything He says." That was a very happy, joyous day in Jerusalem.

But the chief priests and the important Jews heard what Peter said, too. They became very angry. They said, "Jesus is dead! Jesus is gone! But now those disciples are talking about Him again, and the people are listening too. We do not want that. We will not allow it! Those disciples may not speak about their Master! We shall tell them that they are not allowed to speak about the Lord Jesus. Then they will become afraid of us."

The disciples thought, "All the people must hear about the Lord Jesus. They must love Him, He is the Son of God."
The chief priests thought, "The people must not hear about the Lord Jesus. They must forget Him, forget Him completely!"
Would the chief priests get their way, or would the disciples be strong and continue to teach the people about the Lord Jesus?

THE CRIPPLED MAN

There he sat, the poor beggar, always sitting quietly at the same spot near the big, beautiful temple gate. He sat there every morning and every afternoon. For years and years he had sat there. He was a poor beggar. He could not work, he could not earn money for his bread. He could only beg. When someone came past to enter through the beautiful gate into the temple, he would stretch out his hand and ask for alms. Sometimes a small coin would be dropped into his hand. Then he was happy and saved it until evening, when he could buy some bread with it. He sat there at the same spot each day, and he waited and he begged.
He could not walk; his legs were lame. He could not work. He could only ask for alms from the people. In the morning some friends would bring him to this spot. In the evening they would carry him back to his little house. What a poor beggar he was!

There he sat again. He looked and he waited. It was three o'clock in the afternoon. That was usually a good time for him. Many people came to the temple at that time to worship God. They walked through the beautiful gate where the poor, crippled man sat. Often he would get something. Yes, three o'clock in the afternoon was a good time for him.
Two men were coming. They were not rich. Oh, no, the beggar could see that. They were wearing common clothes.

But they looked very friendly. Maybe he would get something from them anyway. Even a little coin would make him very thankful. The poor crippled man held out his hand. Would those two men give him a coin?

They stopped right next to him. The one man said with a friendly voice, "Look at us."

The poor crippled man looked up happily. Oh, yes, these were friendly people. Surely they would give him something.

But then the man said, "I do not have money. We are not rich."

No money? Did these men have no money? Could they not give him anything? Yet they were so friendly, and they had stopped beside him. The crippled man looked at them. He did not understand at all.

Then the man said something else. He said, "Money I do not have. But what I do have, I will give you."

What was that? What was it? The man said, "In the name of the Lord Jesus, I say, stand up and walk!" He took the poor crippled man's hand and pulled him up.

Oh, but he could not do that. He could not! That poor crippled man's legs were lame. He could not stand up. He could not walk. He had never, never been able to walk.

Yes, but now he could! Because that man had said, "In the name of the Lord Jesus."

He looked at them and he believed it right away. He was not afraid at all that he would fall. He was not afraid that his poor sick legs would break. Oh, no. He could feel that his legs were not sick and weak anymore. Suddenly they had become strong and healthy. He stood up. He walked. He forgot all about money to buy bread. He was not sick and disabled anymore. He was better. Suddenly, he was completely better! Yes, that was worth much more than silver or gold. And he went with the two men into the temple to thank God. How wonderful it was! How very wonderful! How that happy man danced and jumped with joy.

But who were those two men? How could they heal this poor cripple? They were Peter and John, two disciples of the Lord Jesus. When they saw the poor man they felt so sorry for him. They wanted to help him, just as their Master had always done when He was on earth.

The people saw it happen. They pushed along into the temple and they looked and they whispered, "How is it possible? See that crippled man who always sat near the gate of the temple? Now he is walking and jumping and dancing. How can that be?"

Peter and John heard what was being whispered by the people. Peter said to them, "Why do you look at us? Do you think that we healed the poor man? No, we are not able to do that. We are only ordinary people. The Lord Jesus has done it. The Lord Jesus who is in heaven. He sees everything, He hears everything, He knows everything. The Lord Jesus healed so many people. Do you not remember that? But the chief priests and important Jews took Him prisoner, and you too cried, 'Crucify Him! Crucify Him!' Do you remember that? The Lord Jesus is not dead anymore. He has risen and ascended into heaven. From heaven, He looks down on us. You must love Him as we do. He will forgive you all your sins and make you happy."

The people listened to Peter. And then many said, "We want to be disciples of the Lord Jesus, too. He is the Son of God. Now we know it. Now we believe it. We want to love Him, too."

That was a very happy day.

But the chief priests and the Pharisees heard what had happened to the crippled man. How angry they were! They had Peter and John brought to them. They demanded, "You may not speak about the Lord Jesus. We will not allow it. The people are listening to you. They must not."

Did Peter and John become afraid? Oh, no. They said, "Our Master commanded that we tell everyone about Him. And what He said, we must do. We are not afraid."

The chief priests and Pharisees became terribly angry. They thought, "Just wait. We will punish those disciples! Just wait!"

PETER RELEASED

It was a very dark night. In the darkness stood a very dark house, called a prison. There were people in it who had done great wrong. Strong watchmen kept guard. They kept watch so that not one prisoner could escape. The heavy doors were locked. It was very quiet in that prison and very dark.

On a little pile of straw lay a man. He was asleep. Beside him were two soldiers, one on each side. The arms of the prisoner were bound with iron chains to the arms of the soldiers. They had to guard him. If he wanted to walk away, he would pull on the chains and the soldiers would wake up. No, he surely could not walk away. The doors were locked and in front of the doors were more soldiers. He could not go away at all. He had to stay in that dark prison and wait. He must have done a very wicked deed. He must certainly have been an evil man. Or was he? Who was he? And what had he done?

It was Peter. What had he done? He had told the people about the Lord Jesus again and again. This had made the chief priests and the important Jews so angry at him that they told the king. Then the king commanded his soldiers to take Peter and put him in prison, there in that dark dungeon. Now he lay bound in chains behind those dark doors. He could not get away at all.

What would happen to Peter? The next day he would be brought before that evil king. And then? Maybe he would be killed. Poor Peter. Was he terribly afraid? Afraid? No, Peter was not afraid at all. Even if the prison was very dark, the Lord in heaven could see Peter. He was thinking about him. Peter was not afraid to die either. He thought, "The Lord Jesus will take care of me. Even if I must die, He will take care of me."

Peter was very tired. He fell asleep that dark night.

But the other disciples, Peter's friends, did not sleep. They came together in a house in Jerusalem. They could not sleep. They were always thinking about Peter. Tomorrow. Oh, what would happen to him tomorrow? Would the king have him killed? Oh, if only they could help Peter! But they could not help Peter. The doors were so heavy and the soldiers were so strong.

But they could do something better for Peter. Something much better. They could pray for him. They asked, "O Lord, help Peter. Do not forget him. The king and the chief priests are so wicked. Help him."

Was it possible? Could the Lord in heaven help Peter? The doors were heavy, the soldiers were so strong, and the chains were made of iron. Was that possible?

PETER RELEASED

Peter was fast asleep when suddenly a bright light shone in that dark dungeon. An angel from heaven was standing there. He nudged Peter awake. That bright light frightened Peter. But then he saw the angel.

The angel said, "Stand up! Quickly!"

Peter did so. But what about the chains? And the soldiers? Oh, look, the chains just fell off. And the soldiers kept on sleeping; they did not notice anything.

"Put on your sandals and your robe," the angel said, "and come with me."

Peter obeyed.

What about those heavy locked doors? And the soldiers by the gate? Undisturbed the angel walked on. And then — then the doors opened, and the soldiers did not even see the angel. They did not see Peter either. And the great iron gate of the prison opened up, too, just like that, all by itself.

There they were, the angel and Peter, outside in the dark night. The angel walked along with Peter down one street, then suddenly he was gone. Peter was alone in the street in the darkness.

How wonderful! He was free! Was he dreaming? Would he wake up in a while and find himself lying tied up between the soldiers anyway? No, it was not a dream. It was true. Very true. The Lord in heaven had sent His angel. He had sent His angel to release Peter. Now he was free. Wonderfully free!

Peter knew the way in the dark city. He went to the house where all his friends were. He knocked. It was a very quiet, dark night. He knocked again. In the door was a small panel which opened up. A servant girl looked through. Her name was Rhoda. She was a little afraid. She asked, "Who is there?"

Peter said, "It is I, Peter."

Rhoda was startled. "Peter? Is that Peter?"

Yes, it was Peter. But how could that be? Rhoda ran inside. She was frightened and yet happy. She left Peter standing outside the door and called to all the friends, "Peter is standing at the door! Peter, himself!"

They said, "Rhoda, that is impossible. What about those iron doors of the prison? What about all those soldiers and what about those chains? Rhoda, you are mixed up. It is not Peter."

"Yes!" she said. "Yes, it is. Listen, he is knocking again!"

Peter was still standing outside. Was he not allowed to come in? He knocked again.

There came his friends with Rhoda. Now they recognized Peter's voice, too. They saw him standing there. "Peter!" they cried out joyfully. "Peter, why are you not in prison anymore? Have you escaped? What happened? Come inside! Come quickly inside. Tell us everything."

Peter came in and Rhoda locked the door securely. He told them everything. "The Lord in heaven sent His angel to release me. He did not forget me."

Together they thanked God who had so wondrously taken care of Peter. How happy they were!

But Peter did not stay in that house. That would be too dangerous. When the soldiers woke up in the morning they would search for him. While it was still night Peter left the city of Jerusalem and journeyed to another city. Some people whom he could also tell about the Lord Jesus lived there. He had to do that. The Master had commanded him. Everyone must hear about the Lord Jesus. All the people must know that He loved them. And Peter wanted to tell about His Master so much. He was not afraid of anyone anymore. He believed that the Lord in heaven would always see him and He would always help him.

PAUL

Horsemen were riding down the road. At the front rode their leader. He looked very stern. Who was that man? Where was he going with his soldiers, and why did he look so strict?

His name was Saul. He was going to the big city of Damascus, far away. There he would take people prisoner. He would tie them with ropes and bring them to Jerusalem, to the chief priests. There they would be severely punished. Saul was very angry with them. That was why he looked so stern.

Had those people done something terribly wrong? No, they had only listened to the disciples when they taught about the Lord Jesus. And they had said, "We want to serve the Lord Jesus, too." But the chief priests would not allow that, and Saul did not allow that either. Saul was a friend of the chief priests. He said, "I will help you. I will catch those people and bind them and bring them to you. And then you must punish them severely."

So there he rode with his brave horsemen, angry and stern. Oh, those poor people in that distant city! What if Saul found them?

Was Saul such a wicked, evil man? No, he was not. Not at all. He wanted to be a good servant of the Lord. But he thought that the Lord Jesus was a deceiver. He thought, "I shall punish all the people who love Jesus. I shall kill them if necessary. Then God will think I am a good and faithful servant."

Foolish Saul. He did not know that the Lord Jesus was truly the Son of God. He did not know that he was doing a wicked thing. Poor Saul! If only he knew better. There he rode, angry and severe.

"Onward! I can already see the city in the distance. Onward!"

Yes, they were coming near Damascus. Then, suddenly, a bright light fell from heaven. It seemed as if that light fell right between those soldiers. Saul was terribly afraid. He fell to the ground. He did not dare to look. He could not look. Oh, what a terrible light!

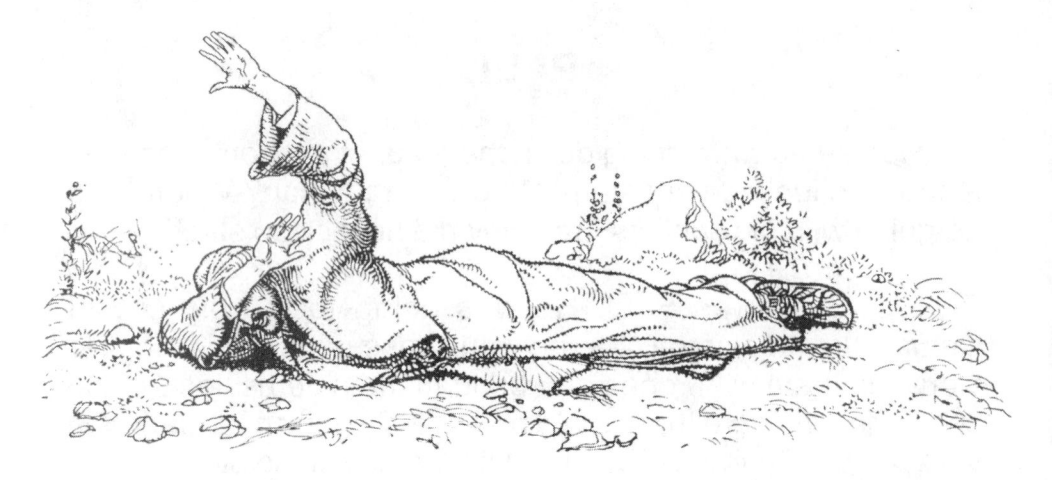

Suddenly Saul heard a voice from heaven which said, "Saul! Saul! Why are you so angry at Me?"

Who was that? Who said that? Saul was so afraid, he asked, "Who art Thou, Lord?"

And then the voice from heaven said, "I am Jesus. Why are you so angry with Me?"

Now Saul became very afraid. Was that the Lord Jesus? Wasn't He a deceiver? Was He really in heaven with God? Oh, and Saul had done so much wrong! Saul had wanted to take the people who loved the Lord Jesus prisoner, even kill them!

In his fear, Saul asked, "Lord, what dost Thou want me to do?"

Then the Lord Jesus said, "Go to the city, and there you will hear what you must do."

Then the voice from heaven did not speak anymore and the bright light was suddenly gone.

There went Saul, not riding proudly on his horse any longer. Neither did he look angry and stern anymore. He rode trembling between some of his soldiers, his head bowed like a pitiful man. They held his hands because he could not see. Saul had suddenly become blind.

They entered the big gate of the city and brought Saul to a friend of his. Were they going to catch people and bind them? No, Saul was no longer thinking of that. He only thought of what the Lord Jesus had said. He sat quietly in a room. He did not eat, he did not drink. He only thought of how wicked he had been. Saul prayed again and again.

Would Saul have to remain blind forever?

After three days an old man who loved the Lord Jesus walked into the room. He laid his hand on Saul's head and said, "Brother Saul, the Lord has sent me to you. The Lord Jesus spoke to you on the way. He has forgiven you all your sins. You may love Him, too. You may become one of His servants."

And then suddenly Saul could see again. How wonderful! And he could be a servant, a disciple of the Lord Jesus. That was even more wonderful. Now he knew that the Lord Jesus was not a deceiver. He was the Son of God. Saul wanted to love Him always. Only then would he be happy.

Saul quietly left the big city of Damascus. Where could he go? To the chief priests? No. He did not belong with them anymore. Saul went to the disciples of the Lord Jesus. He had become a disciple, too. He wanted to tell the people about his Master. If they would listen, if they would want to love the Lord Jesus, they would become happy, just as he was.

That was what Saul did. Later he journeyed to faraway strange countries. The people who lived there had never heard about the Lord Jesus. He wanted to talk to those faraway strange people about the Lord Jesus; to tell them that the Lord loved them and wanted to make them happy.

Now his name was not Saul anymore. He had changed his name to Paul. Before he had been a wicked man, an enemy of the Lord Jesus. Now he was a changed man. Now he wanted a different name, too. He wanted to be called Paul.

Paul went to many lands, and everywhere he told the people of his Master. He had become a faithful servant of the Lord.

One day Paul came to a strange city far away. His friend Silas was with him. Together they told the people about the Lord Jesus. But those people did not want to listen. They became angry, terribly angry with Paul and Silas. They were so angry that they whipped them. They hit them with whips on their backs. Then they threw Paul and Silas in a dark prison. There sat the poor men. The jailer, the man who had to keep watch, was a very stern man. He bound them with chains and put heavy wooden blocks on their feet, then they could not even move. They were so hungry and thirsty and their bleeding backs ached terribly.

The jailer went to sleep. He thought, "Those two men cannot escape. I will go to sleep."

Were Paul and Silas angry with the people of that strange city and with that stern jailer? No. Were they very sad because they had to suffer so much pain and hunger and thirst? No. Paul and Silas thought, "The Lord Jesus, our Master, suffered much more than we. He was not angry with the people. We must be content and patient, too."

In the middle of the night, in the dark prison, while suffering pain, Paul and Silas began to sing. They sang Psalms of praise to God; that was how happy and content they were. The jailer slept on peacefully. Those two men could never escape.

But then, in the middle of the night, something happened. The ground shook, the walls cracked and the doors burst open. It was an earthquake! Everything trembled and shook and broke. The iron chains binding Paul and Silas broke, too. And the heavy, wooden blocks fell off their feet. They were free, and the doors stood open.

With a start the jailer woke up. He heard the trembling and the shaking and the cracking. He got up and then he saw that the prison doors were wide open. He was terribly afraid. He thought, "Now the prisoners have all escaped, and I was supposed to guard them! Now I shall receive a heavy punishment."

Frightened, the jailer took a sword and was about to kill himself. That was how greatly he feared his master. But suddenly he heard a voice out of the darkness, saying, "Do not hurt yourself, we are all here. No one has run away."

Had no one run away? But the doors were wide open! Was it true? Had no one run away?

The jailer called a servant, a soldier. "Bring me a light! Bring it immediately!"

The soldier came with a torch. The jailer walked into the dark dungeon. There stood Paul and Silas, very quiet and content. Their chains were loose, and their heavy blocks were broken. But still they had not walked away.

When the jailer saw that, he knew that Paul and Silas could not be wicked men. He fell down on his knees before them and asked, "Sirs, what must I do? I want to become like you, so content and happy. What must I do?"

Paul said, "You must love the Lord Jesus. Then you will always be happy and content, just like we are."

The jailer took Paul and Silas to his house. Now he was not angry and stern anymore. Carefully he washed the blood from their backs. He gave them food and drink. He called his wife and his children and all his servants. He called everyone who lived in his house and they all listened to what Paul had to tell them about the Lord Jesus. That was a wonderful happy night. All those people wanted to love the Lord Jesus, too.

The next morning Paul and Silas left the city. They had to journey on again to other cities and to other people, teaching about the Lord Jesus. That was what Paul loved to do best. He did it for the rest of his life.

Peter did that, too. And John. And all the others disciples. The Master had said, "All the people in all the lands must hear that I came from heaven to bear the punishment and bring them back to God."

That was what Peter and John and Paul and Silas and all the others faithfully did. But that all happened long, long ago. Paul and Silas, Peter and John, and James and all the other disciples died many years ago. They endured much sorrow in their lives and suffered much pain. Yet they were always happy.

Now they are with the Lord Jesus in heaven. There is no sorrow there, or pain. It is even more beautiful and wonderful there than in the Garden of Eden. And they will always stay there.

And what about all the people who listened to them? And all the people who loved the Lord Jesus? They are also with God in heaven.

And what about us? The Lord Jesus wants to forgive us our sins, too, if we are truly sorry and ask Him to. All the men and women, all the fathers and mothers, all the children who love Him, He will bring to heaven. All of us, and the little children, too.

Yes, the Lord Jesus wants to be our Good Shepherd, too.

We may be His sheep. He will show us the way. He will take care of us.

Always!

The Dort Study Bible
An English translation of the Annotations to the Dutch Staten Bijbel of 1637 in accordance with a decree of the Synod of Dort 1618-1619

The general care of the translators was to express and explain the original text as faithfully and impartially, as could be done, and their language would bear no prejudice or violence to the Truth.
The original English translation was done upon a recommendation of the Westminster Asembly, 1648.

Vol. 1 Genesis - Exodus
ISBN 1-894666-51-8   Can.$24.95 U.S.$18.90

Vol. 2 Leviticus - Deuteronomy
ISBN 1-894666-52-6   Can.$24.95 U.S.$18.90

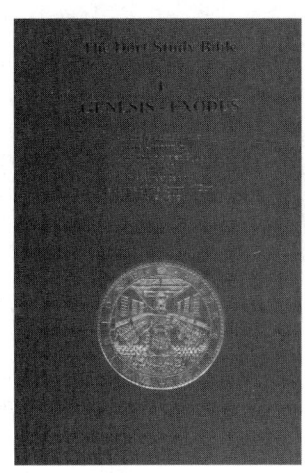

Israel's Hope and Expectation
by Rudolf Van Reest

G. Nederveen in *Clarion*: This is one of the best novels I have read of late. I found it captivating and hard to put down. Here is a book that is not time-bound and therefore it will never be outdated.

The story takes place around the time of Jesus' birth. It is written by someone who has done his research about the times between the Old and New Testament period. The author informs you in an easy style about the period of the Maccabees . . . Van Reest is a good storyteller. His love for the Bible and biblical times is evident from the start. He shows a good knowledge of the customs and mannerisms in Israel. Many fine details add to the quality of the book. You will be enriched in your understanding of the ways in the Old Testament.

Time: Inter-Testament Period   Age: 15-99
ISBN 0-921100-22-1   Can.$19.95 U.S.$17.90

William of Orange-The Silent Prince
by W.G. Van de Hulst

Byron Snapp in *The Counsel of Chalcedon*: Here is a Christian who persevered in the Christian faith when the cause seemed lost and he was being pursued by government authorities. Impoverished, he was offered great wealth to deny his principles. He refused. He remembered that true wealth is found in obeying God.
. . . Although written for children, this book can be greatly enjoyed by adults. No doubt Christians of all ages will be encouraged by the life of William of Orange . . . This book is a great choice for families to read and discuss together.

Time: 1533-1584   Age: 7-99
ISBN 0-921100-15-9   Can.$8.95 U.S.$7.90

The Word of the King Series

These hard-cover Bible story books are wonderful. Children just learning to read can use them as little readers, either reading them on their own, reading them aloud, or reading them along with the narration on CD. Yet what every child enjoys most is being read to. Here are Bible stories written in language which is simple and reverent. These are stories which edify both adults and children. The drawings must also be given due attention: they are simply beautiful. Real to life, they are a great contrast to the modern concept of Bible cartoon characters. There is a great need for good reading for children. Here is a good beginning.

Rev. J. Visscher in *Clarion*: "These books are usually about 40 pages long, are well-illustrated by Rino Visser and are faithful, biblical renderings. They make for good birthday presents to four and five year olds."

Abraham's Sacrifice
by Cor Van Rijswijk
Time: Abraham   Age: 4-8
ISBN 1-894666-21-6   Can.$8.95 U.S.$7.90

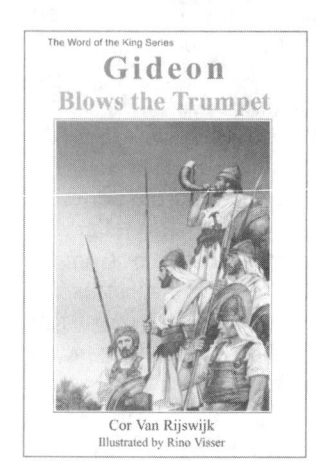

Gideon Blows the Trumpet
by Cor Van Rijswijk
Time: Gideon   Age: 4-8
ISBN 1-894666-22-4   Can.$8.95 U.S.$7.90

David and Goliath
by Cor Van Rijswijk
Time: David   Age: 4-8
ISBN 1-894666-23-2   Can.$8.95 U.S.$7.90

FREE with an order of these three W.K. books:
COMPACT DISC
Bible Stories from The Word of the King Series
read by Theresa Janssen
CD 1-894666-24-0   (Reg. Can.$9.95 U.S. $7.90)